Praise for *How Nature Healed a Broken Soul*

"Penny James presents a real and raw account of her life as a supermodel in the sixties and seventies. Her vulnerability and honesty are not only compelling, but point the way to a healing path of recovery and redemption for those struggling with addiction. Fascinating read that you won't want to miss."

— Rita A. Schulte, counselor, author, speaker, and radio show host

Other Books by Penny James

Muffin, 2016
http://bit.ly/PJMuffin

Real Women's Stories 2018, Chapter 12
http://bit.ly/RealWomensStories

HOW NATURE HEALED A BROKEN SOUL

An autobiography

Penny James

Edited by Sandra Savoia

ISBN 979-8-9866685-1-2 (paperback)
ISBN 979-8-9866685-0-5 (epub)

This is an original print edition of *How Nature Healed a Broken Soul*.

Cover image of author Penny James with her original creation, Bed of
Trees, photographed in Shohola, Pennsylvania. Circa 1990.

This autobiography reflects the author's memories of her life experiences.
Some names and characteristics have been altered, some events have been
compressed, and dialogue has been written to the best of the author's
recollection.

Consider the possibility of loosening up the soil around someone's
heart,
making room for new seeds to grow.

Imagine a voice from your heart so compelling that it causes a ripple
around the world and an
echo into eternity.

It can happen.

~

I believe
everyone has a life story worthy of being recorded and shared.

It is my hope that this book will encourage you
to share your own intimate thoughts,
embracing your uniqueness
as well as your commonality with others.

Table of Contents

Letter from the Publisher

Penny was passionate about sharing her life story so that others could be encouraged by her struggles and healing. While making final preparations for editing, publishing, and marketing *How Nature Healed a Broken Soul*, Penny passed away in April 2019.

Penny spent several years writing this book you now hold. Her writing is powerful. We hope the beauty she brought to the lives she touched is conveyed through each page she is sharing here from her heart. May you feel her loving presence and allow nature to ease any wounds you may carry.

Love and hugs from our dear sister and friend, Penny in Heaven.

—Shanda James Sullivan (Penny's sister) and Sandra Savoia (Penny's friend and assistant)

Acknowledgments

I would like to thank my dear friend and advisor, Beth Kallman Werner, for her guidance, encouragement and support throughout this process. Beth, I could not have published How Nature Healed a Broken Soul without your assistance. Thank you from the bottom of my heart. At last, and together, we have fulfilled Penny's wishes.

—Shanda James Sullivan

Chapter 1
Shohola, PA

I came home to find Darius Rucker's face looking back at me from under a tree. The singer's *Learn to Live* CD was part of a birthday box sent to me by my sister in Colorado. Two days earlier, I'd called the post office and asked them to hold the expected package.

Apparently communication failed — because a new carrier delivered the box straight from his vehicle window to the ground and took off. Muffin had taken my present after it was tossed out the window and carried it in her teeth to her favorite spot. Never mind that it had FRAGILE stamped all over it...

When I mentioned this to the carrier the next day, that maybe a FRAGILE package shouldn't have been tossed out the window, the response was, "I couldn't get out of the car; there was a mother bear with three cubs right next to your door. Mother bears are really dangerous when you get near their cubs."

Muffin's own mail carrier habits had been going on for years. She would tear packages open without seeming to care what was inside. Once I found what looked like a moss bedspread decorated with countless empty packets from my six months' supply of Mountain Home Health supplements. I was worried sick until I saw Muffin again, thinking she might have killed herself from vitamin poisoning. Another time, she tore into and distributed a huge container of legal documents that had already been through hell: divorce papers. Imagine having to go from tree to tree to gather them — now dotted with teeth marks.

Now every innocent creature in the forest could read about my torridly colorful past.

My furry black companion hasn't had a simple or perfect life either. Muffin is thirteen years old and she's been in trouble with the law, but I'll get into that later. I only mention this up front because it's important to know that I have paid a great price for being her mother.

I came to Muffin's territory, the northeast area of Pennsylvania, in 1987 after a suggestion by my voice teacher in Manhattan. I mentioned one day that I would like to invest in some inexpensive real estate to fix up and resell. He said he knew the perfect place and encouraged me to explore the Delaware Water Gap, except for one thing…

"You've got to be careful if you go to a bar. The locals up there don't take to people from New Jersey and Manhattan. They call us *flatlanders*. I almost got my head blown off one night at a place called Rohman's in Shohola."

This was rather ironic because Shohola, named by the Lenni-Lenape American Indian Tribe, means "place of peace." After 9/11 many people fled New York City to small towns in the Pike County area where I currently live. The population of Shohola is less than three thousand. If you love animals, it's the place to be because it has the largest collection of wildlife on the East Coast. The Delaware River runs alongside the national recreation area and it's not unusual to spot deer, bear, eagles, and river rafters. This is a nature-loving place, so if you come to make a name for yourself climbing the social ladder or wanting to hook up with some reality television show, you'd be better off elsewhere.

Many Pennsylvania locals love their guns, hunting, and their blood-splattered history. They never tire of telling newcomers about the Erie Railroad and the famous Shohola train wreck of July 15, 1864, when some sixty-five Confederate prisoners and Union guards were killed during the US Civil War. Earlier, these grounds were Lenni-Lenape territory. The Dutch had purchased Manhattan from a Lenape band in 1626 for almost nothing and then New York City was declared the capital of the United States from 1785 until 1790. This brings up carnal, protective, territorial instincts over land ownership. The locals in Delaware Water Gap enjoy recounting the Battle of Minisink during the American Revolution, where Mohawk Chief

Brant was an officer in the British army. Commander John Hathorn lost that battle partly because of the Iroquois' skill in combat.

A mile and a half from my home, there is an area I consider sacred. It's where the Delaware River divides Pennsylvania from New York. It's a crossing place with thousands of years of history. Many tribes left artifacts behind, which are now being dug up and preserved. Every time I cross over the bridge, I think about their soulful heritage and how they probably would prefer it to be left alone, to rest in peace. But life isn't like that on this earth.

While thinking about all the history and sorting through what had become Muffin's surprise picnic package, I wondered what my sister Sheila would say if she knew this. A few weeks earlier I'd been visiting her in Gardner, Colorado. She makes a living as a baker, and I enjoyed sitting in her log cabin eating my favorite cinnamon rolls with cream cheese filling and fresh cherries. Her desserts sell almost immediately after leaving the oven. She is pretty famous for satisfying people who have a sweet tooth.

The phone rang. It was Sheila. "Did you get your birthday package yet?"

She must have ESP! "Yes. First of all, thank you so much for the beautiful card and message." (I didn't say I could *bearly* read it through the teeth marks!) "Those cinnamon rolls were the best I've ever eaten."

There wasn't a trace left of them or the banana muffins.

"You like those better than the ones with the caramel center?"

Oh God. What else had she sent that I didn't know about? "Uh … I put those in the freezer. I can hardly wait to bite into one of them."

"They're a new recipe. People really love them here. How did the tomato taste from the garden? Wasn't it huge?"

I'd been wondering about those small red flecks scattered on the ground.

"I'll bet you've eaten all of your chocolates. I had my neighbor go to Pueblo to pick up the truffles and turtles you like. You're so spoiled!"

"I can't believe you found those in the Pueblo area. I'm not sharing them with anyone!"

Thankfully, Muffin and her three cubs hadn't gotten to the hot salsa and didn't seem to care for the green zucchini and yellow squash — I was able to wash some of those off and fry them in butter. I remembered Sheila leaning over her stove, adding fresh basil, salt and pepper. I prepared them exactly the same way.

"The vegetables were delicious, Sheila."

Am I spoiled? I can only wish for everyone to have a sister like Sheila.

After the call, I washed Muffin's muddy paw print off the Darius Rucker cover and placed the CD in the player of my Toyota Tundra.

The next day I got in my truck for the long drive to Sloan Kettering in New York City. I'd been diagnosed with cancer and was on my way to hear the test results. I would need my trusted companion to carry me. It was the color of a thundercloud on the outside and had a soft beige leather interior. My truck is my cocoon and none of the recent bad publicity concerning Toyota could have affected our relationship one bit. I turned the heat on and it wasn't long before I felt warm and comfy. I became a bird flying low along the road as nature flashed by.

I turned on the same well-known storyteller who was part of Hootie & the Blowfish in the nineties. I didn't listen to the radio much at that time, so I didn't know who he was until he went country. I'd recently seen a music video he'd done in an open wheat field and it turned me back into a schoolgirl. I needed music like dry riverbeds long for rain. I went to my favorite song, "If I Had Wings" on *Learn to Live*. The soothing, comforting rhythms connected me with Darius Rucker's words. The repeated phrases gradually became meditation, reaching the deepest part of who I am. I have learned over the years to trust in this special, quiet place that always finds the right music.

Chapter 2
Heaven at Grandma's

I had gathered many secrets in life before I'd even reached the age of six. Among them was that my true home was with my grandmother. Mom and Dad would drop my two sisters and me off to stay with her. We would drive south on US Highway 25 from our home in Pueblo, Colorado. In time, we'd turn at a poorly marked cutoff next to an arroyo. That abrupt departure took us to a narrow, seemingly endless red gravel road that led to nowhere and everywhere. The flat, arid landscape was eerie, littered with cacti and wild morning glories that laced around abandoned mines. Crumbling old adobe houses dotted the land. They appeared to be melting back into the earth from too many years in the hot sun.

Every summer I would get real quiet during this part of the trip. I could almost hear the sacred voices of the Ute tribe, Spanish conquistadors, cowboys and, more recently, commune hippies ... the land with layers of stories to tell. The most exciting part was that this haunting, lonely road was leading my heart to Grandma Esther's homestead in Huerfano County, Colorado. As we got closer, trees, flowers and scrub oak gradually closed in enough that they could scratch our car until we reached the wide-open space where Grandma's house sat. To the north of her cabin was the corral, a resting place for her cattle when not threatened by an occasional bobcat or bear. Standing at the top of the stairs leading to the porch of her log cabin, she would invite us in with a mischievous grin. The unspoken message was, "Nothing I ain't been through, and now I'm up to playin' and havin' fun." It was standing on those worn stairs that I once saw an explosion of falling stars that made me wish for a bed of trees to sleep in so I could always look up and see magic in the sky. I remember feeling as though I got swept right up into the stars.

Grandma had become a woman of proud preservation before I ever set foot on her property or carved my name into one of the aspen trees. Her essence was filled with the light energy of freedom. She had bloomed into a colorful prism even though fierce winds had twisted her nearly to the breaking point. The gnarled heaviness of her roots was gone — she had pruned the unproductive branches of her past.

Claw marks marred the frame of my grandma's front screen door — deep, elongated scratches down the side of the new forest-green paint. All of us decided that it must have been a mother bear with her cubs that had tried to break in, looking inside the porch for the fresh milk and the butter Grandma had made earlier. Little did I know that an abandoned bear cub was already woven into the fabric of my heart. She would come into my life, raising her own cubs, to bring joy and soften some of the rough times. It was always destined to be because of the experiences I had with my grandmother, her surroundings and the mosaic that was her life.

A typical day at Grandma's started tucked in bed with many blankets under an open window, surrounded by the smell of fresh air and the sounds of morning. Grandma got up before daylight and I would hear her shuffling slippers as she gathered wood to place into the glazed, green-and-white speckled egg stove. There was always a melting pot of ingredients for the common senses — the clanking of the red hand pump going up and down as she filled the stove reservoir with fresh spring water, the smell of eggs and bacon, and the sound of a spoon stirring biscuit dough in a metal bowl.

Sometimes we made chokecherry jelly, boiling the berries in apple juice, lemon, and honey. We filled little glass jars with the syrup and topped them off with paraffin wax. How excited I was to split a hot round toasted biscuit with steam billowing out and taste the slight residue of soda with the tart jelly.

As children we never let Grandma out of our sight, trailing behind her, tugging at her apron strings. We watched as little yellow flecks formed in the buttermilk she would churn into butter in the combined kitchen-porch area. She would separate milk from cream to make dough, then roll it out and cut thick ribbons of egg noodles one inch wide, tossing them into boiling water. Seeing them come out slightly elastic intrigued us. When flipped, they sprang from the pan onto our plates. We twirled them around our forks and occasionally picked them up with our fingers, testing their endurance and tossing them at one another when Grandma left to go to the outhouse. Perfect behavior would resume when she came back to start a new chapter in nature stories while pressing our clothes with an iron heated on the wood stove.

Early afternoon was bath time, just like clockwork. We were placed in a big oval metal tub and scrubbed head to toe with natural soap she had made from a fusion of lye, lard, and flowers. She warmed the water on the stove to rinse us. On the side was a tin box containing an awesome yellow salve. It smelled like the chest vaporizer she bought at the general store.

The salve was slick and slimy with a fluffed-up consistency that looked like a mixture of whipped cream and raw eggs. Grandma would rub it in our hair, which had been twisted around from the wind and taken on a style of its own from briar patches and scrub oak we had plowed through. With the magic salve our ratty tangles would miraculously settle down and, when rinsed, our hair would get real shiny and flat. Years later when my urban plastic-surgeon husband tried to experience the salve's benefits for himself, Grandma's soothing solution was not able to work any of its magic on him.

To set her clock, Grandma would climb onto the long rectangular kitchen table, which was covered in a green plastic tablecloth with lily of the valley flowers. One day, she set it for two thirty. I was with one of several friends who were staying for the weekend, and one informed me that she had just heard the radio say it was three o'clock.

"No, the radio is wrong. I just set the clock, it's two thirty."

Esther knew instinctively that time is a thief in this world, and she would have no part of it. We all decided right there and then that she was right. It was two thirty.

Most evenings we sat around the kitchen table with a kerosene lantern lit just as the sun fell behind the mountain. We watched

Grandma fiddle with the local newspaper as the day's light faded and the lantern flickered on her glasses, golden, dancing shadows on the darkening walls around us. She would smile at something amusing from the print. Her smile sometimes looked tight in the very center, but then the corners would perk up. It was like someone had told her it was all right to be sad but not to be happy. And yet, happiness always won.

She had straight white teeth. One night after bedtime I saw her in her nightgown tending to them until they were shiny and clean; then she placed them in spring water. I asked her if she had lost her real teeth from eating too much candy. Her wry, knowing grin returned with a long, gritty pause. She didn't answer directly, except to say that George Washington had false teeth and his gums were wooden. I remember having a very hard time falling asleep that night.

The living room commanded respect. In its center was a long, thick oak table once used for important adult gatherings. The outside edging was hand carved with a small, delicate mountain-flower motif that seemed incongruent with the table's massive presence. The mighty oak carried the weight of hidden stories.

In the corner was an old upright piano we loved to pound on for hours. There was an energy beyond the noise that we were drawn to. The old hymn book facing us wanted to stay open to the music "In the Garden." Each time I came to visit, it was always there to greet me. This was in contrast with the dusty Bible my grandfather had preached from, hidden from view on the top shelf of the closet. That book was where I found my name inside with my birthdate written neatly by my grandmother — part of the family tree, bound from the beginning of time. I wasn't aware then that the royal DNA in that grand old, dilapidated Bible was the same our forefathers had used to secure our Declaration of Independence … it was coming apart at the seams.

In the other corner was a hall tree where Grandma always hung her cowboy hat. We never disturbed that hat because we knew she depended on it being there when she had to go out and check on her cattle each day. There was also a handsome radio console from the forties that was never used. She had a large overstuffed burgundy velvet couch under a row of windows. We would climb up and then sink deep into it, side by side. The soft, mushy monster was tricky to stand on, so we had to stretch our necks up really high to watch her as she left each afternoon to go to the corral. She had to cross a stream and walk carefully to avoid swollen mounds, which came with the lush green wetlands after a harsh winter's freeze.

Everything exciting happened at the corral where Grandma mounted her beautiful quarter horse, Browny Red. She was marked with a tiny star on her forehead much in the same way that the model Cindy Crawford has her signature mole. We loved watching as Grandma saddled, groomed, and spoiled Browny Red with horse treats and apples.

One day we saw the horse rear up, whinnying while Grandma was on her. I could see from their body language that something was wrong. It was a few critical seconds before Grandma was able to overpower Browny Red, muscle against muscle. It took all her strength to straighten the horse's head with the bit until she could jump free and make a soft landing on the ground. I watched her get up and run toward the woodpile near the closing bin. Esther went in and came back from the barn carrying a pointed-tip shovel. Without hesitation, she lifted it high above her thin, wiry five-foot-five frame. Her solid, lean legs were firmly separated for balance and precision. BAM! Off came the head of a long, thick rattlesnake. Thankfully, other than getting spooked, Browny Red was unharmed.

Grandma's bedroom was right off the back porch and mostly avoided. The space felt vacant and haunted, and it seemed like only a ghost could sleep there. She rested well in her oak bed with acorn-adorned bedposts but never lingered there. Despite this, the strength and fruits of her life were passed on to us from that bedroom, her highest highs and lowest lows all collected there. She had transformed, but the ghost of her past remained. Broken dreams were just as clear as the fresh air she had come to Colorado for.

Against the back wall was a beautiful black Singer sewing machine with a gold hand-painted floral motif. That machine fascinated us because it was so old, wise, and still in use. We would open a drawer to a regimented army of colorful bobbins and marvel at the long history of stitch work — stars and stripes placed on quilts, blankets, pillowcases, and dish towels before we were born. She must have just kept stitching and mending patchwork until she grew up and out of the bedroom of broken dreams. Grandma had been sewing with the thread that would keep us all alive.

We had become the healing change of fresh air she needed. We would gather Grandma's favorite flowers from the upper pasture and leave a bouquet on her bedside table, along with an apple we had polished till we could see ourselves in its shiny skin. It was a surprise for her when she came back tired after a long day.

Climbing the old wooden stairs to our high nesting place was probably the same experience birds have when they return to their home up and away. Grandma's cabin was an A-frame, and I loved looking up at the sharp-angled attic ceiling adorned with old rose-pattern wallpaper. There was a row of windows front and back that served as our lookout posts.

Grandma pretty much didn't come up there when we were visiting. She seemed to enjoy hearing our laughter and the patter of our feet above her rather than next to her as evening approached.

Upstairs wasn't as clean as the first floor. There were more than a few cobwebs to wander through while exploring. We found a tobacco snuffbox stuffed with rattlesnake tails from snakes killed on her property over the years. The older rattlers looked like transparent buttons that you could use on your clothing for closure, with the extra benefit of sounding like a rattlesnake when you walked! I planned on making a scary Halloween necklace, taking it to Pueblo and selling it to some boys to make money. Girls would never buy something that ugly to wear around their necks.

In time, our interest shifted to the hope chest. It was the only blonde furniture in the entire cabin and the most beautiful with curved, almost voluptuous, large leaf carvings. Nothing was squared off except the opening. We opened the drawer. Neatly pressed embroidered pillowcases presented themselves with soft, sexy-looking salmon blankets and color-matched bedspreads. The sensual bedding was filled with romance and protected in plastic. On the top of it were scarlet love letters written to Grandma by my grandfather when they had courted years earlier. We learned more from those letters than we could comprehend at first, reading them over and over until we were satisfied that all the information had been extracted. We also got into her branding irons, horseshoes, and seed pellets. There was nothing off-limits, including a family of mice scurrying around with us in the closet area next to the bed.

One night, looking out the window, we saw streaking lights that weren't from the stars. We ran down and told her about it. She came up the stairs and looked out. "Them are flares. Them hunters are after my elk."

She went back to the first floor and got two guns from a locked closet, brought them upstairs and placed one flat on the floor beneath the window; with the other, she lifted the window higher, poking the double barrel out into the black sky. She pulled the trigger twice, took the other gun from the floor and did the same thing ... four blasts. The incident was never discussed, and we never saw them flares again.

I can't remember Grandma ever telling us that we had to stay inside when she left each day around three o'clock, but somehow we knew that we should never get near her horse.

Those afternoon jaunts were her alone time, when she would receive refreshment even when steadily at work. Loping along with Browny Red was when her heart soared. Glimpses of sparkling strands of Spring Branch Creek could be seen running right along with them between thickets of fragrant wild rose bushes, scrub oak and Apache plume. And behind them were the Sangre de Cristo Mountains — Spanish for "Blood of Christ." The sacred mountains watched over Grandma as she planted her garden next to the stream — radishes, spinach, green leaf lettuce, string beans and sugar beets. On the range, she had gained wisdom from an inner listening, a quiet stillness for tuning in ... Grandma and nature were married. Two peas in a pod in the garden.

From our windows, we could see Grandma trotting along the crude, uneven road that followed the base of the mountain for nearly one mile before she reached the upper pasture. It had been formed from lava half a million years ago. Browny Red had to avoid big boulders scattered about: some jagged, others smooth and sculpted, looking like they might be filled with nuggets of gold. Over time, nature had molded shapes that looked like vases, bowls and serving trays, mostly the color of homemade vanilla ice cream. Mixed in among them were soapwort plants and giant puffball mushrooms that could weigh over twenty-five pounds! We would slice the mushrooms, sauté them in butter and place over a sizzling steak and crusty pie dough — it tasted like beef Wellington, only with giant mushrooms!

Grandma got off her horse and opened the gate to the upper pasture that held her two root cellars. When necessary, she could fence her cattle in that one big area. This seemed to be the hotspot where all of nature gathered after geographical forces had spewed the perfect blend of nutrients into fertile grounds.

On one occasion I got to watch her from the road; she had a hammer, some barbed wire and wood gathered for posts. Her focus was intense as she sectioned off a small plot of land next to where the cattle were grazing. Grandma was a partner with the earth, protecting it from overgrazing. She studied the mountain grass. If enough rain fell, it would grow about eighteen inches and would protect small tender alfalfa stems from the harsh sun and wind.

Suddenly, a change in the atmosphere, and with it a new life dropped into the meadow. I saw Grandma's hammer go down as she swooped up a wet baby calf, cradling it in her arms. Her small frame slowly, carefully crossed the pasture toward the barn, the calf's big bellowing mama close behind.

Over the course of many years, Grandma must have graduated from partner of the earth to godmother. I would watch the afternoon sunshine as it beamed on her back and shoulders. The memory even now is like living in a different time frame, with Vincent van Gogh painting her in southern Colorado rather than the South of France. His art was in the upper pasture that day. The Sangre de Cristo were before her, Big Sheep and Little Sheep Mountains sloping behind her with the great sand dunes hidden like soft pillows tucked between the rugged hills.

Her love, respect and dedication to all living creatures was well known in the community.

When the calf's mother got sick, I had the joy of feeding the newborn with a bottle, though the calf butted his head with so much strength Grandma had to hold me up. The calf's mother was sick for only a week. Grandma placed an instrument containing large pills down the cow's throat with little resistance, and I was excited to experience and share the whole story with others.

Once the calf was weaned, it was sold to a child in the 4-H Club (Head, Heart, Hands and Health). It wasn't a surprise that this calf later received a lavender Grand Champion ribbon.

One day, Grandma took us on a surprise trip to see the largest hidden sandbox in America! She planned a secret getaway from ranching — a place she could be a child. President Clinton would later name it the Great Sand Dunes National Park and Preserve.

Grandma's vivid imagination kicked into gear, planting seeds in our minds of communicating intimately with the wild animals in nature. She was the leader of the pack in a fact-finding expedition of three young children. We packed a picnic lunch, grabbed a watermelon floating in the spring under the porch and hopped into the back of Grandma's truck, planning to stop in Gardner on the way over to the big dunes. Grandma frequented the little businesses they had opened in town, except for the old one-room beer joint that had been there forever. There was no affiliation with big money and if she or they needed to go to a bank, it was in Walsenburg twenty miles away.

From a kid's point of view, Gardner was filled with adventure. We would always go to the post office first, then past the Methodist church and on to the eerie old filling station. Finally, we would head to the penny candy store, which was what we were most interested in. Walking into the little old store that smelled like bubblegum and fresh green apples was heaven to my sisters and me. My stash of wealth would be a room with floor-to-ceiling shelves filled with different kinds of candy. The creaky brown wooden floors of the store were uneven and hadn't been varnished for years, but the clear eye-level candy bowls were shiny clean, full of Tootsie rolls, candy cigarettes, sugar-covered watermelon slices and black licorice.

Grandma finished her business in Gardner, and we three sisters and a watermelon continued our bouncing in the back of Grandma's old red-and-white pickup truck with the sun warming our shoulders. We worked our way down the narrow red road with the sound of wind and later brush oak scratching the sides of our hay-and-manure-perfumed transportation, barely missing us. But it didn't interrupt us — our imagination kept growing stories as fast as the dust billowing up our noses. We figured out where the bear family lived, pointing up and on our left to a large cave.

The bear family was also attending to some personal business. Mama Bear had her mind set on gathering osha (bear root), a plant crucial to her family's well-being. She had taken it to clean out her digestive system and now chewed the root into a watery paste to wash both her and her cubs' face, body and especially paws, to guard against bodily parasites before playing in the sand. Bear root will not grow naturally in gardens, and she had to leave part of the root in the ground or the entire plant would die. She was careful to leave plenty of roots for others to use for their powerful anti-viral properties.

Mama Bear had once seen her friend Grandma chomp down on those roots when she first started coming down with the flu, making steaming tea from the stems to stop coughing. Any plant considered to be bear medicine is potent and primary. We learned that in many cultures the bear is considered to be the prime healing animal, largely because of their innate intelligence — using plants for their own healing. A male bear uses bear root to make love and will roll around in it for hours, using it for perfume, offering it to his girlfriend and also chewing on it to get high … waiting for the right moment.

But this was the furthest thing from Mama Bear's mind. She wasn't in the mood for anything except moving on. They started off on the same trail as the crow flies — about fifteen miles to the mighty sand dunes — but made a sharp turn and began climbing Little Bear Peak, which is one of the seven mountains over 14,000 feet high partly responsible for creating the 750-foot-high dunes. Mama Bear made the detour to check on her property. Earlier she had marked her homestead with claw marks along the base of the aspen trees until they reached above the timberline.

The time had come for her to teach her cubs some lessons on how to be tough, defend themselves and gain independence. The three cubs didn't like the lecture: she grunted too much, and they were tired of having to stay in one place so long. They started getting fussy and picking fights with one another, so Mama was relieved when she found a loving tree to send them up and away to take a nap on the boughs. After a blissful nap, down they came, one after the other looking like little black inchworms. Soon they hit the dirt, changed their cadence and bounced along behind Mama, approaching the dunes.

We three sisters also bounced along behind Grandma enjoying the dunes, our picnic lunch, and the tales of our bear friends. As we grew tired, we packed up for the ride home and in our slumber drove off to meet Mama Bear and cubs at Ghost Forest, an exclusive part of the dunes, at midnight after all the tourists had gone home. We frolicked with them in a blackout that included only fireflies and millions of stars. The Great Bear and Little Bear part of the magical Milky Way named after them way before we were born, lit our way.

At the end of each childhood summer, I was driven back to Pueblo. It was usually early evening when we had to leave Grandma's homestead, still light enough to see her waving goodbye and dark enough in the back seat of the family car to hide my eyes so no one would see my quiet tears. I would remember hearing aspen leaves swirling among streaks of sunlight, churning up ancient stories in the wind. But my most-loved sounds were from the throats of songbirds as we drove away. Those memories lived in me then and they still do now. I would say goodbye to my collection of friends — the deer, elk, and bears. They were protected by my biggest companion, the Sangre de Cristos. I remember saying to them, *Please don't forget me*. They knew the next chapter had to be put on hold, an unfinished story. I left my joy and freedom with them, but they knew I would return. When the time was right, memories and imagination would allow me to re-enter my secret world in nature where I was free, bold, and courageous … where I could shout out dreams, complete them and fulfill my purpose.

Chapter 3
Grandma's Early Years

My heaven in Grandma's home had been my daddy's childhood hell. The isolated countryside was his prison. When he was only four years old, she became sick, so he didn't have much physical contact with her. I have heard that tactile stimulation is essential for bonding in small children and limitations can occur in later life from not experiencing it. He had grown up learning to survive with almost no affection. His sister later loved telling the story of looking out the window to see my father taking his little red wagon up and down the mountain all alone. She was wrong: he was not alone. His dreams were with him but they didn't involve riding a horse.

Grandma's early childhood was etched into my heart by the memories found in every room of her home. Her mother died from tuberculosis when Grandma was only eight years old; it was called *consumption* at that time. Her father was a horse trader, a breeder of draft horses, as well as a traveler, and he was seldom present at their home in Missouri. After both her brother and sister fell ill with the same disease that claimed their mother, and eventually claimed them as well, Grandma was sent to live with her grandfather. From his wheelchair, he made a living working fine details into wooden furniture, hand carving unusually detailed ornamentation into each piece. Although he never suffered from tuberculosis, his lungs had been severely scarred by smoke residue from coal burning inside his cabin. Much of Grandma's early life consisted of taking care of her grandfather and attending school, which she did until the eighth grade. She enjoyed attending the school that could be seen clearly on the top of the hill. For her and her schoolmates it was necessary to get there in all kinds of weather.

Beyond school, Grandma also loved attending church where she would eventually meet her first boyfriend. It was with him in his parents' barn that she first saw a filly being born, all legs when it came out, clumsy in a new home of straw. Grandma must have felt awkward in the legs, just like the newborn, when she witnessed the foal's birth. She made up her mind that one day she would raise a filly of her own. She would get up in the saddle and they would learn together … prance around the barrels at the county fair to win a Grand Champion ribbon, a dream she stored away.

Friends consisted of families that exchanged goods with one another. They all brought different things to the table: some raised pigs to supply meat for the community or chickens for eggs, while others grew animal feed or provided livestock medicine. They watched out for one another. Agreements were made with a handshake. Trust prevailed — it was called survival.

During that time, neighbors had just completed two root cellars with two-man saws and workhorses. Large bricks of ice were cut from a nearby lake to be placed in an underground refrigerator formed by carving down deep into a cool northeastern bank. The rectangular hole preserved the ice so it could be used in their homes. A strong rot-resistant wood was used for structure, and an underground ventilation tube moved ethylene gas outside to prevent vegetable spoilage. Shelves were built apart from the main structure for breathing room, and then the floor was covered with layers of straw and sawdust. Finally, the ceiling got topped with logs, moss, roots, and plants for insulation. A door was added to complete the framing.

They had unwittingly built an underground bear stock market containing precious commodities — peaches, potatoes, turnips, beans, carrots, and sugar beets — and made a perfect den for sleeping through the winter. It was a market where greed would prevail and there would be no fair trading.

Spring's renewal came with a broken-down door; underground corruption was clearly seen. Bartering was the way of life, but the bears had eaten everything. Without these precious commodities, what could the community do? The neighbors' needs were tightly interwoven. The vastness of their combined human intellect got pared down by a mama bear and her two chubby cubs!

One friend, Harold, had planned on trading his now-missing produce with Grandpa for the hand-carved hope chest he spotted on the porch. Harold had been thinking about the chest for the last year; it was the perfect gift for his new bride. He, like Grandma, had placed a dream in that root cellar. Her secret dream rested patiently in the communal root cellar, along with peas, carrots, and other produce, for the right time, when a harvest from her life would be fed to me.

They couldn't see that something bigger than what they had sowed separately would bring them all together — a small seed of a story waiting patiently to be watered and nourished as I learned to experience life from nature's root cellar.

Grandpa Jesse William James was also born in Missouri, sandwiched in the middle of thirteen. He grew to be tall and handsome, stood out in a crowd and had the gift of making himself the center of attention with poetic conversation. He knew the Bible well and was drawn to Grandma because she earnestly lived what the Bible taught. She grounded him and they joined together as husband and wife.

For a while they were well suited in marriage. Both had developed a love for horses: Grandpa Jesse raced and bet on quarter horses and Grandma would later breed workhorses. Life had been good for them most every day until Grandma became ill. They moved to Huerfano County, Colorado, where the town of Gardner saw her arrive with Grandpa, fighting for her life with tuberculosis and three young children in tow, hoping the pure, dry air would cure her. The town had gotten to know Grandma, peering through a quarantined, screened-in porch extending from the house she stayed in temporarily that was next to the church.

Grandpa Jesse became the town minister in Gardner and taught grade school. The church Grandpa Jesse took over focused on townspeople with hedonistic pleasures like dancing, drinking, and gambling, all of which Grandpa Jesse did well. There had been no tradition of allowing a woman any kind of spiritual title or say in the church, which also applied in the home. I never saw him preach, but always imagined what it was like when he was up at the pulpit ... excitingly dangerous ... teaching the Word from his well-worn Bible, all while living a secret life. There was a movie from 1960, *Elmer Gantry*, about a fire and brimstone preacher. Many people compared that Burt Lancaster character to my Grandpa Jesse. In time, the charismatic preacher, whose name is now etched under the stained-glass windows of the Methodist church in Gardner, fell from grace with some and was heralded by others.

The town of Gardner looked like a downtrodden one-horse town with a few small adobe houses. It was as if a strong wind had come in and blown away the few dreams that had survived the Dust Bowl. There was no new construction happening anywhere, only the occasional tumbleweed and dried out prairie cacti. The Upper Huerfano River Valley, where Gardner was located, was filled with "soddies" — men who live a little like gophers under mounds of earth, next to gold and silver digs. They had finally surfaced to face reality for striking it rich. Their seemingly tenuous position wasn't misinterpreted by the townsfolk, even though they looked like they needed a good wash. The sparkle in their eyes was telling and very much alive. The energy, partly from whiskey, was irresistible because you knew they'd never give up.

Grandma's friends at the post office and my father saw tears I would never see in her eyes. Grandpa would disappear for long periods of time. One day he vanished in the middle of the night with a pretty younger woman in his congregation, leaving my grandmother with no transportation, no money and three children to raise. She had to beg The First National Bank in Walsenburg to lend her enough money to survive. Gardner would also see Grandma cry when the government came into her upper pasture and killed off all her prized cattle during the Great Depression. She was one of the lucky ones who had received a loan before the banks collapsed. Grandpa's horse jockey, who also managed the bank, had secured the loan for her.

Old-timers didn't have the security of banks, the FDIC didn't exist, and folks would line up at a bank that had taken and eaten up their life savings. Soddies supported Grandma until she eventually started a successful business breeding horses after losing all her cattle. They shared her joy when she bought a new herd in Cripple Creek, an area known for superior breeding principles. Later, at auctions in Pueblo that were advertised in the newspaper, she began selling her animals, which sold last because they commanded the most money. She bred and preferred Hereford bulls with strong shoulders, lean hindquarters and square-stemmed tails rooted to their backsides. They were raised on unusually fertile land where they were fed and watered by natural springs, hidden away by mountains.

Grandma's character was strong and her hands were always in motion. With her Singer sewing machine she made beautiful quilts, embroidery work and specialty items for weddings that she sold at the church bazaar. After she passed a civil service exam and became postmistress in Red Wing, a small town nearby, her job was to oversee everyday operations and make sure they ran smoothly. Her Swedish-born father's and mother's DNA produced one of the finest workhorses alive. Eventually, Grandma made the area into a colorful two-horse town that always kept folks talking!

For several years, Grandma also taught farming skills to children at a nearby boys' orphanage and donated funds and the tools they would need to make a living later on. She was to become the tree of life for them. It was as if God had placed her in the middle of the circle of His Majesty.

A bonding took place with a man who called himself Peter Rabbit — a cool, laid-back hippie she met through socializing at the church in Gardner. Rumor was that he and others who were part of the draft dodger movement came to the area from wealthy families who attended Ivy League schools. He would bring his friends to the pasture to learn from a woman who hadn't conformed to society or the industrial revolution, a woman living a lifestyle from one hundred years earlier. Her students embraced her ways of using anise hyssop flowers in tea, preserving meat and drinking from springs around the meadow — fresh watering holes for them and the cattle. Peter Rabbit taught Grandma about the hippies' homes made with tires, tubing insulation and solar panels. Fifty years later, the same materials would be linked with the greening of America.

As she shared her humble work ways with them, Peter saw that her hands were becoming arthritic. He brought her a stash of alfalfa seed that he and his friends had harvested for her to drink in tea. Two years later she would show her much improved hands to my father. "I have to give them hippies credit. They ain't dumb!"

Not long after, a drink surfaced called Peter Cottontail Ale — beer laced with marijuana. It seemed like they may have been harvesting marijuana moonshine! Gossip spreads fast in a small town. How many people knew about it? How many people had tried it? Certainly not Grandma…

"Them hippies have gone plumb crazy! They are a actin' just like my cows when they git into locoweed."

She was right. Some of them ended up in jail.

Chapter 4
Generations That Just Can't Separate

My earliest memory is being up high in a swing with grass below. I don't remember my mother being there, but very early on I became fixated on her. I would watch her body language. She would get sad and cry a lot. I was so in tune with her moods that I would look up to her face and if she wasn't happy, I couldn't be either. I tried not to disturb her. I did whatever I could to get her eyes to light up, by listening to what she said and agreeing with whatever she wanted me to. Sometimes I would brush her hair. It seemed to calm her and take some of her anxiety away. Mostly I tried to just be quiet around my mother and when she would get real bad, I'd kind of hide in a closet and become invisible.

My mother was from a large family of four boys and four girls. Her mother married a baker who worked hard but couldn't make enough money to raise them all. The oldest son, my Uncle Gordon, quit high school to help his father. They were taken care of, in part, by Grace Episcopal Church in Colorado Springs, Colorado where they lived.

This lifestyle caused my mother to be extremely sensitive and fragile. It was almost as if she weren't equipped to live in a world of ups and downs or deal with the complexities of life. Mother still couldn't get past the last words her mom had spoken to her: "Sophie, I want you to stay home tomorrow. You've been gone too much lately."

Grandma Shaw went to bed that evening at forty-six years of age and never woke up.

Mother had been dating my father at the time. They were in Gardner together when Grandma Shaw died.

People who knew my maternal grandma compared her to a saint. She was religious and, even with eight children, did all the embroidery work, edging the cloth covering the altar at Grace Episcopal Church. The gold-thread design from her embroidery needle was intricately delicate, very much like she was.

Every Thanksgiving Grandma Shaw prepared a feast, welcoming many, even from outside the immediate family. Martha Stewart would have loved the presentation of the food, textures and colors at the table, even though their gatherings were far apart in time and motivation — Martha with her own television show and fan base, and Grandma Shaw quietly preparing her large round table with attention focused on one special place setting: an empty chair for Jesus.

She had gotten both her artistic ability and religion from Great Grandpa Phillip Zehner, who owned a well-known jewelry design business in Wyoming. His parents had come by boat from Germany into New York Harbor and settled in New Jersey where Phillip was born. The Gold Rush lured him to Wyoming.

His many customers were from diverse backgrounds. Over time, Grandma Shaw's father became friends with both Sitting Bull and Buffalo Bill Cody. They designed chairs together out of buffalo horns and, later, moccasins with exquisite beading. Their work was shown at a museum in Wyoming for many years. I heard all this from one of my mom's sisters, Gen, before checking further at the Ancestry website. Mom and Aunt Gen's grandfather had passed on detailed memories: "Sitting Bull did a lot of running around. It was like he had ants in his pants. So did Bill Cody, but his was different."

There was apparently discomfort within the clash of cultures, but a deep-seated need to get to know one another won out. All three men were so curious about one another's creative abilities, they would lose all track of time when working together. Then an odd thing happened.

Sitting Bull became spiritually awakened when Great Grandpa started talking about other riches besides the buffalo horns, rubies, silver, and gold around them … talk of commodities they couldn't see and feel. Conversation about Jesus started, how Great Grandpa couldn't live without Him, how he was given strength and power every day from the Bible. Great Grandpa shared the Word with both Sitting Bull and Bill Cody. The planting took place in both of them, but the deep seeds only developed in Sitting Bull. He became a Christian with the eternal DNA of God in his heart and the cross Great Grandpa gave him around his neck.

I wish this was the end of a spiritually uplifting story, but a sad thing happened. Most of the jewelry Great Grandpa designed was stolen in the middle of the night and never recovered. The only jewelry left in our family is what family members were wearing at the time. A fortune lost from a collection of work so delicately refined that you needed a magnifying glass to see the silver etching embedded around precious stones and tiny seed pearls. A mystery never solved; heirlooms lost forever.

In my mom's early years, while she competed for attention with her many brothers and sisters, feeling like she faded into the woodwork, little Sophie Shaw found a friend in Louisa Graham Giles. Louisa was a wealthy patron of Grace Episcopal Church and would watch the Shaw family of ten come in and sit before the service began. The children were well behaved and neatly dressed, even though they were poor. She would say hello to all of them separately, but kept her eye on Sophie and Gen, the two girls in the middle who were small-boned and scrawny. Louisa's heart went out to Sophie because she was clearly uncomfortable around people. When Louisa asked her a question, Sophie would look up with a shocked expression, like she couldn't quite believe that someone would actually be interested in her. Her face would turn red with just a hint of a smile before she quickly looked back down to the floor.

Louisa took the two little girls into her world. Her family had originally owned a sugar plantation in the Carolinas and moved to Colorado Springs with Hostie, her chauffeur, and Bertha, her housekeeper. Hostie and Bertha were former slaves, married to one another. Hostie would pick up Sophie and Gen in Louisa's Rolls-

Royce and treat them to ice cream cones before driving them back to the mansion. Louisa would greet them outside and show them affection with a welcoming hug.

Spring would slip into summer, and Hostie would enjoy meandering along the lane of poplar trees in the front yard, which was framed with fruit trees and a variety of low-lying flowers. He always got out of the car first and opened the rear door for the girls. Was it the large fresh leaves of God's mercy they smelled or was it the strong pillars of His loving kindness adorning the house? Whatever it was, they never wanted to leave.

Once, Gen handed Louisa a small pink-ribboned package with an embroidered handkerchief inside. The name Louisa was needled into the middle. "Did you and your mom make this for me?"

"Yes, we're learning to sew together!"

The noonday sun sifted back and forth through the leaves shining on Sophie's fine red hair. The moving spots of light were playing with the patch of cornflowers next to her feet.

"Sophie, you look so pretty. Do you know what matches those flowers?"

Sophie's downward glance had fallen to the flowers, but they were not yet in her visual awareness because nervousness had kept her from focusing. After a moment, shy blue eyes met Louisa's and the girl's tension began to melt away. Next came a smile, but not an ordinary one. Sophie's grin lit up the entire wooden-beamed foyer as they entered and extended all the way to Bertha, who was standing near the door. She had been watching the interaction and started falling in love with the fragile little girl who would soon be sharing stories and secrets with her.

My Mom and my Aunt Gen lived for the days they could be in Louisa Giles's mansion. There they could have fun playing games in many different spaces. Bertha would teach them silly songs to sing, along with her favorite hymns. The children followed her and Hostie as they did chores.

One day Sophie said, "I don't like my name. I wish it was somebody else's." Bertha passed this on to Louisa.

"Sophie, do you know what your name means?" Louisa asked. "It means intelligence and wisdom. Your mother gave you a beautiful name. You will grow up to be very smart someday."

Inside they would climb the mahogany spiral staircase. From there they could gaze out to green rolling hills layered with mist, orchards and long rows of grapevines that had a vast yet quieting presence.

Sophie and Gen both dreamed of getting married to ministers from the church. They would walk down the curving staircase with long wedding gowns trailing behind and meet up with their husbands below. Years later they both married men with the same biblical name of Joseph. One planned to become a man of the cloth; the other already had a father who was.

My parents met at a post office in Colorado Springs, near a highway-construction site where my father was working with the Civilian Conservation Corps (CCC). President Roosevelt had signed the stimulus plan where enrollees in the program were paid thirty dollars per month, twenty-five of which was sent home to their families.

Mom and Dad were both walking on the sidewalk toward the CCC entrance when a horn started honking accompanied by a long high note–low note whistle. The attention was on my mother, who was wearing a low-cut yellow sundress. Her strawberry-colored hair was wavy and swept back from her face with a thin tortoise-shell band. Her porcelain skin was fair, too much sun would have damaged it, but that wasn't what caused the commotion. Neither was it her beautiful legs accented with high-heeled pumps or her five-foot-five-inch frame and tiny waist. It was her large breasts that had the guys gawking. When my father first saw my mother's shapely figure up close, he decided right then and there he had to have her.

People who knew my parents during the fresh face of their marriage said they made a stunning couple, but Mother wasn't attracted to my father because he was tall with beautiful blue eyes and a fun-loving personality. Her affection for him was mostly because his father was a minister. A charismatic Methodist preacher with a hidden dark side.

In the blush of first love, hidden layers didn't register for my parents. Life was good not knowing one another's underbelly. My father's lonely days were over. He had a beautiful wife to show off in his shiny black Ford Model T. The times they spent in that car were magical. The engine and my father's ego were tied together — no more riding a four-legged animal for him! He wanted to go places and had plans his parents knew nothing about. He would spend hours grooming his pride and joy with the hidden horsepower under the hood till it shone spotless.

With respect, he would gallantly open the door for Mom, hoping she would slide in close to him on the slippery leather seat.

Country life in the way my father had grown up was new and exciting for his young bride, Sophie. He had a city car, country charm and a father who was a minister. She would look out the window with a bright future in her mind as they slowly made their way up the long narrow red road to a nine-thousand-foot elevation adorned with wildflowers and scrub oak. The sound of the motor humming along with songbirds was their music. It was them and the sunset together forever when traveling in the car. They didn't have air suspension like we have today, but they had the spirit of ecstasy that all car lovers are familiar with ... dreams of buying the perfect vehicle to make love in was the same then as it is today. It became the Industrial Revolution's number one aphrodisiac for both sexes.

My parents lived briefly in Gardner and would get up together at five o'clock to prepare for a long day on the ranch. Mother would lean over the wood-burning stove, cooking fresh bacon and eggs while young farm hands would steal glimpses of her breasts overflowing her white ruffled blouse. Their cowboy boots would shuffle around on the floor while they were flirting with her. Mother would give back shy but provocative glances. They would pull their chairs back and go out to bale hay with renewed vigor, carrying secret dreams of going on a picnic, maybe getting a taste of her sweet, smooth breasts. Yes ... nature's irresistible seduction flowed downstream alongside the Orphan River.

To say that my mother and father were not prepared for or looking forward to being parents is an understatement. My mother had been told she was so small-boned that she would probably never bear children. Her doctor was like God to her and she believed everything he said.

Well, Mother got pregnant, and the pink bubble of newly wedded bliss faded with new realities. Bobbie, my oldest sister, came along, and I was on the way nine months after that. They eventually moved into a small, simple white stucco house on Pike Avenue, located on Pueblo's East Side. The house was across town from the steel mill where my father worked.

Time for adjusting to family life was interrupted by a draft notice. My daddy was called away to serve our country — G.I. Joe, another new job to adjust to: being trained to kill humans with an M1 rifle. Before he left for Japan, my mother got pregnant again. Sheila would be born before he came back.

I have no memory of my father ever picking me up or playing with me when I was young.

There are no photographs of him interacting with my oldest sister. I do remember he was very respectful to us, from a distance. He seemed uncomfortable being the only man in the house after coming home from the war. He was happy to get up and out of the house to go to work. But as we got older, things began to change.

Three kids cooped up in a small house without room to play outside prompted the move to Overton Road on the outskirts of northern Pueblo. At least that's how it appeared on the surface. Before moving, I got into Drano from an open container underneath the sink in the kitchen. Mother heard my screams when the Drano activated from the saliva in my mouth. Luckily, a nurse lived close by and knew what to do before taking me to the emergency room.

Moving to wide-open spaces anchored all of us. We were a young family in hometown America with our dreams intact, even though life was as uncertain as the wind blows. The new environment allowed us to be out there on the loose, in a good way most of the time.

My parents were able to buy a small white stucco house on ten acres of land. Behind our new home were olive trees framing Fountain River with a large dump up the road. We would lose track of time rummaging through the debris, hunting for hidden jewels in the mountain of junk. We found old dishes, chairs, bottles, silverware and even a few coins. It wasn't long before we had our own secret hideaway. We also found a deep pond while exploring that was only ten minutes away.

Usually my sister and I didn't have tops on during the summer, and the noonday sun would burn our skin. I remember having on hand-me-down jeans that were too big and a thin belt around my waist that was too loose and too long. I took a sharp rock and made a new hole through the plastic leather so I could tighten it further before going to the bank of the river. The extra length hung down at my side until I jumped from Blue Cliff, flying in midair with the sky until I landed in the soft riverbed. We scattered schools of minnows that tickled our feet as velvet sand made its way between our toes. I fell in love with the wiggly creatures who lived in the water. I had to learn that when I put them in my pocket, they wouldn't be alive when I reached home.

Except for those two areas, the land was dry and flat with cacti. Off in the distance in the opposite direction were the Blue Hills, where large herds of antelope and tribes' echoes lived. My oldest sister, Bobbie, and I would take a massive jug of Kool-Aid and peanut butter sandwiches, knowing we would be gone a long time. We'd follow an arroyo to small, twisted pines that looked old and holy. Along the curving path we found flint arrowheads from those who had lived there earlier. Perhaps they watched for mica: complex minerals that crystallize into translucent layers that glitter in sunshine. Makeup artists now use mica powder for glowing, beautiful skin. There was also an abundance of what Daddy called potato root. We would pull it from the ground and chomp away on it while exploring. It looked a little like a small carrot, only white with stringy roots and a floral aftertaste.

Our small home had neighbors on both sides. On the right, an older couple, and on the left, a very poor family that mostly kept to themselves. Not far from the back of the house were three worn-down sheds with tin roofs and dirt floors. One housed a deep well that provided our drinking water. A few weathered two-by-fours partially covered the opening.

We learned very early not to walk near it.

Most people in the area were poor, except for our neighbors, the Harris family. They had houses sprinkled along the five-mile exit from the town of Pueblo. Together the family owned most of the acreage in the area and knew how to work it effectively. The three brothers in their early thirties and their father were impressive farmers. We would pass by and see the father, getting on in years, working a fourteen-hour day baling hay with his sons. We would get to know them when we received an invitation to watch them make Italian sausage with fresh fennel. We learned a lot from them, maybe too much … one of the old man's sons would become enamored with my mother.

Our dad loosened up a little and even seemed to enjoy us at times. We were raised alongside one big cherry tree, chickens, a cow, pigs, and a goat. Dad planted a garden with us, which was mostly tomato plants. Other vegetables didn't do well in the dry clay, except for some white sugar beets. When they matured, he picked a couple, taking them into the shed as we followed him. He sat in the old chair we found at the dump and peeled the beets with his pocketknife. We settled beneath him on the dirt floor while he hand-fed each of us crisp slices of raw beets. I remember so clearly a ray of sunshine making its way through a hole in the tin roof, draping over Daddy's shoulders. That day G. I. Joe was really home with us. That day we were rich.

A trellis of grapevines defied the odds and seemed to love the soil. Mother canned grape juice and for some reason it fermented and blew up in the basement. We all thought it was hysterically funny — everyone but my mother, who started crying.

My father got a job selling cars in Pueblo, but when times got tough, I could see it on his face when he came home. In those early years he never cussed in front of us, except when my parents would fight. They would argue a lot when money wasn't coming in. I always felt sorry for him when mother complained. We'd get out of the house so she could be alone and have some peace. He'd take us to the feed store in Pueblo. It was located right next to a liquor store, but he never went in there.

Spending on anything but staples didn't happen when we were living below the poverty line. I remember at that time it didn't feel like deprivation. We didn't have a clue as kids what that word even meant. It was normal for us and we were happy. Even though my mother didn't like the struggle, it was amazing what she did with tough times. She made floral dresses for us out of feed sacks that held the grain we bought with Dad. She also made down pillows, encasing chicken feathers in green-checkered print. I still have one of those pillows and looked at it in wonder when it recently survived yet another washing machine cleaning. Fabric, even for feed sacks, was made to last back then!

Mother got us involved in 4-H. Everyone would get together and share their talents. My best friend's father taught square dancing, and Mother taught sewing and baking. A group of girls arrived at our home to make muffins, hoping to win ribbons for the annual event. The muffins didn't turn out and neither did the dress — when a pattern got reversed without enough time to correct it. We really didn't mind much because all our energy was wrapped up in square-dancing dresses. Mom went to the store and bought crinkled turquoise cotton and made my sister and me three-tiered circular skirts on her Singer sewing machine, trimming them in bright multicolored rickrack. The tops were V-neck with shoulder pads and capped sleeves. We had these cool tan moccasins with beading to wear with the dresses while do-si-do-ing. Our lacy underskirts would flip around and go up real high when we felt the rhythm just right. We were really something when that happened!

ADVICE FROM A SINGER SEWING MACHINE
MANUAL FROM 1949

Prepare yourself mentally for sewing. Never approach sewing with a sigh or lackadaisically. Never try to sew with a sink full of dirty dishes or beds unmade... When you sew, make yourself as attractive as possible. Put on a clean dress. Keep a little bag of French chalk near your sewing machine, to dust your fingers at intervals. Have your hair in order, powder and lipstick put on. If you are constantly fearful that a visitor might drop in or your husband will come back home and you will not look neatly put together, you will not enjoy your sewing.

I started first grade in a two-room stucco-and-brick building with no indoor plumbing. It was on two acres of land, but there were no trees and it was enclosed with a barbed-wire fence. There were two swings and a small grandstand on the playground that must have been a seating area for sports at one time. The grandstand was not maintained well, and we never used it except to eat lunch or during recess.

Mother made me a frilly pink dress to wear for the first day of school. I stood out in the stark environment. She had gone to a fabric store and found the prettiest floral pattern on sale. I remember walking in and seeing about twenty desks. They had ornate metal bases with wooden tops and a place for an inkwell, which we never used. A large stage running across the room served as a backdrop for my first-grade teacher. There was a cloakroom to the right as you entered, and further up on the right was a door to another classroom used by another teacher.

Bobbie and I were separated because she was older. I remember looking around at all the school children and knowing right away who I wanted to be friends with. There was only one blackboard, and it was in the second room. We seldom had access to it except on special occasions when our teachers would unite the two rooms for spelling bee and arithmetic competitions.

My childhood memories in that school are as vivid as if they happened yesterday, not when I was six. My best friend and I would search outside for pretty broken glass, then throw our pieces into the squares we drew on the ground to play hopscotch. Miss Pinkerton, my first teacher, taught us Double Dutch rope jumping, very good for body and hand-eye coordination.

I began implementing on the playground what I had been taught at home by my mother.

Even though I had favorite friends, she had told us many times to be nice to the poor people down the road from us whom we passed by most every day. They lived in a curved warehouse made of tin with no insulation. The children from that family were listless, a little dirty and had sad eyes. The girl was about two or three years older than I was, and so skinny. I remember going up to her and asking her to play with me when she was sitting alone. We went to the swing; I sat in the middle and she stood on the swing with her two worn-out shoes on each side of my body. Her toothpick frailness changed as she kept gaining momentum from swinging. I swear she got happier and happier as we went higher and higher before almost flipping over the top.

This friend seemed to flower over the months as we played together, and it wasn't long before other kids started to include her in games at recess. Those games could really get crazy! One time someone was chasing Bobbie too aggressively and she ran into the barbed-wire fence surrounding the schoolyard. It made a deep gash in her throat. Fortunately, she was taken home and eventually got stitched up. It wasn't much later when she fell onto some hot coals outside that were used to heat the school — off to the doctor again!

Even though my legs weren't as long as Bobbie's or the boys', I could outrun everyone. I had pent-up energy inside, and it all got released when I ran. I felt free, like a wild horse. I fell only once, early on when I had just started going to the school. I clearly remember being picked up by a tall boy. I didn't know him; he was from the second classroom. He carried me in his arms up the steps to Miss Pinkerton. It felt just right. His name was Tim, and I developed my first crush on him, but a month later he was gone. His parents had moved to town.

My oldest sister and I always got up early. Sometimes Mother would pack us lunch in a brown paper sack, and we'd travel on the dirt road about half a mile away from school, passing orchards and groves of sweet-smelling lilac bushes when it was their season.

Sometimes the bookmobile would schedule a stop on a Saturday, and we would meet up with it parked at the side of the road. We jumped up three steps to get inside the large vehicle that looked like the caboose of a train. It was there that I found the *Black Stallion* books, *Nancy Drew*, *The Little Engine That Could*, and *The Boxcar Children*, the book I most identified with. That particular book was very musty and dusty. The paper felt coarse and mysterious. I wondered where it had come from. I loved getting lost in the stories and touching the paper. It took me into other worlds.

Miss Pinkerton was a tall, thin woman with reddish-brown hair who looked to be in her midthirties. At that time, she was single and could have been considered an old maid. I don't know how others remember her, but she had more of an influence on my life than any other person at that time because she helped so many around her. She instinctively knew how to bring about plasticity in the brain, sixty years before the scientific data surfaced. She never missed a day of school. I can remember her being sick one day during recess, vomiting outside, alone. We came back in and she resumed teaching.

Then there was the time when my younger sister, Sheila, told everyone that it was her birthday when it wasn't. She came home with a lot of presents and Miss Pinkerton had bought her a special gift. Miss Pinkerton wasn't just good to our family, she was good to everyone. She was always planning Christmas pageants and parties, finding children with musical talent and showcasing them. She would be sure to give everyone a part in these productions. The large stage inside the school became our heaven. For Halloween parties, we would all bring disgusting, slimy things from home and set them out in separate bowls. She'd place blindfolds on us and served as a prankster. We knew she wouldn't disappoint, and she always made Halloween the really gory day it was supposed to be!

Miss Pinkerton would give us poetry to learn for the following week. I remember knowing I had to start memorizing it immediately at home because it wouldn't stick without going over it again and again, every day. When my turn came to recite it, I would start to sweat, my hands becoming cold as ice. I was terrified. My brain would shut down but, because I'd gone over it so many times, I could get through it without thinking. Still, many students learning at the last minute did much better than I did.

The biggest event in the area was the yearly National Spelling Bee in Pueblo. Miss Pinkerton spent hours after school preparing us for it. Unlike trying to memorize poetry, I didn't study at all but got almost perfect scores. I knew how to spell words even when I didn't know what they meant. I would just look and remember. I became runner-up in the contest. Miss Pinkerton's name wasn't in the news. Mine was.

One day she wanted us to memorize "The Children's Hour" by Henry Wadsworth Longfellow, but she knew I couldn't concentrate, so she took my hand and placed me in the cloakroom, thinking that being alone would help me. I sat on the floor and memorized, focusing on one word at a time with no distractions. I will never forget that poetry, the round-tower of Miss Pinkerton's heart melding with Longfellow's words, or the importance of placing the patter of little feet on a pathway with grounding underneath. Miss Pinkerton is now in a special place deep down inside me. I want the whole world to know about her … I don't even know her first name.

At school functions and 4-H, my classmates started nominating me for things I knew absolutely nothing about. I became secretary and was supposed to record minutes of meetings and keep records in order. When it became clear I didn't know how, my parents dropped me off at an old man's house in our neighborhood. He was an old-timer who had founded 4-H in the area. His name was Fish and he lived alone, down next to the Fountain River. He was brisk and clearly didn't want to be bothered with teaching me what I needed to know. When I didn't understand quickly, he called me stupid, confirming what I secretly thought of myself.

At home, Mom and Dad never read bedtime stories or any kind of book with us. We weren't a family tucked in bed with goodnight kisses or even taught basic skills, so when I first started school, I was behind many of my classmates. My way of getting along in life was to smile at everyone, to treat them special, to never talk about them behind their backs, and to keep my mouth shut and act like I understood everything. I was convinced that I was living a lie. The amazing thing was that people began to look up to me! I was always busy participating in every new project the school offered and didn't have time for the bad seed of negativity. There was simply limited space for it because it was crowded out by school activities.

On a hot July night at square-dancing practice, we ended early because of the heat. I went outdoors to get some fresh air. The stars were out and there was magic in the air. I thought I was imagining things when I heard soft music coming from the grandstand. I moved closer.

There was a full moon out. I saw Mom in the parking lot between cars, dancing with a man who had dark wavy hair. He looked a little like Dean Martin. I hid so she couldn't see me. I watched his movements, so smooth and elegant. The moonlight would catch their silhouettes as he turned her and tipped her up close to him. The song coming from the newly hooked-up car radio was "Embraceable You" by Frank Sinatra. There are only so many dances that can be streaked across the sky. They weren't about to pass this special moment by. I became the audience.

It wasn't long before Mr. Harris started coming over to the house to build closets for us. I watched him on the ladder, sawing and pounding away on the wood.

The smell of Old Spice and fresh sawdust was mesmerizing. He would always leave before Daddy came home.

At night I would lie in bed and dream of him kissing me and marrying me someday. When he was around, Mother's mood changed. She was energetic; her eyes would shine. I remember her writing a letter to a radio station when they were having a weekly program on "Best Neighbor in Your Neighborhood." The elderly couple next door to us had so lovingly taken us in as a family and helped us out on bad days. Mother expressed herself on paper like she had a college degree. The letter was read over the air as we all sat and listened. It was the only time Mother ever received recognition in that way, but it was quickly forgotten by her and us, as if it never happened.

Our family was not emotionally cohesive. Bobbie, the oldest, spent most of her time outside alone. Daddy would leave early for work and

Bobbie's job was to take care of the farm animals, and us if she was told. She and Mother weren't close. I stayed in the house a lot and spent time taking care of Mother when she was like a broken doll. Since I was born a happier child and didn't complain a lot, I was favored. Mother would say, "Why can't you be more like Penny? She's so much easier to raise."

When we got into mischief we would all get condemned. It became a pattern with our parents that if they didn't know who had caused the mischief, they wouldn't try to find out. There was no detective work done. We all got blamed equally and were punished. (None of us could ever pass a polygraph test if we got into trouble!) We all started feeling guilty about things we didn't even do. This, of course, would cause sibling rivalry. We started keeping a healthy distance from one another, except for one time — we became unified when we found out Mom and Dad were planning to move. We told them we were unhappy and were going to run away.

"Fine. We'll pack your bags for you."

Mother packed a large lunch and we put it in a burlap bag tied to a stick. Bobbie placed it on her shoulders and we left the house together. Sheila was always the feisty one, impulsive. She took off on her own, got lost and we couldn't find her until nearly nightfall. We finally made it back home in the dark and hid in the basement. There was a trapdoor that opened separately from the rest of the house and the steps into the basement were nothing but hard clay, the floor was dirt, and the walls were covered with old wooden shelves. Spiders attached their webs to the electrical wiring and pipes. We felt their architectural designs as we made our way through the dark, before hiding next to the coal furnace. There was a leak above us that kept dripping on our hair. We finally got so uncomfortable that we went upstairs. It was probably ten o'clock. Mom and Dad would surely be relieved. After all, they had played a game with us and packed our lunch sack. Were they afraid something bad had happened? They might be happy to see us … but what we saw and felt was anger. And we knew they knew how to get back at us.

Every year there was a school picnic with a bus ride going to the park — life is always fresh on a picnic bus. We would sing, "Ninety-nine bottles of beer on the wall, ninety-nine bottles of beer … if one of those bottles should happen to fall … ninety-eight bottles of beer on the wall…" It was our chance to harmonize and learn new social languages outside a structured classroom. It was always so important who sat where. I could see myself sitting close to my secret love interest and also right next to my best girlfriend, who loved music. Looking out the window wasn't as important as the atmosphere inside. The whole world without homework was on the bus, where anything could happen. Anything. We lived all year long for that day.

The picnic arrived, but my sisters and I were grounded. We spent the day together at home. It hurt. We never forgot it. Going to the movie *Picnic* later on and hearing "Moonglow" on the soundtrack made it even worse! Mom and Dad got their revenge.

We never strayed too far from home as a family, except for the long trip to live with Grandma each summer while Mom and Dad took a vacation. Warm spring days, spent alone in our front yard, were a common occurrence. I remember one day, one of the Harris boys came into our yard. He was about three years older than me. He would watch when my sister and I had our bathing suits on, spraying one another with the hose. He started touching me inappropriately. He gave me the creeps. I felt superior to him and would have nothing to do with him. There had been one previous episode when he wandered into our yard with a friend and followed Bobbie and me down to the riverbed. The boys relieved themselves over Blue Cliff while Bobbie and I watched, being judges. Which one squirted the farthest? I remember not liking that game. It felt dirty, and I was right. Seeds were being planted in the boys' imaginations.

My father heard from one of the teachers at school that one of the Harris boys had said he was planning to make a baby with one of us in the arroyo behind his house. My father was very even-tempered unless he was drinking or fighting with my mother. When he heard what the teacher said, he went into a rage. He took a long stick and made a switch by nailing strips of tire tubing to it and then took off. There was no doubt he was planning on using what he had made. No Harris boy was going to make a dent in one of his precious girls …

plucked like a cherry from his cherry tree. That Harris boy came very close to hearing the sound of my father's anger through a switch … down deep in the arroyos.

One time Mother insisted that I curl Sheila's hair, even though she had the flu. I didn't want to catch it because I was proud that I had not missed a single day of school. But when I became too sick, Miss Pinkerton sent me home. I asked her if she would put on my report card that I only missed half a day. Miss Pinkerton agreed but it turned out that I would be gone for a long time. Neither of my parents realized how bad it was. On top of the flu, I developed an infection that reached my bloodstream. I had severe pain in my stomach and became too weak to get out of bed. I finally begged Mother to take me to the hospital. I knew I was dying. My father wrapped me in a blanket and carried me to the car. That was the only time I remember being in his arms.

My hospitalization became the talk of the neighborhood. When they heard I needed a blood transfusion, all the Harris brothers donated blood. I was then placed on penicillin every three hours by injection and the doctors wanted to perform an exploratory operation. My father refused and within a few days my fever finally subsided. I was sent home the day after Christmas, after being there for eight days. I still didn't feel well and became nauseated from the smell of my father's cigar in the car. I felt guilty for what I had put them through and for all the money they'd had to spend on me in the hospital.

When I got home and was placed in bed, Mother gave me a gift. It looked like a rectangular cookie tin and had a chicken attached to a rolling magnet that went up and down. I couldn't understand why anyone would want something like that. I didn't ask my sisters if they had received presents. I feared they were angry with me for ruining Christmas. I decided from that day on to stay away from anyone who looked like they were sick. In total I was out of school for about a month and thought I would never catch up with the rest of my class. I remember thinking, "I'm eight years old now. It's too late to be a singer like my best friend."

Life on the farm was so good and so bad. Our cow's name was Bozo. She was loved by the entire family, including Mitten, our black-and-white kitten that someone had dumped by our home. We all learned to milk Bozo and would take turns spraying milk on Mitten's whiskers so we could watch her wash her face. Then we'd fill a dish for her right next to Bozo's hind legs. Mitten followed Bozo everywhere and they would take naps together when it got hot in the afternoons.

Bozo would get lonesome being the only cow around and would break out from the barbed-wire fence to go down the road to find a boyfriend. This happened several times.

Bozo finally bore a calf. Daddy found the tiny animal exposed to the cold and not moving. He covered her with blankets and brought her into the basement of our house, next to the coal heater. He warmed bricks and wrapped them around the animal's legs. After a few days, the baby finally stood up. Family pets got a lot more attention and affection than we did. We all became more interested in the animal's life and care than we were with each other's.

One day, Sheila was standing by the fence. Her hair was the color of straw. I'll never forget the image of Bozo reaching out, taking one of Sheila's braids in her mouth and yanking it out by the roots. It's hard to imagine that an animal could do something like that so fast, to have that much strength and coordination. It took about six months for Mother and me to make Sheila's hair look fairly normal. All these experiences, good and bad, shaped who we became while growing up, similar to the prickly cacti and soft morning glories at the side of our house.

Life at home might have been a little easier if Daddy had had a son. He didn't realize the trauma involved when he took me out to the chicken house, grabbed an ax from behind the door and picked up a roosting hen. He held her firmly in his hands, placed her neck alongside a rock and chopped her head off. The head fell to the ground but the body flew up, flapping over us in the air and spraying blood everywhere. In that moment, I became the chicken with my head cut off. Would this have been easier for a young boy to experience? Was this a natural part of being prepared for manhood in a father-son relationship?

We were a unified, happy family concerning one thing — we all loved Uncle Gordon, Mother's oldest brother. Gordon was a gentle soul who came to live with us for a while after going through a bad love affair. He had been hurt by an unfaithful girlfriend and never got involved with a woman again. Uncle Gordon arrived on our doorstep vulnerable and not prepared for the rude awakening of farm life. He got invited over to the neighbor's place early on when the farmer was slaughtering pigs to make sausage and saw him slit the animal's throat. While my uncle was drinking his beer, the old man with bravado took a shot of whiskey and washed it down with a glass of fresh blood.

Gordon, who had the nickname Uncle Buss, taught us the basics of golf and played baseball with us. He slept on the couch and went to work every morning with my father. Every night he would bring us candy — mostly licorice and cinnamon drops. We would all eat it together while he was drinking his beer. He would line the empty cans in a row, sometimes up to a dozen, knowing they were getting the best of him. The next morning was hangover time. He eventually stopped cold turkey. I asked him later in life how he was able to quit on his own…

"I wanted my mother to be proud of me."

After Uncle Buss left, the fights between Mom and Dad escalated. There was no one to curb life's rawness. The fights were a part of our life almost every day. To get away from them, I would go out to the tin shed behind our house that stored paint cans. There were white, pink, and blue colors to concentrate on. I gathered small dried flowers from the parched land and dipped them in the fresh paint to make a bouquet and made a sign: Flowers by Penny. I would go to the road to sell them and then come back to the shed. I made curtains during the day with the burlap bags stored there and hand stitched a thick hem with a hole in the corner. In would go the coins. I was saving money and my dreams in a secret place deep in the fabric.

John and Alice Harris invited Mom and Dad to their house to celebrate the Christmas holiday while my sisters and I stayed at home.

Our parents came bursting back through the door late at night, waking us all up. Both had been drinking, and Mother was in a yelling rage.

"I saw you in the corner with Alice, giving her your handkerchief!"

"Well, her brother just died, for God's sake!"

"When was the last time you offered *me* your handkerchief? I think it's about time I find someone who appreciates me."

My father's body stiffened and his voice became as loud as hers. "It looks like you've already done a damned good job if you ask me. What about him coming over here during the day building closets? He's built a goddamn closet in every room for Christ's sake!"

"Well, you never do anything around here. I have to have someone help me."

"Why in the hell doesn't he build closets in his own house? I'll bet Alice doesn't know anything about this."

Mother ended up throwing her high-heeled stiletto with a delicate bow at Daddy's backside, but we all survived that night.

Mom and Dad's fights were how I learned the meaning of being lonely. When the bell rang at school, I didn't want to go home. At night I didn't want to go to sleep because of the nightmares. I was a child looking at the reflection of my mother in me, but I was the grown-up. I had to keep an eye on her, be respectful and responsible. She was the tree I had to keep alive. I began watching the whole world, wanting to hold it up for her so she could have a good day.

Some mornings I went to the shed and put on the ice skates she had worn when she was a child. They were already too small for me, but I didn't care since I was still able to squeeze into them. It was about a quarter mile to the pond. Seeing the slick ice surrounded by trees was magical to me. I loved being by myself, away from noise, learning how to skate backward. I wanted to be a professional skater someday … and most of all, I wanted to sing on stage.

On Mother's good days she was peaceful and loving. My father would say, "When she is *right*, there isn't a finer woman than your mother."

On those days she used me as a messenger. She sent me over to our poor next-door neighbor's house when their newborn was sick. I took over a roast fresh from the pressure cooker. When I knocked on the screen door, it was ajar with a missing hinge. I could feel in the atmosphere how bad it was. The young mother took the roast. The baby was on a cot right next to the kitchen door, in need of air. I accidentally hit the edge of the bed because there was no pathway, and the rough edge of my jacket snagged the newborn's sock. The baby was blue and not moving until my movement made it cringe in pain. I became sick to my stomach. I was so sorry for what I had done.

There was no welfare at that time. It came into existence under Lyndon Johnson. This proud family, ashamed of being poor, had slipped through the cracks with a baby left to die at home. I wandered out of their yard and then back in just one other time, and again encountered death. Their reddish-brown collie was lying flat on the ground, motionless. When I went up to it, blood was coming out of its mouth. It must have been hit by a car. I couldn't stand being there and ran as fast as I could back to our property. My foot got entangled in a low-lying prairie bush and I landed flat on my stomach, unable to breathe for a few seconds. I never went near that house again. Was I too young to be sent out as a messenger? I didn't tell my mother about either incident but I lost my appetite after that. Mother would make me sit at the table until my food was eaten. Sometimes I would be there for hours before going out to play.

Mother was either really up or really down but always had three meals prepared. She did an amazing amount of work — cooking, washing and drying our clothes, ironing and then paying bills. She would do all of this without speaking to anyone, sometimes three days at a time. Her only form of auditory communication was crying. We all knew she was building up to an explosion. Then words would come flying out. We all tried to duck from the onslaught. I would go out to the shed and put my hands over my ears. As a child I didn't know what was wrong with her. As an adult I call it demonic depression.

"What am I doing with a house full of kids I never wanted anyway? My mother had eight and what did she ever get out of it? She died in her sleep at age forty-six. No one ever appreciated her either — the last thing I want is to be pregnant again. Sometimes I think the only reason I was born was to raise a bunch of kids. I told you we should have used a rubber.

"Marlene got pregnant and got rid of hers with a coat hanger. Men are so lucky. They never have to go through the shit women do. They just get up in the morning, go off to work and never have to worry about anything. I wish I had been born a man. How can we afford to have another kid? I'm always scrimping and saving as it is, making dresses out of feed sacks…" (pause) "and all this washing and ironing … you don't know all the things I have to do to make ends meet."

Dad sighed. "God, how did I ever get into a mess like this? I wish I could take off and never come back."

"That's the way I feel right now, just so you could see what it would be like without me. You certainly don't appreciate all the things I do. We probably would have lost this house if it wasn't for me. When things get tough you take off on your motorcycle … why don't you ever talk to me? I think it's about time I find someone who appreciates me."

"Who can talk to you when you're like this? You're always in a rage for no reason. You're the one who always wants to get together with those people. I go with you and end up catching hell."

"I haven't been happy for a long time."

Things usually blew over, but this time they didn't. Mother came into our bedroom late at night and turned on the lights. "I'm leaving your father. Which one of you kids wants to come with me? Penny, you look the most awake. Get dressed." I had been sleeping with Mitten purring next to my chest.

"Go on, get dressed. Leave the cat here, it's better off here. It's just one more mouth I'll have to feed. Let this be a lesson to all of you to marry someone with a lot of money so you don't have to go through what I'm going through."

We would experience the same threatening ritual, over and over again. Each time we would think, *This time it's for real.*

Mother never left, and her last pregnancy was hard on all of us. Life was hell for nine months, but miraculously it got better after Shanda's birth. My father started bringing home more money, and my parents bought us a spinet piano. Mother played a song she had memorized from childhood. Until then I hadn't known that she played piano.

Life with a new baby was fun. We all enjoyed being around her. My parents were more relaxed and gave her affection the rest of us never had. You'd think that would make us jealous, but it didn't. There wasn't much Shanda didn't like doing. We would cut out a window from a box, place her in the box in our wagon, then close the box. Her little face would peek out the back with so much joy in it. We would spend hours riding her up and down the driveway.

Looking back, my sisters ended up being the greatest gift I ever got from my parents. We had the usual sibling rivalry, but when things really got tough there was unity. When we felt we had no one else, we knew we had each other.

Mom and Dad had friends from town named Chris and Marlene. They would get all dressed up and go dancing. This was always planned by Mother. Father, like Grandma, couldn't dance well, so Mother would find partners who did.

Marlene began coming over to our home regularly; she helped Mother sew some of our clothes. They enjoyed one another's company and Marlene seemed to blend in with the offbeat décor of our living room. The inside of the house had spurts of newness counterbalanced by cheap, old furniture. Organization within the home and general housekeeping didn't exist, so anything fairly new stood out. There was a rather nicely shaped paisley-print couch from the forties sitting on a large area rug with a rose print. There were drawstring curtains with an oversized morning glory print in a shiny, sheer, cheap-looking fabric over the windows that were noticeably uneven in length. Two floor lamps with shades in similar fabric stood alongside the windows. A garish plastic cigar stand sat next to a worn La-Z-Boy, and what really got attention was a brand-new Zenith radio phonograph console in blonde wood — Mother's new gift. Her favorite singer was Nat King Cole. Her favorite songs were "Unforgettable" and "The Ruby and the Pearl." When they were playing, she would get a faraway look in her eyes … far, far away from us.

There was a corner knickknack stand filled with family photos. Everyone was always dressed up and all of the photos were in cardboard frames. Plastic religious hangings were on the wall with additional photos hung haphazardly next to them.

Mother and Marlene would get on their knees and pin patterns to fabric on our red, bubblegum-speckled linoleum floor. Marlene was tall and beautiful and her husband was impressively handsome. I remember seeing her flirting with neighbors when Chris wasn't there.

One day the phone rang and I heard Mother talking to Marlene. She accused Mother of having an affair with Chris. She had discovered Mother's lipstick and perfume on his shirt. That was the last time I ever saw Marlene. It wasn't the last time I saw Chris.

As a family, we all got tired of country life at pretty much the same time. Bobbie, Sheila, and I were approaching our teen years and wanted to explore city life. Mom and Dad were able to find a family living on the east side of Pueblo in a fairly new housing development that we traded houses with. It was interesting that we were all happy moving there. Daddy and I painted the living room the color of bright salmon. We thought it was beautiful. Our entire family life together had always been with only one bathroom, and our new home was no exception.

Bobbie and I never had separate rooms and we had to share closet space, which was always cramped. Because we were in such close quarters, there was always an uneasiness. Sheila and Shanda shared a room in the basement.

Across the street from us was a vacant lot but we had neighbors on both sides. The houses were close to one another: we were on a quarter of an acre. We had a long clothesline going across our backyard. It collected a lot of energy. Mother would put her short shorts on with a low-cut blouse — boobs on the top, cheeks at the bottom — and go out to hang clothes. It wasn't long before cars were circling our block screeching their brakes. Mom would stretch up real high and bend over real low to the clothes basket containing all of our personals. We heard loud whistles. Hey … with five girls there was a lot of underwear! Sometimes I would carry petticoats out that I had rinsed in sugar water so that they would get stiff when dry. It kept my circular poodle skirt out. One time in the fall, the washing was left out overnight. It froze and someone came and snapped off all the long sleeves from my dad's shirts. You never knew what was going to happen next. Sheila and Shanda, watching from inside, loved the excitement and added to it by placing a large piece of paper over their bedroom window. It said: "We have the hottest Mom on the block."

They made a song up about Mother's breasts: "They swing high, they swing low, they swing everywhere we go." This vocalizing would generally go on in the back seat of our car all the way to Dairy Queen. We were always in a new demonstrator Cadillac or Buick. When Mother had had enough fun, she would turn around and look at them. "Would the two of you shut up?" We all had fun in the car together.

Bobbie and I started attending Risley Junior High. We walked approximately sixteen blocks every day. The neighborhood consisted of fairly new stick-frame one-story houses costing about eight thousand to twelve thousand dollars. Risley was a sturdy old red-brick structure in need of renovation. I remember the wide hallways lined with lockers and room after room with teachers inside teaching many different subjects.

The school had a music department with instruments in the basement. The orchestra conductor eyed me looking at the instruments. There were flutes, violas, violins, cellos, a bassoon, and many I knew nothing about. He realized I didn't know one from the other. "You look like you have the intelligence to become a good cello player."

I started learning to tune the strings. The A-string was catgut, and I fell in love with the cello bow with horsehair, needing just the right amount of tree resin to produce a beautiful tone.

There was a girl much more advanced to learn from. Her name was Ruthie and I watched how focused she was and how the music affected her whole body. Her wrist curved, then loosened to make mellow, deep, rich tones as the bow moved back and forth over the strings.

A few years later I would be playing the cello with her in the Pueblo Symphony Orchestra. There were no cello players in Pueblo to speak of and they desperately needed us for a concert. The music was advanced, and I remember having the greatest time performing before a big audience, faking my way through the hard parts with aggrandized gestures and emotions. I was careful in trying to keep my bow going in the same direction as everyone else's. The orchestra was so large, I felt secure knowing that less than perfect playing would never be heard. Now I know that the conductor probably heard every bad note!

I would carry the cello home every day and practice for hours. School and home were so different. The noise bothered everyone in the family, including Corky, the next-door neighbor's dachshund who had come to live with us because we gave him so much food and affection.

Corky would lift his head and howl when I played high notes. Everyone would laugh and then complain. I asked for a new cello bow for Christmas, but it never made it under the tree.

Risley had an English teacher who was well known in Pueblo for preparing students to take and pass college-level tests. She was heavy set and threw her weight around. A strict disciplinarian who taught sentence structure with an iron fist. Everyone feared her, even other teachers. She wouldn't tolerate anyone speaking incorrect English and would make students sit in a corner facing the wall when she wasn't happy with something they'd done. When she would temporarily leave to deliver something to other teachers, all hell broke loose. Students would break the chalk and throw erasers out the window. She would come back to a roaring noise followed by complete silence. Nobody would fess up. After that happened a few times, she never left us alone.

Ruthie, my cello-playing friend, was also in the class. We sat across from one another and the two of us became teacher's pets. She would always choose one of us to deliver messages and papers to the principal and other departments. One day she had me leave to plant geraniums. I remember being outside in the back of the school with the sun, feeling peaceful and loved. Hope sprang eternal.

Every Christmas seemed to bring on new drama. I heard "I Saw Mommy Kissing Santa Claus." Then I saw Mommy kissing Chris under the mistletoe in the basement. I was becoming a master detective as I observed a man who came by a little too often to sell Mother groceries and household items from a truck. The company was called Jewel T. He would stare at her Dolly Parton look-alikes, and then start dropping the things he was trying to sell. That poor man didn't realize there was too much fire in those bosoms he was peeking at, and he would get burned if he didn't continue down the road with his truck and bagged groceries.

Life was exhilarating most of the time, except for Mother's extreme mood swings.

We started noticing a change in father ... a distance. But he was a great teacher when he taught us to drive. It was his anchor, his comfort zone. When the winter was too cold to walk to school, my father served as chauffeur. He picked up all of my friends and me at Risley. He was always quiet, and I remember the girls would blush when he opened the door for them.

They would talk in hushed tones about his deep cleft chin.

A wealthy entrepreneur named Buck Owen became interested in my father when Father won awards for being the top salesman at the Buick Cadillac dealership he worked for in Pueblo. Mr. Owen set Father up in his own business, and they remained friends even after my father eventually bought him out. When Buck later died of a heart attack, my father came home with tears in his eyes. Buck Owen was the only person I can recall who ever clearly exercised faith in my father and treated him with admiration and respect. It took a long time for Dad to recover from the death of his friend.

The basement of our house in Pueblo was a large open space without a lot of clutter except for Sheila and Shanda's bedroom. The floor was smooth concrete, painted a high-gloss gray. One time, Mother was alone in the basement, ironing and singing. I only heard her sing that one time. Her voice was so soft and sweet. Most evenings, Daddy sat in his chair with a cigar watching Groucho Marx and laughing.

I had spin-the-bottle parties and would invite about fifteen kids over. We'd sit in a large circle with one person who would spin the bottle in the middle. Whomever the bottle pointed to when it stopped spinning got kissed. If it ended up being someone of the same sex it really didn't matter, it just made it crazier and funnier because you had to kiss them. Then the kissed person sat in the middle and the game continued. We would have the only Black student at Risley join in, but there was a gang of Mexican girls who never came. They would tease their hair into pompadours, where they concealed small knives. Mom and Dad had to pick me up at school one day after I had been cornered in the restroom. Those girls were not good spin-the-bottle candidates!

There was a cool drugstore just a few blocks from school that we all hung out in. When we went there, we knew nothin'. Nothin' but music from the fifties. We would go to the counter and sit on these round red bar-like stools that swiveled around. They had silver studs in them that made them even better. We ordered root beer floats from the soda jerk serving us behind the counter. He was a Jehovah's Witness by the name of Tommy Anderson.

We listened to the jukebox playing "Be-Bop-a-Lula," "Tweedlee Dee," "Earth Angel" with "Great Balls of Fire"; "Twilight Time" — "It's Only Make Believe" because there's "Lipstick on Your Collar." Then we heard Johnnie Ray and his "The Little White Cloud that Cried," and Johnny Angel, like Tommy Anderson, had ducktail hair to die for; both were cute and both were Earth Angels. Well, sort of. They were a few years older than the rest of us, full of energy, totally into music, and loved to make out.

Tommy fell in love with Bobbie and started coming home with her. The whole family took a liking to him. He would dance in our salmon living room to "Rock Around the Clock," "Hound Dog" and "Wake Up Little Susie." His moves were almost as good as Elvis Presley's. Bobbie started skipping school to be with him. My father finally went nuts and plucked Bobbie and Tommy out from under the Fourth Street bridge. All I can say is that young love is strange … it won't give up … it keeps coming back for more, especially when there's resistance.

Television was the new energy plugged into wall sockets. One television, one day at a time, gradually changed culture and the course of history. It blurred one reality and brought in another, revealing global diversity. Privacy slowly eroded, but as we started learning what other lives were like, ours widened.

Television introduced us to Groucho Marx, Hopalong Cassidy, *I Love Lucy* and *Your Hit Parade*. Celebrities came into our household. We knew them intimately. They were with us while we watched from bed or in our living room. I would make up conversations with them in my mind and because I knew their personalities from being around them so much, I just knew how they would answer. Because they had bigger-than-life television-and-movie personas, they would become intimate idols, more perfect than the rest of us. I wanted a boyfriend like Rock Hudson when he was Jane Wyman's gardener in the movie *All That Heaven Allows*. I became obsessed with how movie stars kissed each other. In the movie *The Rains of Ranchipur*, Richard Burton slaps Lana Turner in the face after she becomes hysterical from a poisonous snake preparing to attack her in the bush, then follows with a melting kiss. It was one of the hottest scenes ever. Hysteria, a snake, a slap, and a kiss — all in one frame. Wow was he good at making out! No wonder Elizabeth Taylor married him twice!

As a teenager, I was focused on movie romances like Steve Jobs was probably focused on building computers in his garage a few decades later. His preparation made a fortune.

Meanwhile, I had only sugarplums dancing around in my head.

In the fifties, roughly 6 percent of doctors were women. Mother volunteered at the local hospital to get close to the other 94 percent. A mere three decades before I was born, women weren't allowed to vote and most didn't think about careers. The world was run by men, and for the most part a woman spent her time dreaming about the man who would someday take care of her. What a waste. Mothers would unite with their friends, gather at Tupperware parties, share recipes and small talk about turning their men on with food. This was before aprons were thrown out with bras. At slumber parties we were up all night practicing the latest dance moves, laughing and talking about boys … how to turn them on.

The worst unspoken nightmare for all females was to be left alone, to become an old maid. This was worse than the Cold War threats requiring underground bomb shelters. The Russians are coming! The Russians are coming! We weren't particularly interested in bomb shelters. We were focused on the nearest prince charming, a man in shining armor who would sweep us up onto his black stallion and save us when the Russians came.

I moved on to Centennial High School until my brand-new high school, East High, was built. These high school years were a whirlwind of events for me. I was nominated to the student council, became basketball queen and a year later, football queen, and then starred in the school play — *The Crucible* by Arthur Miller. I became a cheerleader at East High. Oddly, I would come home in disbelief, somewhat tense and uneasy. When I became prom queen, the orchestra played "Pennies from Heaven." Everyone was seated and as I went up to be crowned, with each row I passed, students stood up to honor me. It felt surreal, really out there. I couldn't connect with the celebrity-like experience. It felt like something out of *The Twilight Zone*, like I was dreaming and about to wake up.

In time I concluded that my early instinct of choosing to smile no matter what was my perfect formula for being popular. I decided to treat everyone like they were someone special and not talk about anyone behind their back, and to act like I understood everything.

Life at home was grounded. At least once a week we heard, "As soon as you graduate, you're out of the house."

Bobbie and I started working at Sears after school, and on Saturdays I would clean the house of Eleanor Alt who was a schoolteacher. Her daughter, who had been a Valedictorian at Centennial, was already off to college by the time I started working in their home. Ms. Alt would always entertain me while I was ironing clothes and vacuuming, and we had a lot of fun together. She offered to send me to college. *Thank you, my dear friend.* I still remember, fifty-three years later.

School is the centrifugal life force. Everything stems from there in one way or another. There were always activities listed on the bulletin board. Bobbie and I, along with a neighbor, joined the Civil Air Patrol (CAP). It was held at the hangar near the airport and had a military atmosphere. We were the youngest inductees; the older officers were intellectual, no-nonsense leaders focused on helping others who needed rescue by air. At first I was a total blunderbuss. An officer placed a stone in my hand so I could remember right from left when learning a military drill. That experience matured me.

Bobbie and I went on dates with the cadets from the Air Force Academy in Colorado Springs when they had their yearly dinner dance. For the most part, they had little time for leisure outside of that one scheduled event. A cadet that I did get to know gave me a tour of the entire academy. What I remember most was a large room with nothing but sound equipment. I heard music with clean crispness and rich, vibrating base tones that I had never known existed; I was introduced to quality. I also got a glimpse of the omnipotent power of nature combined with the Air Force Academy's cutting-edge glass cathedral. It was breathtaking.

There was a well-known photographer living in Pueblo by the name of Bob Chinn, who had been on *The Linkletter Show*. Bob would canvas the schools to find photogenic models and was a great contact because the newspapers welcomed his photos. He was always involved with fashion shows and beauty contests. He nudged me into several of them and was the one who paved the way for my modeling career. Also, guys from different schools would find out who I was through Bob and then call me.

Bobbie and I got involved with a group of wild guys from Central High School. They were in a band called John Valente. We went to the prom with two of them and I remember feeling like an outsider. The guy I was with was very sought after by the girls; he played the drums and was a great dancer. Their beautiful prom dresses stared me down on the dance floor.

We took our dates to Grandma's in Gardner a few days later. The trip was loaded with intrigue because of the long drive on Highway 25, which was boring until we turned off onto the narrow red road with cacti and abandoned houses. We then wound our way up to the peaceful isolation of mountains, flowers, and streams. Top it off with a grandmother who lived all by herself, no one within miles of her, who raised cattle, had no electricity, and loved baking pies and talking to young people. In Gardner with Grandma, I always ended up happy. It was the only place I felt really alive.

In my senior year I became involved with a boy named Pierce Ford, whose father was a wealthy business owner in Pueblo. They lived in a beautiful contemporary home overlooking a park. He was cute and popular with the girls. He was the first wealthy boy I dated and would pick me up in a brand-new bright-red Ford truck. During the Christmas holiday he had me over to his house to meet his parents. They had a horse-drawn carriage that we took out after dark. The glistening snow and night air were filled with the sound of bells. It was a fantasy land that I wanted to last forever.

Pierce's father didn't like his son dating someone from the poor side of town. After a while, Pierce started complaining to me about the color of our living room being too bright and about my sisters not speaking proper English. I started correcting everyone's grammar. Pierce Ford was not a date that I would take up to see my grandmother. This started a pattern with me that would last over the years. Later on, when I met my husband, I treated my family the same way. I had some growing up to do. Dolly Parton speaks just like she did when she lived in her childhood home in Tennessee and the whole world embraces her; people are comfortable with her family roots. It makes for good music!

Pierce soon faded out of my life.

We attended church services with Mother at the Episcopal Church of the Ascension, joined the choir and received confirmation. Our whole lives became rich in that we were surrounded by caring people. We served as counselors on church outings held at open-air chapels in the woods, surrounded with the sweet smell of pine trees and church harmonies. The roots of that kind of charmed life must have originated with my mother's patron, Louisa, and her housekeeper, Bertha, who had passed it on to us.

As a child, Mother had played on Louisa's grand piano, which had a spiritual pathway. Hostie, Bertha, Gen and Louisa must have become a choir, though not consciously aware of it. Louisa was Mother's godmother and, in a sense, our Grand Godmother. This part of my life insulated me from drinking, drugging, or smoking. I simply wasn't interested in it. I took pride in being pure and always hung around with girls who were religious, even though there were no Bible readings in our house.

We lived a spicy salt-and-pepper life. Sometimes we would go to the Church of the Ascension, get picked up after singing in the choir, then go to the circus and walk into a big tent to look at "carnival freaks." It was our family entertainment after the formal, sanctimonious service, following the minister down the aisle with the large, jeweled cross in his hand.

Daddy refused to go to church. He had absolutely no interest in anything spiritual. I realized as a teenager, starting my own dating life, that Mother must have been in a state of shock when that pink cloud of early marriage faded away … when they had married, Sophie had no idea what her life would really be like.

The boys I dated, for the most part, weren't pure. They were interested in drag racing on Main Street and "Standing on the Corner" — being cool with a pack of cigarettes folded into the sleeves of their t-shirts. The lucky ones had cars and would pick up girls to take to the drive-in. They would get out of their cars, hang the movie sound speaker on their window and get popcorn for their girls from the refreshment area. Usually scary movies would play, like *Horror of Dracula*. The girls would scream, get close to the guys and then hands would slide under blouses — up, down, sideways, under and over our bras. Everywhere. All in the name of protecting. The good girls made out but wouldn't go all the way.

One day, Grandpa Jesse came to the house unannounced in a shiny new Cadillac. My father hadn't seen his father in eighteen years. He was no longer a preacher and had come back from Missouri to take care of a legal issue. His interest in dropping by seemed to be primarily to take a look at us, his granddaughters. He spent the night, and early in the morning while we were still in bed, he came into the room I shared with Bobbie. We both looked at him in disbelief. The ice-cold reception gave him no opportunity to start a conversation. That was the first and last time we ever saw him. It was hard to imagine Grandma being married to that man.

Bobbie graduated from Centennial and attended a trade school in Omaha to become an airline stewardess. After graduation she was hired by United Airlines. It was the first time I had been away from her. I graduated in 1960 and shortly before leaving home, I started getting frightening telephone calls from what sounded like an older man. He would tell me what time I had arrived home and what I was wearing. I would hang up and he would call back. And then Bob Chinn's studio was broken into and a photograph of me was stolen. The police were called and they monitored the phone conversations. The person wanted to meet me at the movie theater and the police told me what to say and do, but he never showed up.

I left for Denver shortly after graduation. The man was caught a week later, parked in the vacant lot across from our house. It turned out he was married and had children.

In the fifties, in our hometown, almost everyone had trust in the police and all public officials. We looked up to them. They were our heroes. They always protected us and caught the bad guys.

Chapter 5
The Miss USA Pageant

Fast forward to 1962. The Supreme Court had just passed a law banning prayer in public schools. I was standing on stage of the Miss USA Pageant, using my three minutes on national television to tell the world why the star on the flag, representing the state of Colorado, shines brighter than the rest.

Talking about nature took away most of my fear, but I still felt a million butterflies fluttering around inside. "It's the only state where all water flows out … because of the mountains. Nothing flows in!"

Words of waterfalls and flowering meadows spread sacred healing into the large darkened audience around me. For a brief moment I felt as if I was no longer on stage with artificial light, nature's light filled me with energy and joy … I was simply present to share what I had grown to love so much.

The preparation of the pageant was much more practical. Behind the scenes we each had watch dogs coming in and out of our dressing rooms. One girl was found stuffing her bathing suit with toilet paper; she was disqualified. The woman assigned to me was a Cuban refugee. The Cuban missile crisis had not yet made history and she, along with many others, escaped by boat from a tough and challenging homeland most Americans would never experience … in search of a better life in the USA. I felt support from her and remember her proudly pinning the Miss Colorado sash to my bathing suit like she was my mother.

Once adorned with our ribbons, we were all herded out to meet up with a large group of photographers. I felt like the little calf with the Grand Champion ribbon that Grandma had weaned and sold when I was a child prancing around. Cameras clicked away as we paraded along the beach in a long line, with nature providing a beautiful backdrop of the ocean next to the hotel. Finished photos would be released to newspapers throughout the country to provide publicity for the upcoming pageant.

There was no time for making genuine friendships, even though all the women in the pageant seemed to be wholesome and likable. I felt my competitive side when looking at the clothing I was wearing next to theirs. My outfit didn't look new and fresh, but rather like it had a history of many dry cleanings. Each state dressed their contestant and I was the only one without a beautiful dress or gown. I had been driven to a small rental-costume business on the outskirts of Denver to be fitted with a pink cowgirl outfit with matching boots and hat. I remember sitting outside under a palm tree among clusters of girls, feeling like I was part of a beautiful painting ... ruined because I didn't fit in. The painter's brush had unfinished work.

It seemed like my uncomfortable thoughts were addressed immediately after surfacing. I was going up to my room in the crowded hotel elevator with my faded pink cowgirl outfit still on after rehearsal, when one of the judges blurted out, "I put you in the top fifteen." He turned out to be Burt Bacharach's father, a well-known journalist. He said it with bubbling energy like he had fought for me and won. I smiled and thanked him. He had been a gift from God.

During the evening ceremony, the top fifteen contestants were nationally televised and asked different questions relevant to current social issues. The question given to me was, "Do you feel that there should be more government regulations, and if so, why?" My answer was for less government interference and citizens pitching in to help one another rather than depending on the government for everything. Decades later the same question came up — different topics... same fear.

Dr Pepper was one of the sponsors during the pageant that year. The drink was bubbling up everywhere and I loved it. The aftertaste was a little like chocolate and cherries. There were many businesses in the audience looking for a beautiful face. I ended up doing a Pert shampoo commercial that aired shortly after the pageant ended. The exposure would launch me into a new career.

I was in Miami for ten days during the pageant. Every second was filled with preparation for national television. There was no time for reflection. My parents didn't attend but my oldest sister, Bobbie, sat in the audience to support me. I never told my current boyfriend, Jack, about the talent scout who had approached me to try out for Miss Colorado. After winning the title, I ended up in Florida so quickly there had been no time to explain the whirlwind experience that was to follow. Jack found out about it when his mother came across it in the newspaper. He was hurt but came down to surprise me anyway. I remember feeling oddly uncomfortable that he was there and watching me.

Hawaii recently added a new star to the American flag and also ended up winning the crown. Everyone was shocked when Miss Hawaii won, but we wished her well before going our separate ways.

My trip to Denver from Miami involved getting back to work. Since Bobbie was a flight attendant and an excellent employee, it was easy for me to connect with United. When I got my interview, I knew I would have to take an IQ test and remember getting on my knees and praying to God that I would pass. I had trouble taking tests and couldn't remember reading material because of the many anxiety-provoking thoughts that kept me from focusing on what was in front of me. I was popular and people valued me, but I always feared that if people knew how slow my mind was, they wouldn't have anything more to do with me. My negative thinking told me that all my accomplishments in life really meant nothing. These thoughts were a heavy burden and carried over, to some extent, to all areas of my life.

How and when was it determined that the testimony for self-worth is a piece of paper with a high IQ score?

I became a telephone operator for base operations at United Airlines. I would get ballast information, flight configurations, mechanical failures and weather problems from large computers encased in a room of their own and would distribute the information to over sixteen men who controlled United Airlines basic functions. I also got them donuts and coffee every two hours throughout the midnight shift.

My boss, Jim Doty, was a thoughtful, caring man who would serve as a father figure. He watched over me and one time, even made sure that the tires on my car were replaced. He encouraged me to travel abroad and, in the future, stood up for me at my wedding.

People always seemed to set themselves in the foundation of my life when they were needed. Mrs. Mott, Jack's mother, was another example. She was a secretary for a CEO in a large company, and divorced. She was pretty, petite, and intelligent. Her home was small but very sophisticated with stylish décor from the forties. She had an upright piano, and I remember seeing the sheet music for "Moon River" from *Breakfast at Tiffany's*.

Jack was living at home in the basement and had a rectangular fish tank filled with tropical fish in a colorful array of shapes and sizes. It sat parallel to his bed and was approximately the same length. I remember his sheets had a beautiful design of fish complementing those in the tank, and they were crisply ironed without a wrinkle, such a contrast to my upbringing. After being mesmerized by the interesting markings on the fish and the movement of their fins in the water, I remember being picked up in Jack's arms and placed between the sheets as if I were weightless. The fish knew what they were doing; I was swimming around in oblivion. I was in a dark seductive dungeon. He kissed me lightly on the forehead — it felt like a fatherly kiss — and then he made his way down to my lips. He teased me with light butterfly kisses cascading down my neck and then came back up for a few more on my lips. His elegant, relaxed fingers lightly stroked my face then traced along my shoulder and up through my hair, gently going for my mouth to open it wider for the long, deep French kiss.

He spoke in my ear with a soft voice. The sound of him … his words made me weak … "I need you. I need you … I need you now. I know you're having your period. It'll be okay."

His hands slid down my body, removing my underwear. I felt him really close to me on the bed, naked. He cradled my hips, tipped them up to him and found a hot spot. I lost control. I was prepared for the very first time … penetration … bullet shot through flesh. It hurt … but it felt so nice. You do it once, you'll do it twice. Life in that moment was heaven. The aftermath was hell.

Jack's mother invited me over for dinner after she returned from her business trip in Detroit. She was a ball of energy, excited to hear all about my trip to Miami. "I agree with you on having the government out of our lives as much as possible … I also saw you on television doing a Pert commercial! You looked adorable. There was a big close-up of your face. I noticed that you have a tooth a little shorter than the other one next to your front teeth. I'm going to take you to my dentist. He's very good and he will fix it for you."

I looked at her and saw so much joy in her face, joy in wanting to help me. I didn't yet have her sharp, developed eye — I hadn't even seen the uneven tooth — but loved the attention. The dentist was young, handsome, and good. I left his office with a perfect smile.

Jack's Mom would also teach me how to fold stationery properly. I had written her a thank-you note that was at least two pages long after my tooth was capped. "What a beautiful letter I found in the mail from you. I'm going to save it." She went to her desk. "I'm also going to teach you how to fold stationery the proper way. Jack, you watch this too." Her professional hands glided down the cream stationery, folding it with quick artistry and precision. Her fetching personality was entertaining, and like her finely-tuned son, she was spellbinding.

"I saw blood on the sheets downstairs. Did you sleep there while I was gone?"

"Yes."

"Did my son take advantage of you?"

"No."

"Were you a virgin?"

"Yes."

"He's turning out to be just like his father. Did he protect you with a condom?"

"No. I was having my period." I felt such shame. "I'm so sorry. It won't happen again."

I had disappointed this woman whom I had placed on a pedestal. Mrs. Mott had been so loving to me. Her directness and courage to search for truth was somehow calming to me after the initial shock of all the questions. A bond formed between us that didn't include her son.

During our friendship, I never asked any personal questions about her divorce because I knew she would answer me truthfully and I was much more comfortable being in a fog. I didn't want to know the story behind "like father, like son."

A few weeks later, I was brushing my teeth and I gagged on the toothpaste. My entire body felt tingly — oddly ungrounded. When I would lie down to rest, my stomach seemed to adjust … like it was settling after movement. It was telling me that the fire of menstruation hadn't worked; Jack had planted his seed. Nature. Pollination had taken place.

I couldn't go to my mother but remembered a doctor who had become a friend of hers.

My mother and father had gotten to know him when Bobbie ran into the barbed-wire fence in the schoolyard. I'd had the misfortune of watching him when he stitched her up. His fingers were fumbling and unsure. With each pierce in the skin, she let out a scream. I was so glad when he finished. I remember thinking that he didn't seem like a real doctor even though he had an office. Was he another person who had been placed in my life?

I traveled to Pueblo after setting up an appointment. "I can't believe this has happened. I just became Miss Colorado a month ago and will be doing work through the Chamber of Commerce soon. I don't want my mother to ever know about this. Can you help me? I just know I'm pregnant."

I looked at him with grim determination. There was a long pause. His dark-brown beady eyes darted around a little, but the lines around his eyelids were sympathetic and compassionate. "I can't personally do anything, but I've heard of a woman in Gunnison who is an osteopath; she has helped girls in your position. I'll try to find her phone number."

Things happened quickly after that. I didn't tell Jack I was pregnant. Mrs. Mott took me to the Greyhound bus center in Denver. I clearly remember looking down from the bus window at her small, delicate face looking back up at me. The tears in her eyes waved goodbye.

The bus ride was long — a good time for reflection — except there was none. I didn't experience that until many years later. I only knew I didn't want a baby. Babies had offered no value to my parents. Babies had no value to me.

The country outside the town of Gunnison was lush. I watched the many shades of green streaking by, fusing with sprinkles of flowers, making a rainbow of colors in the grass. I was near-sighted and didn't have my glasses on, so it was a Monet painting ... but this was before I knew who he was or learned the technique that blurred his canvases.

The cab driver found the white farmhouse stationed back from the road among a grove of cottonwood trees. We turned in. I knocked on the door to see a face I will never forget, the face of a woman approximately sixty years old with wavy silver hair combed back ... a beautiful, ethereal face with no makeup. I looked into her eyes and knew I would be okay, but I was to pay later for the grace given to me that day.

The foyer was large and smelled of mercurochrome. There was a long table with stacks of what looked like medical records. She said little; I did all the talking. "I've only been pregnant for about a month." I showed her all my newspaper articles from the *Denver Post* and *Pueblo Chieftain*. She read them, then smiled in a disinterested way, laying them down among her many other papers.

She led me to an open back room next to her kitchen where she had prepared a table with sterilized instruments. They were laid out meticulously in a row. There was white starched cloth under them.

I lay down on an operating table and she propped a pillow under my head. "Are your head and neck comfortable at that angle?"

"Yes."

"Are you sure you want to do this?"

"Yes."

She picked up a long instrument that looked like it had a small spoon at the end. "I am going to insert this. It will probably hurt a little as I clean you out." Why were the words so soothing, to have her clean me from the inside out?

"Take a deep breath and relax as much as you can…"

In a very short time it was over. I spent the night in a white bedroom with an open window. I heard the gentle gurgling sound of water outside and though very tired, didn't want it to end with sleep. The song on Mrs. Mott's piano, "Moon River," kept repeating itself over and over in my mind, comforting me into a quiet lull.

Sun filled the room the next morning. There had been no anesthesia, no pills of any kind, not even aspirin the night before.

"Take it easy for a few days. Everything went very well."

I cried — not from sadness, but relief. "Thank you. I'll never forget what you've done for me. How much do I owe you?"

"Whatever you can afford."

I paid her two hundred fifty dollars from the money I'd made from my job with United. It had become clear to me that she would have been willing to perform this dangerously illegal, clandestine task at her own peril and expense, for someone she didn't even know.

The memory of that doctor is deeply etched into my body. The truth is, she performed a procedure that would forever haunt me, yet there is no doubt in my mind that inside of her was an angel. With some people you just know. She was filled with love.

Leaving Gunnison brought new freedom to my life. I was always scheduled to celebrate something new — opening shopping centers, cutting ribbons, breaking champagne bottles on ships — flashbulbs lighting up my world. Store owners would place hats on my head at odd angles, skirts around my waist and shoes on my feet. I would model them and smile for the cameras. I also had the job of giving Mr. Universe his trophy for having the most developed muscular frame. He was scary looking up close. I wasn't used to seeing muscles being flexed and veins popping out like that. Men working on a farm didn't do that.

I lived with my sister Bobbie in Aurora and felt I was a burden to her. When I received the shocking news that base operations at United would be moving to a suburb outside of Chicago, I could tell she was relieved that I would be separating from her, moving east and embarking on a new life.

The plane ride to Chicago was beautiful, filled with golden rays from the late afternoon sun. I had fallen asleep on the flight after catching up on *Dick Tracy* and *Superman* in the newspaper. I wondered if the creator of *Superman* realized the tremendous influence he had on our culture when the image blossomed in his imagination. How it would evolve, gaining momentum with each generation, creating an idealized man with supernatural powers, regarded as the ultimate goal of male evolution.

Part of this momentum caused some of the pageant contestants to have plastic surgeons disassemble and rearrange their bodies — removing ribs to make waists smaller, reshaping noses, performing breast implants and liposuction along with belly button tucks, so curves would be curvy and firm while at the same time appearing soft and seductive. Even the public was corralled into the beauty market, thinking they had to compete in some international contest of their own to be sculpted into the perfect image of their icon. Some would fly to Brazil for the latest butt lift to get the hottest booty. Even more bizarre, America was becoming a nation of obesity. This led to eating disorders of anorexia and bulimia, as well as stomach surgery and de-bulking through suction and excision. These images would continuously show up on my living room television. I was consumed with information overload. I would need a new, clean channel for knowledge within this surreal glimpse of life.

My youth gradually faded away after reigning as Miss Colorado, but the state's beauty remained. It would stand alone for many years, winning the title for being the healthiest state in the country. Homegrown Colorado citizens had the lowest obesity and the highest vitality, yet it was fertile ground for some of the worst crimes in history. *Why does evil always attack the stronghold?* Colorado's pristine quality attracted the rich and famous. They would construct beautiful homes using nature to help lift themselves up onto Aspen's highest peaks of prestige.

I took off in the opposite direction, with new stilettos that would click on the sidewalks of Chicago flatlands. I built a greenhouse that sprouted boy-crazy buds, meeting on blind dates with the flower generation of the 1960s.

Chapter 6
New Beginnings

The group of girls I worked with at United were assigned to take care of an all-man crew. The company hired an interesting mix of characters to serve them. One of the girls, Penelope, was originally from England and had been a professional ice skater. She was cute and had a pixie haircut and an English accent that became much thicker when talking to boys on the phone. We were all between the ages of nineteen and twenty-three and lived together in a large apartment complex in Des Plaines for about six months. We worked rotating day, afternoon, and midnight shifts.

Another girl by the name of Peggy looked a little like Audrey Hepburn but had a very bad acne problem. She would clear it up with a pink lotion she wore around the house during the day that would dry on her skin like a thin rubber mask. She had a boyfriend who was crazy about her but she always seemed to develop a crush on *my* boyfriends. Jack was one of them; he had also been transferred from Denver.

Peggy would see him going to the parking lot after work in his trench coat, collar up just so and a cigarette hanging from his mouth like Humphrey Bogart. She'd go crazy over him just like her boyfriend was going gaga over her. She would talk about Jack's full, pouty lips. She didn't know my history with him or the spark she was rekindling — moth to the flame. Her father had been a drunk and disappeared when she was six. Her boyfriend had been employed by the CIA and he finally gave up on her because she couldn't commit. He flew back to Washington, DC and Peggy became obsessed with getting him back. It was like she was always looking, yearning … a constant craving for something she couldn't have while discarding what she did have on a cold night, when she really needed it.

My other roommate was like a den mother. She was overweight, didn't date and had great insight into people. Someone called me an airhead when I left the room one time, and I overheard her say, "I saw that smile she had on television. It wasn't the same as it is here. She's sly like a fox."

Was she right? She was about the smile. I had read about Marilyn Monroe lowering her smile because too much of her top gums showed and I decided to try the same thing. At the time, I secretly liked what she had said about me being like a fox.

We were all different, carefully checking one another out, but since I had grown up with three sisters, those roommates filled a void I would have suffered from otherwise. Now I had the gift of new sisters to explore. We all got along quite well, mostly because we were to go our separate ways fairly quickly.

United had good benefits for its employees and paid well. I bought a powder-blue Triumph Spitfire and would drive it on the expressway. My plan was to attend John Robert Powers Modeling School where I had won a scholarship for winning Miss Colorado. I called one of the three biggest agencies in Chicago and was told it was unnecessary to go to school. They preferred to send me to photographers for test shots. I would need a portfolio to get started.

Al Seaman's Agency gave me a list of Chicago photographers after I signed an exclusive contract with them. They took me around town and introduced me to clients. I spent my days off going to auditions. Before long my agent asked if I would consider quitting my job with the airline to model full time; they would guarantee the same amount I was making. I talked it over with my boss thinking he would discourage me, but it was just the opposite. He said he thought it would be hard to get promoted unless I switched to another department, and I would have many more opportunities in modeling. He recommended I make the transition gradually. I enjoyed both jobs so it was an exciting time for me, but I ended up working almost nonstop.

Chicago was fairly easy to get around as I went on bookings for commercials, catalogs, newspaper, and magazine ads. I would go shopping at Marshall Field's buying the clothing I needed for different jobs such as a housewife standing next to a refrigerator or stove.

Playboy was the only major magazine published in Chicago that booked a lot of models.

I was tested for a cover right away, driving a bright-red sports car convertible down a Chicago alleyway. The cover wasn't used, but it started a professional courtship.

I met a woman by the name of Marilyn Grabowski who worked closely with Hugh Hefner.

Hefner had received a degree from the Chicago Art Institute, became an entrepreneur and planted one of the seeds of the sixties' sexual revolution by creating what turned out to be an iconic magazine. He filled it with art, politics and culture and placed Marilyn Monroe on the cover. She was and still is the personification of male sexual fantasy. Hefner had been clever, buying photos of her prior to launching the magazine, which became an overnight success in 1953. Years later, Marilyn Monroe is still so embedded in his psyche, I've heard he has plans to be buried beside her. I wonder if the rest of his family will be buried next to them.

Hefner's daughter, Christie, was only a year old when his business started to take off. By the time I started going in for bookings, she was working for the magazine — a pretty brunette, neatly groomed young woman, with a no-nonsense hairdo; always hovering over the books while running the office like a well-oiled machine.

The employees at *Playboy* were all educated and business oriented. There was never even a hint of lewd or lascivious behavior. It was always a fun, entertaining atmosphere with an abundance of creative people. I enjoyed doing advertising for *Playboy* within the magazine and at parties, introducing new Bunny Clubs, and promos that included atmospheric shots. I was usually booked by a photographer named Larry Dale Gordon and would get up at one o'clock in the morning to be at the beach along with Hugh Hefner's party guests. We waited for the sun to rise; sometimes it would be magical with many layers of color tinting the sky. If it wasn't, there would be a re-shoot.

Those were special times in Chicago. There was something downright exhilarating about being with a crew of all-nighters and then experiencing the humid dawn of Lake Michigan. Our faces glowed. Nature's first light and *Playboy* together made life seem surreal. I worked with many photographers over time but Larry Gordon became a real friend. He was drop-dead gorgeous — tall with dark wavy hair, clean, all-American looks and an easy-going personality. I didn't realize when I first saw him, with his long, slender legs in Levi's, walking around Hugh Hefner's studio with a handheld camera, that it was my first introduction to a real urban cowboy! Click … a photographic memory to last a lifetime.

I did a fashion spread with Larry in a secluded, wooded area wearing mini-dresses. It was summer and the outfits had flirting cutouts at the waistline front and back — a circle around my belly button allowed light and Larry's camera eye to wander down my silhouette, to compliment waist curving into hipline. Slight dimples on either side down my lower back filled with shadow … masterful light for a sensual photograph.

This caught the attention of Hugh Hefner and he sent a memo to Marilyn Grabowski asking if I would do a centerfold. Prior to this, I had done innocent, all-American modeling, and dresses with peek-a-boo holes were as racy as I got. I was shocked that he'd asked, even though from his point of view it was simply what he'd seen and wanted to see more of. Duh! Shortly after that, he booked me at his beautiful Chicago townhouse along with two other girls for a shoot in his bedroom. I remember sitting in the center of the room on a large round bed covered in red velvet. It was revolving and I was getting dizzy. As the bed turned it revealed a fascinating room filled with deliberate, eclectic décor. I half expected to see Hugh Hefner and his pipe suddenly pop out from one of his closets or to see his image in the mirrored ceiling.

Hugh Hefner and I never met face to face. To me he was the phantom of the *Playboy* empire — a ghost who appeared unexpectedly at night with his pajama-party outfit on. I later saw photographs of him winding down a long staircase from his bedroom, creating fantasy — unforgettable iconic imagery in the minds of men and teenage boys all over the world.

Even though I turned down the offer to do the centerfold, I ended up doing five covers for *Playboy*. One was on the beach with several other girls. In another, my face was a bunny with my hair held up in the shape of bunny ears. My other covers were equally as innocent — one flying a bunny kite, another with freckles on my face and one the shape of ... you guessed it — a bunny!

I got my first booking with photographer Victor Skrebneski, who lived on LaSalle Street across from Carl Sandburg apartments where I eventually moved. His studio was hidden from view, next to a parking lot with a trendy bar called Al Welsh's. In the future, I would never be able to completely free myself from the unforgiving cement quicksand my high heels sunk into on the path called Skrebneski Way.

I opened the door to what I thought was the photographer's studio and met up instead with a nice-looking young man wearing green scrubs and a bronze tan. "I'm looking for Victor Skrebneski."

His burnt-sienna eyes flashed back at me with a wave of diverse, intense energy. "You've got the wrong building. This is a sanatorium. It's right behind here."

"Oh, I'm so sorry."

"Don't be. This has happened before."

A client of mine would later give this man my phone number, thinking we'd make a good match.

The events occurring within this one block radius — the meeting of this well-known photographer hidden from traffic on LaSalle Street, a civil rights fire with Molotov cocktails, the sound of breaking glass on Wells, and an accidental meeting at the sanatorium — would all end up permanently changing who I was.

Victor's studio was not impressive on the outside. Even the ironwork was nondescript. In contrast, walking into his immaculate black-and-white studio was intimidating. I knew I had entered another world that only the privileged had access to. The entire space had a sharp-edged coolness that matched the woman sitting at the desk. Her name was Jovanna. She was tall and large-boned with defined muscles — a handsome Greek. You had to get past Jovanna to get to Victor. She was like a big stern bodyguard who flawlessly organized his day-to-day schedule.

Victor didn't like to talk much (forget socializing) and Jovanna's presence together with the icy atmosphere kept me on my toes with nervous energy which I hid well. He had booked me to do a back-to-school ad for Marshall Field's. It appeared in the *Chicago Tribune* five days later. After that he continued to book me a couple of times a week for newspaper ads. I'd never met anyone like him. He wasn't much taller than I was, small-boned with an Adonis presence. He had perfect proportions, a chiseled face with beautiful wavy brown hair and a refined haircut where locks would rise and fall in exactly the right places. My heart would jump whenever I saw him.

Victor was thrilling. He filled me with dreams. He was always dressed the same way, in freshly pressed Levi's, a matching shirt and loafers. *Women's Wear Daily* was always a fixture in his studio. Jovanna seemed to represent his cold and mean side, and he was then free to be slightly silly and flirty. He would pop into the dressing room with beautiful blue teasing eyes, like he always had a funny joke to play on me. I had a face that looked like I'd come fresh off the farm, and he knew I didn't know what was happening, especially on the mean streets of Chicago. Almost all the other models he used were taller, more gaunt looking and street smart, tailored for *Harper's Bazaar* and *Vogue*. Because I was different, he seemed to delight in wanting to remake or reinvent me. "Get rid of the bangs." "I want your hair back from your face."

On set he used only one large round light source, a GE 1000-watt incandescent bulb. It was covered with white butcher paper, which filtered flattering light into the beautiful faces of revolving door women who entered daily. One sentence of instruction was the norm for all of us.

He preferred black-and-white photography over color. The dark room was his companion.

That was where he magnified the delicate interplay between shadow and light. He did all of his own retouching on photographs, and when his first book, *Skrebneski*, was released, I was surprised to find out that he was mostly self-taught. He was Chicago's Richard Avedon and once he started working with a model, it separated them from the others.

During the time I was modeling, it was rare to have a hairdresser or makeup artist. I remember ironing outfits at Victor's studio that I wore for Marshall Field's. One time he asked me to put my false eyelashes on upside down. It was for a film he was experimenting with, out in left field somewhere. It was the only time Victor seemed to lack focus. It was during the era when Andy Warhol's slow-motion underground films surfaced and were shown in commercial theaters. Was Victor influenced by them? He got spooked after viewing his own work and scrapped it. I had never known him to waste time and money on special projects. But one thing I do know ... I looked weird. He took one look at me and burst out laughing. Our bonding was childlike silliness and we would get the giggles together. It was those moments when I was convinced he had become attracted to me.

Victor hung out with Bruce Gregga, an interior designer. The ambiance of their surroundings taught me style, compositional balance in art, and sartorial acumen. I began to pursue designs by Le Corbusier, Mies van der Rohe and Marcel Breuer to place in my home. I also learned from him the art of sensuality — how to shyly tease, quietly draw in heartstrings and then not deliver ... all good for the camera and Victor was a master.

When I first started working for him, a rumor floated around that he had gotten involved with his favorite female model. He suddenly stopped using her and she was never seen around again. I lived to be at his studio, and for that reason I was always walking on eggshells — careful not to do anything but please him professionally.

I remember one day when we shot five outfits in one hour with neither of us saying a word. "Angie" by the Rolling Stones was playing in the background and it was like we were doing a contemporary ballet together. All the steps were choreographed. I would move and he would shoot. If Victor wanted my hair changed or the collar of a blouse adjusted around my neckline, he would walk up and place his hands on me in the most loving way. He would just take my breath away. The turn-on for him was to find composition in a photo using a fluid model to emote, curve, bend, and shape into a stunning art form. When the booking was over, he would simply walk out of the room. Never was there a hi, goodbye or thank you.

There was an iron spiral stairway leading from the studio to his home on the second floor. Every once in a while we would use it for a background in a photograph. The entire floor was white veinless Carrera marble with what looked like original Greek Corinthian columns sitting on it. His bathroom commode was made of gold contrasted with black marble. The living-room area, which led to an outside terrace with an iron railing, had a spacious, sparsely decorated Art Deco feel to it.

One time he threw a party for some male friends who had just flown in from England. It was held on the main floor of his studio and, looking back on it, I was a lollipop prop. I was standing below his staircase with a drink in my hand and lofty dreams in my head. Suddenly he came out of nowhere and kissed me gently on the lips, then walked away. I was stunned, but watched his body language as he turned. It changed back into the shy, don't-touch-me posture I was used to in the studio during the day. During the party we talked a little. He told me that he'd once had a Rolls-Royce and it drove like a truck, so he got rid of it. Sharing that with me was major intimacy! By that time, my powder-blue Triumph Spitfire had been upgraded because a boyfriend told me it was a piece of junk and recommended I buy a white 911 Porsche Targa.

Maybe he was impressed with that?

When I went home that night, I remember placing my hand on the telephone. I longed to call Victor and ask why he kissed me and to tell him I was falling in love with him. Had the party become more exclusive in the upper room and terrace that I wasn't a part of? Why had he given me his private phone number? I never dialed it. Down deep I knew the truth. I was now his favorite model. Wanting more than that would ruin my career.

We did shoots on location only six or seven times. He preferred the comfort of the studio where he had control over both light and wind. One time after a shooting, we were alone in a cab together. I remember sitting next to him feeling electricity between us. I lingered there, waiting for him to make a move before opening the door to get out, but he never budged. Our private moments were an emotional cat-and-mouse game.

Just as soon as I locked my feelings away there would be a little note scribbled on my daily release voucher. "Pretty Penny, be careful while you're driving. Love, Victor."

Then there was a time when he had seen me on television modeling furs for a morning show. It just so happened that the camera man took a liking to me that day. I must have really looked good. I remember Victor's eyes sparkling when he told me he had seen me on television, and again my heart started opening up. Then two weeks later I heard from Jovanna that he'd gone to California to shoot Vanessa Redgrave on location. When I saw him a couple of days after he returned, the sparkle in his eye was for Vanessa. It was the only time I ever saw him without his feet firmly touching the ground. He ran all over the set showing the photographs to everyone. He placed them high on the wall, along with many women from Estée Lauder ads he was fond of. There was also a shot of Audrey Hepburn and me with another girl doing a hair ad. The wall set us apart, yet placed us together as "elevated" women.

In the hallway, Victor also had a huge black-and-white nude of what looked like a male boxer. Sharply contrasting light and shadow bathed his muscular frame, drawing attention to the beauty, power, and energy of the male body each time you walked past.

I didn't work for a single female photographer during my entire career. Men controlled the puppet-on-a-string actions during booking time: "Turn your head a little to the right ... look up ... separate your legs a little ... more ... Great. Straighten out the right collar. Turn your inner thighs into the light ... yes, right there. Now come on to me ... beautiful ... straight into the camera!"

I was booked on the West Coast for a hair commercial with a man named Fred Glaser. He was Barbra Streisand's hairdresser; very nice looking and bisexual. We became close from frequently working together and eventually got involved. Victor found out about it and told me to stay away from Fred, that he was dangerous. Fred was becoming famous; he had recently opened a hair salon and the press was all over it. The hair dryers were raised to different levels in a wide-open space, looking like pods on a Ferris wheel. It was unique, impressive, and only open for a short time. Fred suddenly left town. No one knew why. We wouldn't see one another again until years later, in New York City.

Soon after I received a surprise phone call … the man who had answered the door at the sanatorium was on the other end of the line. He had just finished medical school at the University of Illinois and would be graduating in a couple of weeks in the top 10 percent of his class. He had considered being a psychiatrist but felt uncomfortable with that specialty and switched to Otorhinolaryngology (ear, nose and throat or ENT). His father was from Czechoslovakia and his mother from Italy, both with humble beginnings. They were a stable, loving Catholic family experiencing new life in America. He did a lot of talking on that first phone call. When there was a pause in the conversation, I invited him to a party I was planning that week for two of my roommates celebrating birthdays.

I was working the afternoon shift at United which ended at eleven o'clock. By the time I got off work, most of the guests had been drinking for three hours. I opened the door and the first thing I saw was my roommate Peggy sitting on the floor against the wall. She had on a light-pink crepe mini-dress that was very pretty, and she was drunk. My new friend from the sanatorium, who had revealed his entire history a few days earlier, was on the floor with her. His arm was around her waist and a hand on her thigh. Her dress was hiked up almost to her panty line. I was stunned. Peggy never drank around the house. We'd had conversations about alcoholism and the pain it inflicts. My date for the evening had been enjoying her vulnerability and beautiful legs. I laughed and shrugged it off on the outside. After all, everyone was just having a good time. I had gotten there late and hadn't been a part of it.

Before the evening was over, my date asked me if I liked mushrooms. He wanted to sauté some for me the next night, so we agreed to meet for dinner. He then leaned me up against the refrigerator, getting close to my face.

"I think we have something special together." He didn't have long to cast me in a spell. It was only three months before he had to do his internship in San Francisco and he didn't waste any time.

In the evenings, he'd pick me up after he finished work at the sanatorium, where his job was to pick up wealthy drunks and dry them out temporarily. We spent an evening at Al Welsh's bar, which was located right next to Victor's. Al Welsh's was a dark one-room secret hideout with a jukebox filled with jazz. My date prided himself in knowing the latest, coolest jazz artists who "just the elite were familiar with." He preferred a blend of offbeat Brazilian — Stan Getz, Charlie Byrd, Dave Brubeck, and Santana. "Black Orpheus" was added to the mix. He needed to educate me. I knew nothing of jazz at the time and it impressed me, the way he loved the music. I felt elevated, learning from this smart, educated, cultured doctor. I watched his darkened silhouette as he lit a cigarette, finished his wine and recited to me.

"Remember this: In Greek mythology there was a musician whose magic ability on the lyre affected animals, and even rocks and trees. His wife, Eurydice, died and he obtained her release from the underworld on the condition that he would not look at her until they reached the upper world." Part of his knowledge came from the 1959 Cannes Film Festival where a "haunting narrative of the Orpheus was told against the backdrop of Mardi Gras in Rio, where African rhythms fused together to make contemporary Brazilian music. Only the intellectually elite could fully appreciate the special quality in the blend of Latin with African rhythm tapped with the American jazz of Vince Guaraldi."

Going to his graduation from medical school at the University of Illinois was awesome! I met his entire family at his aunt's house afterward, and fell in love with his parents and grandmother. Being on campus, watching him walk across the stage and switch his tassel from one side to the other was something I felt I couldn't do. He was a young man from a fairly poor background, graduating at the top of his class. I was proud of him, but it only made me doubt myself more.

I met him in San Francisco where he moved for his residency. He had planned everything in great detail for the entire week I was there. We went to Mount Tamalpais for the day, before driving up sparkling hills in his open convertible to Twin Peaks magic in the night. I stayed with him and his two roommates. They were all smokers, edgy, and seemed to live life in the fast lane. I fixed all of them breakfast, bacon and eggs, but I was uncomfortable. I was still a wholesome girl at heart. I tried to hide my uneasy feelings.

My boyfriend didn't like my prim and proper behavior; he wanted to loosen me up. He mentioned when we were alone that he wanted me to dress "more tweedy." I guess that meant more casual. He also told me that as a doctor's wife I would have to be more sociable (the word networking wasn't used at that time).

After returning home from San Francisco, I waited for and cherished his letters. I saved every single one. He would express concern about how hard I was working. He also asked if I could lend him fifty dollars for something he needed, and that it wouldn't be long before he would be making a lot more money.

Many doctors have handwriting that is barely legible, but his handwriting was architecture in print, every letter in majestic uppercase like an interesting building, a tall cathedral with complex capital columns. I got hooked. It was the energy of his words as he scripted those beautiful letters on call in the middle of the night at San Francisco General Hospital. They contained information about his city, San Francisco, the magic of her nights, statistics on how she lured in the highest suicide rate and collected desperate people seeking the last oasis for happiness.

I looked forward to each day's mail; I was seduced with each new letter. One ended with, "I have miles to walk before I sleep … miles to walk before I sleep." Robert Frost had said it first, but it didn't matter. The words were from him. They never left my mind and dropped down deep in my soul. In time, writing from the emergency room while on call at all hours of the night slowed down. We were starting to feel the distance of being apart for almost a year.

I received a booking in Europe and, because of the duration of the trip, I had to quit my job with United Airlines. The modeling assignment was with International Hairdressers, a team of four men and women creating haircut trends worldwide for the following year. My personal hairdresser was a woman named Joanne and she was good at creating hairdos that were flattering to my face. There was another hairdresser named David who I was very attracted to and came very close to having an affair with. I also had the pleasure to meet and briefly talk with Dave Brubeck only a few months after being enlightened about his jazz. He and Paul Desmond happened to be staying at the same hotel while we were both working in Basel, Switzerland.

Our team went on to Madrid, where my passport was stolen. The American Embassy had to be called in order to get me back into the United States. When I arrived home I saw that the *New York Times* had written an article covering the photos of hair trends for the following year.

Upon my return I moved to Carl Sandburg apartments on LaSalle Street in Chicago. My new roommate was a sophisticated German businesswoman who had heirloom vases she placed on the windowsills. They complemented the beautiful view of the city. Life was good even though I had no quiet time.

Carl Sandburg had a sunroof where tenants would socialize. I met a man by the name of Harvey Goldman who had a friend named Ellen. She was a gourmet cook and they often invited me for dinner. She wouldn't just fry chicken. After crisping, it would go into the oven at a low temperature, baked to melting-in-your-mouth perfection. I had never tasted food prepared with so much love. For some odd reason she seemed interested in getting Harvey and me together. He worked for Helene Curtis and we started spending many evenings together as friends.

My boyfriend came back from San Francisco and began spending the night too frequently to please my roommate. She didn't take a liking to him. Sometimes he would cross from the sanatorium and go up to the sunroof when I was out modeling. I found out later from him that one afternoon Ellen and Harvey happened to be up there, talking about me and the fun we all had at dinner, along with some personal tidbits. Like Easter Sunday when we went to a college campus in Wisconsin. Harvey mentioned I had become tired, placed my head on his shoulder and fell asleep that way coming back in the car. They had no idea the person listening to them on the roof was involved with me, and the chance encounter would expedite the marriage proposal.

The next day my boyfriend came over. "I've stopped jumping through bay windows.

You're a great lady and I'd like to spend the rest of my life with you."

The time with Ellen and Harvey dwindled, and this made Harvey pursue me more aggressively. He left a dozen roses at my door one day, and the next day I came home to find a big Helene Curtis hair dryer blocking the entranceway.

My fiancé was not impressed. "If that guy doesn't leave you alone, I'm going to do something. I'm not going to let him hurt you."

By this time, I was really busy modeling, with no time to do much else. My fiancé admired my work ethic, my stability, that I had national exposure on television and that I was working with Victor several times a week. What he didn't know was that Victor had become my god. We had just finished shooting a sensual hair commercial that ran during the NFL series and he told me how sexy I looked!

Chapter 7
Distant Rumblings

About six months after leaving United Airlines, Al Seaman's Agency recruited me to do a commercial for them. I also did one for General Motors. It was shot inside an all-glass high-rise building. I had a large painting under my arm while sliding into a roomy Chevrolet. The commercial aired frequently during the series *Bonanza* and my family would look forward to viewing it weekly. Chicago was good to me! Commercials included Evans Furs, Florsheim Shoes, United Airlines and many others.

Twiggy, the model from England, would be visiting the Windy City, and I would be photographed with her for the *Chicago Tribune*. All of this exposure came to the attention of Wilhelmina Cooper, owner of Wilhelmina Models. She contacted me to come to New York.

That same week, I took my first zippy yellow pill as I was cleaning the apartment at Sandburg. I thought nothing of it at the time, but one sip of water permanently changed the direction of my future. I got one of my roommate's expensive round bowls from the window, filled it with pink water made from food coloring and added floating candles and flowers. My roommate wasn't thrilled with my behavior and didn't appreciate my intense pleasure in what I had concocted. I was like a newborn puppy following the zippy pill around, playfully rolling over belly up, vulnerable and tickled with what would become my new master. I didn't have a clue what this new pattern of false energy would cause long term. Over time I started looking forward to being in the state where eating food wasn't needed. The pill's energy was abundant and satisfying, boosting my passion for whatever I was doing in the moment. One pill was fuel for twelve hours. It was incredible!

My fiancé wrote a beautiful letter to my parents, asking them for my hand in marriage. We decided to get married in East Moline, Illinois, where he had been raised in the Catholic Church. My father was upset I wasn't having the wedding in my hometown and prejudice reared its ugly head. "I'm not going inside any *Catlicker* church"; the term must have come from his father. He also didn't like that my fiancé was half Italian. In the end he refused to come to the wedding.

My fiancé and I met with the Catholic priest for three sessions. The priest explained responsibilities and loving gestures that become part of a successful marriage. I remember feeling guilty about having had an abortion. Later, it came out. My fiancé needed to know what I'd done. He responded like I had briefly pulled off an expressway, taken the exit ramp to a rest stop and gotten back on the road again. It simply didn't matter to him. I was so relieved!

We found a nice apartment at 3950 North Lake Shore Drive. Two days later, after we were married, I was booked for six weeks doing bathing suits and junior dresses for Montgomery Ward in New York City. Before I left, Victor told me I should switch from Seaman Agency to a new agency called A+. I did it without asking why. Al Seaman was puzzled and hurt, but whatever Victor said, I did. While I was gone, my husband attended a medical convention in Dallas, Texas. That too, had implications I wasn't yet aware of.

When I returned from my trip, I received a phone call. There was a woman on the other end of the line asking for my husband. "Who am I speaking with?"

"This is Penny, his wife."

There was a long pause. "Oh, I didn't realize he was married when I met him in Dallas.

I'm sorry." She hung up.

When my husband arrived home he had a beautiful gift for me from Neiman Marcus. "A woman from Dallas called asking for you. You didn't tell her you were married."

Another long pause as his eyes fell to the ground. "I would never, ever do anything to hurt you."

One moment in time; marriage without trust. The incident wasn't mentioned again.

A few weeks later, we drove to Woods Hole and took the ferry over to Martha's Vineyard. While approaching the shoreline we saw colorful Victorian houses. Mesmerizing widow's peaks seemed to jump out at me. I could feel past times when young, beautiful women would longingly wait for their husbands to return home after long, grueling days at sea, fighting the waves for food that would later be placed on their table.

One of my husband's patients rented us their vineyard property located along Menemsha Pond. We stayed in a white farmhouse surrounded with daisies as far as the eye could see. I fell in love with the area. The remoteness and purity of the land reminded me of my grandmother's, especially that little section of land where wild roses bloomed along the road, though much of the terrain was different. There was a stretched-out, clean white sand beach with a huge lighthouse to look up to. Menemsha Pond had a unique personality of its own with jagged rocks, sea creatures and barnacles I had never seen before. The pond habitation was totally foreign to me, like exploring another world. I wanted to linger there, underwater with my new mysterious friends. Just like in those early summers at Grandma's, I never wanted to leave.

We drove toward Zach's Cliff and ate at a restaurant that served only lobster. We wore big bibs to protect our clothing as we dipped our lobster in melted butter. Afterwards, we returned to Zach's Cliff, home to a nude beach with large pockets of clay climbing up the ridges. People would rub the clay all over their bodies. Jacqueline Kennedy Onassis later bought the entire area of the beach for her and her family's personal use, and it would no longer be available to the public.

I didn't want to take my clothes off and felt really uncomfortable being there. My husband had his camera and was aggressively taking photos of a tall, beautiful woman adorning the beach. I felt a gnawing separateness being next to him without clothes, like an endangered walking stick bug.

"You've got to open up more, like a free spirit."

I remember I finally got clothed in a blanket of fog. I was relieved … the Sympathetic One had covered my shame.

After we had been married for about a year and a half, my husband became ill with the flu. It was around New Year's and I remember the night before watching him at a party with a tall dark-haired girl who was engaged to a lawyer we met at Al Welsh's.

Whenever he drank, his behavior was hurtful but I was careful not to show vulnerability.

I remember him with a terrible cough and congestion the next day. He was out of work for three days and always seemed a little embarrassed about being sick. I was relieved and happy to have him at home and in our bedroom.

"I have a heart murmur. I'm going to stop smoking." He said it half-jokingly, but after that he did stop.

During my marriage, Victor continued his provocative, flirty playfulness and seemed impressed I was doing so much work in New York City. My husband was planning a facial plastic-surgery practice in Chicago. He had two colleagues that had established themselves as highly talented surgeons. They knew how to use a scalpel to carve elegant noses that didn't look "done." He learned from them how the angles of each face could direct the shape of what a perfectly proportioned nose should look like.

Dr. Phillip was not considered politically correct, so celebrity status never reached him the way it did others. Dr. Roger and my husband ended up being world-renowned facial plastic surgeons, with Dr. Roger frequently asked to speak at plastic-surgery conferences. Jealousy between facial plastic surgeons and general plastic surgeons raged as many otorhinolaryngologists performed ENT procedures without being board certified as plastic surgeons typically were. It was highly unusual at that time for the crossover to take place.

I eventually set Dr. Phillip up with Jovanna. He was intense and complicated, with coarse salt-and-pepper hair and an offbeat personality.

In social settings, Dr. Phillip could be assertive and charming, confident even, but at times that persona would change in an instant; a fleeting thought might cause his chin to recede and his feisty spirit to disappear. Dr. Phillip must have struggled with inner conflict and confusion, which often robbed those around him of his true authenticity.

He had an endearing smile that would sometimes get squirrelly, making it difficult to know exactly what he was thinking, but I remember he had a passion for opera. I thought he and Jovanna made a handsome couple but the evening turned out awkward and they ended up as good friends. Because he was a single doctor, many women pursued him and we double dated with a long string of those women while enjoying Chicago's nightlife. Second City Comedy Club was one of our hangouts. We generally bypassed Rush Street neighborhood bars like Butch McGuire's, even though it had become hip because people experimented with "poppers" there. (Poppers were amyl nitrites in small glass ampoules wrapped in a cloth.) We as a group were too high-minded to follow that kind of crowd. We were best-seat balcony elites with new, high-power opera glasses.

My husband got front-row tickets to see Herb Alpert and the Tijuana Brass at the McCormick Place Convention Center. We were enjoying the concert when I smelled something burning. No one else detected the odor so it wasn't mentioned again. The next morning my new agency A+ called to tell me my morning appointment was canceled. The McCormick Place Convention Center had burned down; there had been an electrical fire inside the walls. This was the first of many fires that I would narrowly miss.

Dr. Phillip eventually began dating a beautiful model named Paulette, who had also done a cover for *Playboy*. Once in a while, a model's face is so stunning, even if she does not possess the height or perfect model's body. A photographer might pursue her for her face only, and this was true of Paulette. Victor used her in his book, *Skrebneski*, and Dr. Phillip, after just a few months of dating, asked Paulette to marry him.

My husband was required to serve in the Armed Forces for two years. Because I was booked so much in New York City, he joined the

Navy Medical Corps and enrolled into what was called the Berry Plan at St. Alban's in Queens. He became a Lt. Commander and looked handsome in his naval attire. We planned to return to Chicago when his tour of duty ended.

We received an invitation to Dr. Phillip and Paulette's wedding just as we were placing a down payment on a beautiful old townhouse with seven fireplaces near Grant Park. We flew from LaGuardia to Chicago for the wedding, but Dr. Phillip didn't show up. No one knew where he was. Paulette and the rest of us were left standing there. After about two hours we said goodbye to Jovanna and the other guests we knew and went to see the brownstone. We found out that the owner no longer wanted to sell it. This was disappointing, but I decided it was not meant to be.

Before catching the plane back to New York, we spent our last few hours at the Art Institute of Chicago. It was here that I had my first introduction to Georges Seurat. He shaped life by filling canvas space with delicate, organized tiny dots of color. The paintings had a serene, calming effect, the antithesis of what could be used to paint a picture of the life we were living in … except in my imagination where the dots burst from the frame like shrapnel in a decade without boundaries — Timothy Leary spotted next to Allen Ginsberg, and in the opposite direction, a little Woodstock speck of a town became famous worldwide. Andy Warhol's underground smoking gun moves into the scene alongside *Easy Rider* drifters with motorcycle attitudes: *I know it all. I'm young. I'm making up my own rules. Get out of my way.*

A dotted, psychedelic whirlwind appears, bringing a montage of ménage à trois ingredients: open marriage, marijuana, LSD, Dexedrine, and birth control pills: an unprecedented sexual revolution gone wild. Gasoline absorbed in a rag ignites the civil rights movement, creating a fiery paint that spreads to later generations. A tornado unexpectedly roars through an unstable atmosphere, spewing out a new infection of deadly microscopic AIDS droplets for future generations while we digest Love-Ins, *Laugh-In* and *Saturday Night Live*. Author Rachel Carson seeps in with Gloria Steinem, adding color contrast to an all-man landscape. Cancer from the sobering effect of DDT appears without a brushstroke. Crimson red: blood-splatter cutouts of Martin Luther King Jr. and the two kingly Kennedy brothers stick to the painting, almost overriding a collage of newspaper articles about man on the moon, the Beatles and Vietnam. Various colors of life mix together randomly, battle it out and are shaken up into the atmosphere, producing odd, mesmerizing mayhem. Family disoriented. Family disregarded.

Camelot invented. It's all hurled into the painting of us ... acid into the eyes, a handprint of who we were becoming.

How did this all happen? How did it happen so fast? America had just started experiencing the seemingly fresh, charismatic dynamics of the Kennedy family. We weren't really prepared to wake up to the aftermath — the shock and awe of simple life crumbling in America. Traditional, deep-rooted values got dug up and thrown out while we sang songs about wearing flowers in our hair.

Did I come into a big city without the capacity to adjust to its complexities? Although Chicago was good to me, I never liked it except for Lake Michigan. I unconsciously separated myself from city life, I felt trapped in its flatness, not being able to run away to the mountains. The urban political environment felt hardcore and corrupt. It was a city with a history of fires before I was born, and I was there once again experiencing fire. Between the riots and the 1968 Democratic Convention, I hardly knew what was happening. No one did.

Mayor Daley gave a shoot-to-kill order to police when the riots started. The entire surrounding area was dangerous and I remember two of my modeling jobs on Pulaski Street were canceled. From Victor's studio I could hear glass shatter from windows while fire ate at the heart of Wells Street. The violence had started with civil rights issues and continued later when anti-war protest leaders tried to get permits to sleep in Lincoln Park. When the park was officially closed, Chicago police bombed protestors with tear gas and forced people from the park with billy clubs. By the time it was over, 589 arrests had been made. There were 11,900 police; 7,500 army troops; 7,500 Illinois National Guardsmen; 1,000 Secret Service Agents and of course, Mayor Daley. On the last day, he printed one hundred We

Love You Daley signs and orchestrated a pro-Daley demonstration to counter the negativity.

During the last two years of the 1960s, a moral meltdown was going on, not only in Chicago but across the United States. Cultural icon Andy Warhol was shot in New York while Ted Kennedy swam ashore, leaving Mary Jo Kopechne under water in a car he'd been driving on Martha's Vineyard. Since his two brothers no longer had voices, Ted Kennedy was the man Daley wanted to run for president ... but it was not in the cards. Despite Joe Kennedy Sr., Chicago's mafia and corruption within the court system, another Kennedy would not be leading our country.

During all the unrest in 1968, *60 Minutes* began ticking its way into our American consciousness with investigative reporting. How did they cover these events? Reporter Mike Wallace had a watchdog presence stronger than — if you can imagine this — the CIA, FBI and Secret Service all working together. Wallace's interviews were focused questions, finding the way into the heart of a crooked man, then scalding him with a follow-up of his indiscretions that would climax into transparency. The camera closed in for "the kill," revealing a sweaty face and murky eyes. I took such pleasure in watching evil squirm. You could tell Mike Wallace wouldn't like politically correct legal terms like "affirmative misstatements." "You are lying" suited him and the format much better. In my mind, *60 Minutes* could keep the world in order and catch all the bad guys right on camera. The program made me feel more grounded. It became my comfort zone and must have resonated with many other viewers as well, since it has now been on the air for nearly fifty seasons.

Later on another show would originate with the same power, even though the format was totally different. Chicago would soften with the arrival of a woman — Oprah Winfrey would be a beacon of light in the middle of a large crowd. Through her program each afternoon she empowered women, addressed issues that had never been discussed in the open, helped people to heal themselves and their families, got people reading who had never read before and not only played a man's game in a man's world but, as a Black woman, beat them paving new ground on her own terms. During the Oprah era of the early nineties, I felt dread over what seemed to be the impending derailment of US leadership. I wrote two letters to the popular daytime host which were never answered, but in time, Oprah helped a Black man become president of the United States.

Lyndon Johnson's unexpected presidency lacked the drama of the Kennedy administration. Ian Fleming's James Bond allure fizzled for at least a while, only to come back full force in later generations. Lady Bird Johnson didn't command the attention that Jacqueline Kennedy Onassis had with her youthful beauty, couture designer fashion and savoir faire. Lady Bird thrived in the garden and through the Highway Beautification Act, made driving more enjoyable for decades.

Only once did the Johnson White House take on a soap-opera ambiance. It happened with a brief love affair between George Hamilton and the president's daughter, Lynda Bird.

George's golden tan and dazzling smile glistened briefly in the garden behind the White House. This was while an unpopular war lingered, before coming to an end. It took until 2011 for the government to finally reveal that the public had been lied to about the Vietnam War. Was LBJ a good president? Some people remember him by an uncouth gesture, lifting up his shirt, showing his scar after surgery. I remember him because he signed a bill so we would have access to a public broadcasting system. None of us at the time knew how important this was. Because of him, we have quality television with meaningful subject matter to inspire children and adults alike.

Free spirit reigned. I remember watching nudity onstage while listening to the energizing music from the production of *Hair*. During intermission, one of my friends told me she had gone that day to "Dr. Feelgood" in Manhattan for a weekly amphetamine injection. It was administered along with an injection of vitamin B complex. Dr. Feelgood was finally written about in the *New York Times*, then disappeared underground; his clientele had included President Kennedy.

The atmosphere, at least in large cities, had changed to "anything goes." Was Andy Warhol's influence interwoven with President Kennedy's promiscuity? As women's panties got tossed over the

White House fence, yet kept under wraps with a sly smile in a Secret Service box, were the rest of us left vulnerably naked in later generations?

In *POPism: The Warhol Sixties,* Andy Warhol was our hip Jay Gatsby. A shadowy, voyeuristic, charismatic figure addicted to publicity. He wanted to be known as an oracle and prophesied that each one of us would experience fifteen minutes of fame. Andy Warhol presided over a mélange of kinky sex and drugs with people desperately needing recognition. He hung out with his crew in Greenwich Village networking at Max's Kansas City, the unofficial club of New York artists, underground filmmakers, rock musicians, poets, and pop intelligentsia.

As I wrote about Andy Warhol's influence on culture in the sixties, I received a 1968 *Playboy* magazine to autograph and came across an article written by Paul Carroll. Warhol had started out as a highly successful commercial artist, and *Women's Wear Daily* hailed him in the late fifties as the Leonardo da Vinci of the shoe trade. In the early sixties he did a Lord & Taylor window display featuring painting blowups of *Dick Tracy* comic strip characters; it was considered by some to be the first chapter of the book of Genesis according to Pop Art — assembly-line character art. When enough of his Campbell soup cans and silkscreen portraits sold for five thousand dollars apiece, he said he was retiring from painting.

Was he a victim of his own "oracle orgy"? Did the term *great society* include assembly-line art? Had he become culture itself, passing on his own lifestyle as art?

Where is this past "artwork"? Is it placed safely away — waiting to be celebrated in a newly opened New York Metropolitan Museum of Art, American Artist Wing of the future? The truth is, Warhol's art had a tremendous impact on our culture. Why were so many of us lost, mindless followers, opening the door wide, buying tickets for pornography in commercial theaters? I went to see *Deep Throat* with all of our friends. It was hip porn, the thing to do. "Sophisticated culture" spread quickly to the street. Larry Flynt got famous, then shot, like Warhol. Flynt's porn magazines sold openly, sandwiched between *Screw* and the *New York Times*. Racy Calvin Klein ads surfaced under the same sex-driven theme years later — at bus stops, billboards in Times Square and in many subway stations. During this time, pornography also ended up inside my home, *Screw* magazine and a large collection of pornographic films with names like *Debbie Does Dallas* and *Behind the Green Door*.

Once Andy Warhol seeds started sprouting into later generations, young people were seduced into believing they deserved their fifteen minutes of fame. Kim Kardashian and those like her came into being, making nude images the rule of the day. New icons and a new America emerged within the self-celebrating worlds of reality television and YouTube.

My life in that sixties' atmosphere included a girl from Bogotá, Colombia. I never met her but knew her haunting allure from my husband. He would drop her name at odd times in conversation. This happened over a period of years and etched eerie Seurat dot patterns in my memory that began repeating themselves over and over.

"I have a deep soul connection with her," he said. "We share wild spices together, spices that blend with rosemary and thyme."

A young hobo of a man captured some of the uncertainties and longings of this period through song. He seemed to rise out of a mysterious garbage site somewhere, a rough, rare jewel transforming himself into a national treasure. My husband certainly hadn't brought him to my attention — he wasn't upscale. He was a musician with a quirky voice and haunting, strange arrangements. His lyrics portrayed gypsy life with broken cups and harmonica sounds that carried our great-grandparents ashore. Rich, poor, elite, young and old, all listened to Bob Dylan. He captured an elusive yearning within our heartland with songs like "The Times They Are a-Changin'." His music rattled our consciousness and forced us to look at what it is to be human. But even Dylan's powerful, poetic imagery couldn't stop the fading of American life as we knew it. How do these chapters end? They don't. We experience the aftermath going forward.

With Dylan on the radio, my husband drove our white Porsche convertible into Manhattan in the wee hours of the morning. We caught the sun's playful, reflective patterns on the backdrop of New York's tallest buildings. I started to lose sight of where I'd come from and who I was becoming. Many of us would start losing our way, including President Nixon. Soon he would come crashing down with Watergate. During his presidency he had publicly focused on cracking down on marijuana and drug immorality, but we weren't listening. Before long, we were in Billy Joel's "New York State of Mind," grooving with Big Apple buoyancy. The next decade was fun. The next decade was challenging. The next decade revealed quiet desperation.

Chapter 8
Moving Up the Ladder

We found a two-bedroom apartment at 230 East 48th Street in what is called the Turtle Bay area of New York City, a few blocks from the United Nations. When we started moving our furniture in, the elevator man welcomed us. "Bette Davis used to live in the corner apartment. She was very quiet and almost no one ever saw her." I could just see wise Bette Davis eyes spying through the peephole of her door to make sure no one was in the hallway before escaping to the street. We smiled and thanked him for going out of his way to help get furniture safely into our apartment.

A couple of weeks after we settled in, Wilhelmina called me into her office. I had never met her in person. She reminded me of a rare, elegant bird swooping over my portfolio, changing all of my photos to her liking. She had recently quit modeling at the height of her own career after being on the covers of *Vogue* and *Harper's Bazaar* so many times it no longer mattered. The week before I happened to see her on the *Tonight Show*, juggling at least eight different styles of hats on her head at different angles while at the same time arranging her hair to suit the garments. She looked like a magician because she was able to do it so fast. That evening she met a man by the name of Bruce Cooper, who was an executive producer of the show, and fell in love with him. They were married soon after and together they started Wilhelmina Models, which later became Wilhelmina Agency.

I was a good workhorse in the early days of her business since I had already done catalog work in New York many times. I had an advantage because of face recognition through television exposure, doing many new commercials not only in the United States, but in other countries such as Japan and Mexico. These included beauty products, perfumes like Jean Nate and Hai Karate, and feminine hygiene deodorants. I was one of the few models in New York City who didn't go on endless interviews. Things were fun, new and exciting at first. As one of Wilhelmina's top money-makers, I felt there was no limit to what I could achieve and was generally booked about three weeks in advance. It wasn't unusual to do three or four one-hour bookings at different locations in one day; I even took jobs on weekends.

Wilhelmina and Bruce had a party for everyone to celebrate the new successful agency located at 527 Madison Avenue. I remember wearing a long burgundy velvet dress that accented my small waistline, something I took pride in because so many guys had mentioned it. I wanted to resemble Juliet; I was always into some fantasy. In this scenario, Romeo, my husband, had eyes for all of the beautiful models in the room. That was the real part. But that night he was respectful to me, kept his hands to himself and seemed uncomfortable.

Wilhelmina stood at the entrance of the agency and greeted her guests. Her tall, offbeat elegance was grounded in business with an exceptional memory for names. Over time I would be taught some of life's painful lessons through this rare, genuine woman with masterful networking skills. When the party was over, she again stood by the door, shaking everyone's hand as they left. I was surprised to find her husband walking us out to our status symbol. He, not my husband, opened the car door and whispered in my ear, "You stood out in the crowd."

My career with Wilhelmina remained strong for a couple of years even though I wasn't happy being part of the herd of working models. *Woman's Day* booked me for a fashion shoot in the Caribbean, but generally speaking, I was not the IT girl in New York City like I had been in Chicago. *Ladies' Home Journal* scheduled me twice for a cover, but they ended up not being used. My popularity was much more prominent in Japan where I did several covers.

Asian culture had a profound influence on me and what I would be doing artistically in later years. Being able to experience Kyoto's artistic Japanese gardens opened up new worlds of unexpected creative energy. I was also blessed with being booked in remote areas throughout the world, going to unusual places like Cat Island only reached by a small, private plane. The local natives were married to the sea, but feared it. Their beaches were untarnished by commercialism. I experienced the vastness of Heaven there. I later found out Sydney Poitier, when interviewed by Oprah, was born on Cat Island and retained some humble, homeland roots:

"Are you self-taught?"

"I don't like the use of those words, there's arrogance in them."

Shortly after I saw the Oprah segment, Hurricane Sandy's path went directly over the terrain. I wonder how time has changed the island.

I was getting frustrated, unhappy. I wanted to work for *Glamour*. I wanted to work for *Vogue*. I wanted to work for prestigious magazines and receive name recognition like Cheryl Tiegs, Lauren Hutton, or Twiggy. At twenty-seven I was way too old for *Seventeen* and didn't fit in with the look for *Harper's Bazaar*. Forget *Vogue* and *Glamour*, I was too short. At five foot five and a half, I was one of the shortest models in New York City. I passed for five foot seven because of being long-waisted and wearing really high heels. No one questioned it. Models that were around the same height and body build would get booked together. Cheryl Tiegs and Cybil Shepard were large-boned and booked together a lot. Lauren Hutton was not that tall but was over five foot seven and *Vogue* loved her offbeat look. The agencies wouldn't even look at you if you weren't at least that tall. I had a certain amount of power with Wilhelmina because I was booked so often that she didn't want me switching agencies. She tried her best, recommending me to a magazine called *After Dark* that wanted to do an article on interesting people in New York. I refused, thinking if I put enough pressure on her I would finally get in with one of the fashion magazines, but I didn't understand the process. It doesn't work that way.

Eileen Ford of Ford Models became very competitive with Wilhelmina. She had been set back from her throne when Queen Wilhelmina opened the agency and reduced Ford's successful business. I had been in the city for a couple of years when the rumor started floating around that Wilhelmina was being dishonest in record keeping. I almost switched over to Eileen Ford at that time, but Wilhelmina found out I was planning to leave and called me into her office. She had her bookkeeper, Fran, review my records and compiled a mile-long tabulated receipt to show there were no discrepancies. I was told that Eileen Ford had started the rumor to lure models to her agency. Because they had gone through so much trouble and my records were accurate, I stayed and would not end up switching to Eileen Ford until three years later.

My husband met a couple in our building that had also recently gotten married and we ended up spending time together socially. Alan and his wife, Enid, worked together. They were the young darlings of a well-known advertising agency, written up in news magazines for writing the best television commercials. Heinz pickles was one of them. We had much in common because they had just purchased a silver Porsche, and we were interested in taking a trip to see Paul Newman racing his Targa in Connecticut.

We had our tops down along the highway, driving about one hundred miles an hour. I was always uncomfortable in a vehicle with my husband. He had installed a unit to detect police radar and always drove way over the speed limit, tailgating other vehicles within inches of their back end before passing. I would yell at him every time we got too close. It didn't do any good. He was always impatient with slow drivers. Then there were the fast truckers, he spent a lot of his time communicating with them on the highway. His handle was "Italian Stallion." He also developed a pattern of picking up female hitchhikers. At least that didn't happen when our newly wedded friends were following us.

When we finally reached the raceway, Alan and Enid got out of their car laughing. They had seen my hair blowing all over the place but from the neck up my husband looked like a bronze bust — nothing flapping but his shirt sleeves. Alan wanted to know what kind of hair spray he was using thinking it would make a great commercial for the agency.

Alan and Enid were friends with two men, Sean and Christopher. They started a company named Glorious Food and used Alan and Enid's refrigerator on the ninth floor to store some of their products. They began catering to the rich and famous, became successful and were written up in various magazines. Looking back, those contacts were important to my husband. He would buy the *New York Times* and read the society pages carefully each Sunday as we relaxed by the fireplace. At that time I didn't know he was preparing a life that I would not be a part of.

I didn't realize then what climbing the ladder of success entailed. Even as his wife, I was naive about what it meant to be part of the Who's Who in New York City society. My husband had become a social animal with purpose. I loved and preferred being around four-legged animals like dogs, cats, and cows, and going to the zoo when I had time off from work. For my birthday he bought me a seal point Siamese cat that I named *Katsu* (it means "victory" in Japanese). Spending time at home with her was comforting.

I remember going to a fundraiser at Lincoln Center with Sean, Christopher, Alan, and Enid. It was exciting for all of us because Grace Kelly was spokesperson for the event and had flown into New York City from Monaco. I can't recall what the fundraiser was for; it didn't matter to me. I just wanted to look sensational. I had recently bought a long, soft, slightly diaphanous dress by the designer Stephen Burrows. It had small pink and blue clouds within the polished fabric that sensually accented the curviest, most flattering parts of my body. The bottom hem was unusual in that it was stretched out somewhat, like crepe paper could be, with red stitching along the edge to ground it. I made a white satin hat that hugged the shape of my head with a Gatsby flare, matching the mood of the dress, and put on five-inch, burnished, crisscrossed, silver-and-gold heels bought at Henri Bendel's. All that time with Victor in Chicago had given me a cutting-edge fashion sense that most New Yorkers didn't have.

I was the first to get out of our new maroon Mercedes Benz as it pulled up alongside Lincoln Center and the paparazzi started chasing me, taking photos of me in all of my sartorial splendor. They were in a flash-bulb frenzy like nothing I'd ever experienced. I ran past the fountain toward the entrance with Alan, Enid, Sean, and Christopher close behind.

"Who is she?" Long pause. "Who are they?"

The running continued. There was no answer to the questions. Silence. Then, "She's nobody. They're nobody!"

Not exactly nobody … Enid was a librettist and had worked hard to obtain the rights to do a musical on the *Diary of Anne Frank*. Everything had come to fruition for her in her new career. Sadly, not long after this night at Lincoln Center, she and Alan wound up divorced. Enid moved to 249 Central Park West and helped us get into the same landmark building.

I remember looking up at Grace Kelly's porcelain skin. She was incredibly beautiful, even more so in person. Her face was flawless. The speech she gave lasted only a few minutes and I don't remember what she said. Afterward we went to Sardi's restaurant, close to Lincoln Center. I brought up the paparazzi incident, laughing hysterically. Sean and Christopher glared at me. "I don't think that's funny."

It seemed to bother everyone but me. By this time I was popping pills that served as a cushion for whatever went on in life. I was prepared for anything. Dexedrine for energy, Valium to keep me mellow and a drink of bubbly champagne now and then to share in the fun of the day. I was a "happy addict" without a clue how drugs dull the senses, change the brain and distort reality. The truth is, the New York paparazzi saying that you are a nobody is a big deal in New York City! There must have been a part in all of us that believed what they said. We all long to be somebody.

Agencies fulfilled needs other than booking models for photo shoots. They were also used by men to meet beautiful women as dating escorts. People like Ted Kennedy — T. K. as he was called by the many models who experienced his one-night stands. One girl brought in a pair of his glasses. He had left them at her apartment for all of us to see! Ménages à trois that a certain actor orchestrated in the middle of the night were whispered about in our dressing rooms. Book celebrities seemed to have new girlfriends every night.

Then there was a different kind of man, an outsider not interested in dating women. He started editing for *Mademoiselle* magazine and later on, his pen leaked unflattering personal tidbits about people he associated with. He transformed himself into an F. Scott Fitzgerald-esque, glamorized fictional character. The real-life twisted, bizarre ending found Truman Capote dead in Los Angeles, with nothing more to write.

My husband met an ear-nose-and-throat doctor who was well respected by his colleagues and was looking for a partner in his practice. We decided to move from New York City into a beautiful French Normandy house in Larchmont near where they would share a practice together. The practice picked up quickly as my husband focused on facial plastic surgery and his partner dealt with ear, nose, and throat problems.

Our home looked like a castle. My husband resisted buying at first, preferring to rent a place. But I wanted the home so much that I placed a forty-thousand-dollar deposit on it, money I'd saved from modeling. The dollar amount would be equivalent to about seven hundred thousand dollars today. We purchased the house for eighty thousand dollars (in today's market it would probably go for millions).

This was the busiest time of my career. I commuted back and forth by train everyday with pep pills that gave me enough energy to totally renovate the house after I returned home. White marble was brought in and placed in the vestibule, which led to a sunken living room with beamed ceilings. I purchased the same couches that Yves Saint Laurent had in his living room from a company called Italier after seeing them in *Vogue* magazine. I pickled all of the floors after finding a high-grade, non-yellowing polyurethane made in New Jersey. It cost ninety dollars a gallon and turned out to be highly toxic. Seven years later I started showing symptoms of the auto-immune disease Scleroderma and realized those toxic chemicals most likely had been a catalyst.

It was a dangerous time for me. I was ingesting many different chemicals and didn't know how they would affect my health ten, twenty, thirty years later. Ignorance was bliss. I was young, naive, and invincible. I would take a birth control pill, Dexedrine, and Valium in the morning before my bookings, a combination that made me feel victoriously tranquil like my feline companions, Katsu and Miso. After all, we were all Leos!

The more I worked the more lost I became. I was either manic, working on the house in a frenzy at night or almost catatonic. What was happening? On the outside, my husband and I had the perfect house, perfect cars, perfect marriage and two perfect Siamese cats. The song, "Our House" could have applied to us, we were envied by many. But I can remember doing a television commercial that featured close-ups of my eyes. I was to show emotion when different scenes were introduced and the photographer became irritated.

"Your eyes look vacant. Can't you give me something better than that?"

It would take many years before I would know that vacant eyes reveal disengagement from the heart.

While in the Navy, my husband practiced the plastic-surgery procedures he loved doing so much by gathering everyone who would let him operate on them. He started refining some of the rough edges of the military with his scalpel. He would bring photos of their many faces home, showing before and after. Some started out with huge noses and ended up looking like movie stars. When preparing for battle, they needed to look good, just like in the movies! My sister Shanda came to visit and we went shopping at Bloomingdale's with my husband. He pointed out everyone who needed a nose job while we shopped. As we dined at prestigious country restaurants like the Box Tree and Emily Shaw's the same topic came up. He would point out people who could look better and how he could transform them. We were a parlor room of profound discussion; well-focused, on our way to getting a Nobel Perfect Face Prize in superficiality.

Chapter 9
Downward Spiral Staircase

My modeling career with Wilhelmina came to an unexpected and sudden halt. I sang a few lines from a television commercial for National Airlines with a lot of dialogue afterwards.

They gave me a new script during the shoot inside LaGuardia. I remember being apprehensive because I didn't have time to practice. The director had dark glasses which he never removed while we were filming — a bad sign. They kept changing things around, which usually doesn't happen during a commercial, especially of that magnitude.

Another woman was booked along with me, also playing a stewardess — now called flight attendants. She happened to be Pam Dawber's roommate. Pam played opposite Robin Williams on *Mork and Mindy*, then later married Mark Harmon. Pam and I worked together once in a while because we were around the same height and weight.

Even while on camera filming the commercial, they changed the lines again and again. I couldn't memorize fast enough to complete the commercial. I tried many times, but couldn't make it work. They were very nice to me but finally gave the lines to Pam's roommate. I was embarrassed in front of a lot of people. The drugs hadn't worked. I was no longer "tranquilly victorious." I was drug-altered, and in my mind, stupid. The game was up. I called Wilhelmina the next day and told her I was quitting. When she finally realized I was serious, she canceled the remainder of my bookings. A week later I sent her a bouquet of flowers to say goodbye. She called back.

"I've never had anyone send me flowers under this kind of condition. Thank you. I am so sorry you made this decision. I don't quite understand. If you change your mind, you can always come back."

I would return to modeling two years later with Eileen Ford's company. Eileen could be ruthless but luckily had a soft-spoken husband, Jerry, who helped smooth over the sometimes cutthroat agency, Ford Models. I got one good commercial and did the usual catalog work that I had done with Wilhelmina, but as we entered the eighties my relationship with the seventies' drug scene still controlled me and I lost interest in modeling for good.

There was very little discussion between my husband and I over ending my career after only a year and a half with the Fords. His one comment was, since I was no longer bringing money into the household, it was unfair. It brought about an abrupt power shift within our marriage. I began spending my free time painting and designing furniture while he was expanding his practice and the name he had built. He left his partner, who had been so good to him, taking along his secretary.

When he went into solo practice, my husband and I created a beautiful Art Deco environment for his new office within the large space he rented close to the hospital. Before switching to medicine, he had studied to be an architect, so it was a fun, creative time for both of us. I designed a desk made of white oak that he placed in his consultation room and a streamlined couch for the waiting area. I brought in white marble for the scheduling counter and complemented it with elegant marble pedestals to place magazines on. I got on my hands and knees to pickle his entire office floor using the same toxic non-yellowing urethane. About a month after it was finished, a pipe burst on a weekend and the entire space was ruined. I went back in and did it all over again without even thinking to open one window for ventilation.

Looking back, how could I have disrespected my body that way?

I was still on a combination of drugs — Dexedrine, Tranxene and Valium. Later, I switched to cocaine, believing it wasn't addictive. My husband remained drug-free while my disease progressed. I was an addict and cocaine wasn't as satisfying as Dexedrine. It made me anxious when it started wearing off. But alcohol and cocaine together were perfect partners.

In the sixties and seventies, unlike the fifties, it was en vogue to be a little crazy, a little humorous, lying on a couch talking endlessly about yourself like a fucked-up Woody Allen. It was my friend Enid who first noticed my behavior and recommended that I go to her therapist. Enid knew something was wrong, but didn't realize it was drug related.

I became obsessively focused on my face. With the help of my cocktail enhancers, I started believing that I was more beautiful than Elizabeth Taylor. She was IT in the face department of the sixties, after Grace Kelly left. Luckily, some of my habits included painting and playing the piano, so my brain was still somewhat productive, but I would become fixated on one thing, then move on to another and another while never finishing anything. I couldn't remember lines, so I couldn't be an actress ... maybe I could learn to paint something impressive ... or learn to speak French ... there was desperation.

When my husband came home from work he would ask me, "What have you been doing all day?"

I was always feeling guilty because no matter what I did, it didn't matter. We both knew it wasn't enough because I wasn't making money. I was getting older and knew that soon I would no longer have a fresh face, the gift that had given me success. This started the facelifts, silicone injections and plastic surgery. What a perfect setup, married to a plastic surgeon. I had age-defying surgical magic at my disposal in my home, all at the end of my husband's tenacious fingertips.

I started doing abstract drawings with an Art Deco influence. Babe Shapiro, an artist friend, stretched out a canvas for me, was very encouraging and really seemed to like my work. My husband bought one of Babe's contemporary paintings. He lived in Soho and was loosely associated with many artists in the area. It was an exciting place to be — non-commercial with large, ironwork factory buildings being transformed into loft spaces. I remember one night a group of us walked the damp streets after we had gone to CBGB's to listen to punk rock and get bad attitudes. Wet cobblestones filtered through polished darkness and held stories from a century of faded footprints. There was a mysterious force in the air that seemed to create a collective humming, like an old well-oiled sewing machine.

Wheels started turning for Babe and our friends, including Ellen Staller. She started a company called Terrafirma. Her unique ceramic designs sold well and the company became very successful. It is still a working pottery studio on 35th Street in New York City. Eric, Ellen's husband, became a fixture in Central Park at night. He was written up in *People* magazine for using small lights like a paintbrush, etching his journey on a vintage two-passenger bicycle as he rode past tree shadows into the wee hours of night.

Another good friend of Ellen's, Judith Lieber, ended up making evening bags for Bergdorf's and Bendel's. Work and play were married in the early seventies. Babe's huge, wide-open loft space at 31 Walker Street was filled with art, recipes, and sinful desserts. Babe and Ellen did the cooking. I'd settle in to smoke a little grass later in the evening.

Babe taught art classes in Baltimore at Maryland Institute College of Art and his students would visit periodically. His studio was always filled with people. Because my husband "discovered" Babe, he took great pride in knowing him and his friends. When we all went out to restaurants, he was always generous, picking up the bill, ordering the most expensive wine. He even bought Babe a beautiful watch. Babe and I would speak on the phone almost every day.

He became my best friend, someone I felt comfortable with and visited often. When neither one of us could kill a little bug or spider, we would take it outside together where he had planted mimosa seeds on the loft building roof. We watched the tiny trees grow their first blooms before I placed one in the backyard of my home in Westchester. Twenty years later that tree survived the worst fire in Larchmont history.

Enid introduced me to a deep muscle therapist named Joan Witkowski, who was a follower of John-Roger, founder of MSIA, Movement of Spiritual Inner Awareness. I started reading his books and realize now the information was planted along my pathway, preparing me for the free fall of my life.

I would go for massages once a week, and Babe later followed with some shoulder problems needing treatment. My muscle therapist was well known in New York society. I remember Ariana Huffington coming in after my session and showing me a book that she had written about Greece. Ariana later started the Huffington Post on the internet and was a follower of John-Roger until he fell from grace. Yoko Ono and the late Georgia O'Keefe also frequented Joan's office.

I planned parties so we could be together as a larger circle of friends. We spent a fair amount of time in each other's company and Joan had a wonderful depth that I did not yet possess. There was nothing superficial or materialistic about her. She was more spiritually aware and enlightened than anyone I had ever met, then or since. I can remember her going through a hard time when her younger brother died. She said she had a soul connection with my husband and needed him when she was in mourning, counting on him because of this bond; but he didn't devote the time so I would always try to make up for him, wanting to be soothing and upbeat, but ineffective. Too much of my spirit in those days came from drinking, and I wasn't able to comfort her.

I remember walking up to her apartment one time and seeing two men having sex behind shrubbery next to her building. It was a time when gay people were starting to come out of the closet. Many men on Christopher Street were wearing a sports cup that could be used like a woman's bra to attract attention and enhance what they had below the waist. After being pent up for so long by society's judgmental codes and notorious, inhumane treatment, many gay men became more public with their sexuality in bath houses, discotheques, and night clubs. Bette Midler would perform her shows sandwiched in between the sexual escapades of the men diced with their "poppers."

New York City attracts young, creative people from all walks of life who are full of dreams. It's contagious and spills out into the streets. "I will work hard. I will be smart. I will meet the right people and be famous."

We started hanging out on the Upper East Side at restaurants like Elaine's near Bloomingdale's, the Rainbow Room at Rockefeller Center, the Four Seasons and Windows on the World at the World Trade Center. It is true that there are famous people around almost every corner in New York. I took pride in being cool — would simply acknowledge them with a subtle "hello" gesture that makes them see they were understood, that you knew they didn't want to be bothered, unless of course a social situation presents itself that they can benefit from.

New York City celebrities are left alone by the public for the most part. There is very little bad behavior, even with the paparazzi, except for one obnoxious photographer who was constantly stalking Jacqueline Kennedy Onassis.

Vladimir Horowitz, the great pianist, was a fixture on the streets and frequented the restaurant Sign of the Dove. He was a celebrity exception in that he very much enjoyed mingling with autograph seekers in his elder years when his fingers started failing him. He was a sight to see as he walked down the street accompanied by a beautiful silver cane with the spirit of the city around him.

I once saw Mike Wallace walking alone and wanted so much to tell him about my grandmother, hoping that he would realize how unusual she was and want to place her on *60 Minutes*. His body language told me he was unapproachable, but his legs told me that he was made to ride a horse. They were curved just right to get on Browny Red bareback! The Gotham metropolis is an exciting blur of happenings because of people like him.

New York is hard to define logically. People with the most money and influence aren't asked to pay much for anything. And magazines like *Vogue*, *Seventeen* and *Harper's Bazaar* would give models fifteen dollars per hour to work for them because they knew they could launch lucrative careers and we would gladly do it for nothing if asked. Movie stars and people like the late Jacqueline Kennedy Onassis would receive complimentary invites to benefits and movie openings.

The Big Apple is a rather succulent fruit filled with nuance. What variety of apple would you choose to best represent New York after experiencing it in person or through film and television? I pick Fuji, which is known as *antique* and traces back to Thomas Jefferson's plantation. It was bred as a hybrid in Japan by crossing Ralls Janet with Red Delicious. This new apple, with the perfect balance between sweet and tart, juicy and crisp, was named after the town it was founded in, Fujisaki, Japan, has sacred wisdom and exhibits color variations that blend into one another.

The city filled with libido comes on as red hot, but is tempered by mature people who have worked or lived here a long time — those who have gotten past the ego and into wisdom. Citizens of the city like Mike Nichols, Charlie Rose and Diane Sawyer lay a good foundation to inspire others through the media. Their fragrance lingers with us walking the streets, taking a big juicy bite of the Big Apple.

I began meeting up with some New Yorkers, the likes of which I had never met in the protected environment of my early years in Colorado. People who would hop over the homeless lying in the streets like they were a puddle of water. The other extreme were those unable to develop alligator skin because of their tender natures. They walked around protecting themselves with their companions of unconditional love — dogs in particular. (God is dog spelled backward!)

Manhattan is an island comprised of thirteen miles jam-packed with people speaking hundreds of languages, strolling with colorful pets. It is not unusual on any given day to see parrots, skunks and even snakes! I was shocked to see so many four-legged animals on leashes in such an unlikely environment. They are everywhere with little but cement ground to walk on. It was hard always looking down to avoid stepping in some mess. The pooper-scooper law eventually changed all that, and most people gladly honor it. One thing I never questioned is how much people living in New York love animals and protect their pets. It is a beautiful thing to experience.

There are particular parts of society that don't feel comfortable with spirituality. This was true in the sixties and hasn't changed. You're out of their circle if spirituality is part of your life.

Faith is considered a weakness and New York City has an underbelly that can be cold, lonely, and cruel. It's no secret that the rich rule the city. Mayor Lindsay was in office and someone everyone wanted to be with. His story was unique in that he would end up forgotten years later and would die a poor man according to rich standards.

I was told by New York photographers more than once that I was too sweet-looking and needed a tougher essence. I learned that it was cool in some circles to never crack a smile. I met a woman on the elevator going up to the Horticultural Society who was the spokesperson for the Metropolitan Museum of Art. She didn't have a smile to crack. I remember her tough exterior, like alligator skin, and looking at her as if she were an alien from another planet. I wonder how many years it took being isolated within her particular social circle to take her smile away. Did she know the curator who was best friends with Andy Warhol? I wanted to get to know her and find out what had happened, to pinpoint the exact moment when she was robbed of childhood's joyful, playful innocence.

I would look down from my terrace on Central Park West to see large numbers of rats crawling around the park. There was a phone booth outside, under the window. I learned that New York never sleeps, and neither would I. My husband stopped staying at our pied-à-terre after two nights; the endless, desperate phone calls with cursing, drunken crazies drove him out. Drug dealers were in full force and it seemed their office was beneath our window.

One night around three o'clock. I heard a loud but cushioned thump, then the sound of screeching brakes. I knew without looking out the window that someone had been hit, and hit hard. Usually you hear screeching brakes and then a loud crash. I looked down to see a woman spread out on the pavement with no vehicle around. The driver had left the scene. I called 911 but couldn't bring myself to go outside to be with her. The ambulance arrived. She didn't survive.

Cultural stereotypes emerged from seeds planted back in the sixties, sprouting in the new decade of the eighties. The eighties became known as the ME decade. I would walk through Central Park and observe the hippies, yippies and yuppies. Hippies were still into nature and low-key living, while yippies were self-proclaimed intellectuals and yuppies commanded the corporate mindset of bigger, better, more.

Entitlement started to set in. Having children wasn't en vogue. Women started competing in the man's workplace, forging progress for professional equality. Female lawyers started to become commonplace. Family values for the most part not only weren't popular, but at-home moms were, sadly, even ostracized. Babies were not coveted and were seldom seen on television. Avant-garde art took the place of sentimental family photos on your wall if you wanted to be cool. The décor of the day was stark simplicity — a style called minimalist — the home, a huge picture frame with nothing in it.

The counterbalance was somewhat of an art explosion from different genres. There were unforgettable films like *Lawrence of Arabia* and *Saturday Night Fever*, and fresh sounds from bands like the Bee Gees. Their song, "Stayin' Alive," is now used for hands-on CPR. With a103-beats-per-minute rhythm, it's perfect to start failing hearts back up!

Victor invited me to an event for Estée Lauder, I think it was for her birthday. I found this unusual because Victor didn't like New York City. He typically stayed away and left his rep in East Hampton to make all the necessary connections. I had only seen him on two occasions since leaving Chicago. After his book signing, I visited him in the Hamptons and remember being out by a pool seeing Victor in swimming trunks that looked a little like boxer shorts. They had elastic underneath, around his muscular thighs. He had taken the bottom fabric and folded it under so the snug fit would hug his handsome legs.

Victor and Estée were seated on a platform at the head table, isolated from the rest of the guests. Joe Lauder, her husband, was seated next to me on the lower level. I remember watching him write a nasty note and give it to the waiter to pass on to his wife. That was my first experience seeing the importance of people placement at social functions in high society.

A few weeks later, I was walking down a Manhattan street and saw my photo on the cover of *Screw* magazine on a newsstand. The picture was taken from Victor's newly released book, *Skrebneski*. I was with another model and underneath the image the caption said, "Lesbians Page 9." At that time, our society had not yet granted gay people the right to be themselves. That magazine cover claiming I was a lesbian was scandalous. I lacked awareness and empathy for the difficult challenges gay people faced each day, having their authenticity stifled. When they put me on that magazine cover with that caption, I was horrified. I called Victor at his studio in Chicago with tears streaming down my face. "I'm going to sue *Screw* magazine."

He started laughing and couldn't stop. His response shocked me. I felt as though that sleazy magazine had taken advantage of both of us. But I hung up the phone thinking, *It can't be that bad. Victor viewed it as a funny joke...*

Chapter 10
The Ugly Face of Narcissism

Modeling in my case had taken on a strange twist. Putting on makeup for an ad versus putting on makeup to attract and seduce men came from two different motivations. Looking in the mirror had become an addiction that had not yet fully manifested in Chicago. Now, all of my self-esteem came from how I looked. New York City had a sophistication that Chicago didn't. I became swept up in it and was able to comb through a store like Henri Bendel's and coordinate an outfit from the best designers the world had to offer. Geraldine Stutz was president of the store. She had worked for *Glamour* magazine and knew just how to fill the space.

I remember sitting next to Ali McGraw in the rear of Bendel's first floor trying on shoes. It seemed as though she was caught up in the same joyless trap I was. She had been a stylist before landing the leading role in the movie *Love Story*. I watched her carefully measured gestures. One was with her mouth parted just so and then sliding the tip of her tongue from one side of her top lip to the other. It was seductive and worth trying at home in the mirror. Had she used this gesture to catch the attention of Robert Evans, the film producer?

I would run into Cher, Jacqueline Kennedy Onassis, and Ali McGraw the most while shopping at Bloomingdale's, Bergdorf Goodman and Bendel's. At that time, it was those three stores that were frequented by women with a highly tuned fashion sense. It was like an obsessive mental cat fight, getting the most sensational bag, pair of shoes or eye-alluring outfit, to snatch it up first. Now trendy fashion resides mostly in Tribeca.

The atmosphere in the stores brought almost as many men as women, buying gifts for their girlfriends from the lingerie, jewelry or fur departments. We've all seen the influence of a woman who knows how to dress in order to make herself alluring. There is an art and intelligence to it. Having a keen fashion sense can attract royalty. Crossing legs at the right angle when sitting and sensually using body curves to full advantage while wearing an Yves Saint Laurent garment could be far more effective than a college degree in "getting a man." A marriage proposal from a rich, powerful gentleman promised the peace of mind that comes with financial security and being taken care of, not to mention an exciting lifestyle. Knowing how to dress was a free ticket into the newly opened Studio 54, part of the Donna Summer disco craze.

Where did this bizarre stream of consciousness come from? The common lie: *If I can just have a perfect face and figure and the most outstanding jewelry, house, man, and car, then people will look up to me and I will be secure and happy.* I was already married, but as youth faded, that sense of security was lost. Was I afraid of being tossed out with the trash? Drugs propped up my self-esteem, then turned on me, bringing desperation and insecurity I hadn't known before.

My universe became a prison. I was caught in the thorny briar patch of self-indulgence. I had graduated into the ME generation. Narcissism blocks the process of purpose until painful abnormalities are addressed through awareness, acceptance, and new behavior. Narcissism can be described as self-love, an excessive interest in one's own appearance, comfort, importance, and abilities. In psychoanalysis, it is a mind-dysfunction regression linked to the first stage of sexual development in which the self is an object of sexual pleasure.

Did my husband have his own narcissistic tendencies? He spent a lot of time on call in the emergency room at the hospital. They would have a yearly gathering. I wasn't invited. I remember feeling uncomfortable, wondering if other wives were also excluded. I never checked to find out but felt a loneliness that ached right through my bones, a loneliness I never felt when I was single.

During this time, a former medical school roommate of my husband's contacted him.

Michael started joking with him, reminiscing about crazy, wild times they'd shared, the strip clubs and scratches down my husband's back while hanging at parties with nurses. I would be on the other phone, listening. My husband stopped the conversation in a low steady tone.

"No, not into that."

It wasn't long before a new nurse came into our lives. I heard through the office staff that my husband had done a rhinoplasty on her; she had a crush on him and they were hanging out together. It turned out that it was the best nose I had ever seen him do. She was much younger than I was, married to an attorney, and when I first saw the two of them together it reminded me of two moths and a flame. I knew my marriage was in trouble. My way of dealing with the attraction was to become friends with her and encourage their friendship. My strategy was to act like it didn't matter to me, like it was no big deal. Maybe that would break up their intensity. I never asked my husband any direct questions.

Because I was on birth control pills, my husband never used a condom and I didn't address what he did when we weren't together. The thought of catching a sexual disease never entered my mind. He got very sick two times and I took care of him at home for over a month, but in the twenty years we were married I was never sick in bed. Somehow I knew that he would not be there to take care of me, so with an iron will to never be vulnerable in that way, I would secretly hold my breath while giving him food and being near him when he was ill. I remember one of his associates calling during that time, thinking I would be upset.

"It's part of the marriage contract."

The truth is, except for fear of getting sick, it was the only time I felt secure in our marriage because I could always keep an eye on him at home.

Since I had been on birth control pills for years and there was a recent news release stating a possible health risk associated with staying on them too long, I asked my husband if he would start taking birth control measures so I could get off them.

"No."

"Why?"

"I don't want to."

Why didn't I have the strength to tell him that was an unacceptable answer? It is equally hard to believe now that I didn't realize I was developing an auto-immune disease. There were so many red flags. My husband's doctor friends would smile when looking at the flushed butterfly shape across my face. It was a knowing, almost cynical look, as if to say, "You're on top of the world now and feeling good, but just wait." They did tell me I had Raynaud's, a disease associated with scleroderma. I could see in their eyes that they were amused about something. This was before the internet was in the palm of everyone's hand and I didn't have access to important medical information. Even if I went to the library, I had no idea what I was looking for or how to find the information.

After being nursed with bed rest, my husband returned to his practice and was contacted by producer Philip Gittelman. Philip was looking for a doctor to star in a syndicated series for television called *Today's Health*. He would be working with a woman by the name of Carlin Glynn. She is the mother of Mary Stuart Masterson, who starred in *Fried Green Tomatoes*.

Carlin received a Golden Globe nomination for *The Best Little Whorehouse in Texas*, which she and her husband produced. Carlin is a member of the Actors Studio and was connected with the White House as a lobbyist for Consumer Action Now (CAN), the first public-interest program run solely by women. The office in Washington, DC was devoted to promoting solar energy, and Robert Redford's first wife, Lola, was co-founder of CAN.

My husband brought the script home to read a week before production started. He had not had any acting classes and no help at all before production time. I knew there was no way he would be able to be natural without a tremendous amount of work. I couldn't believe that he wasn't prepped in some way. I worked with my husband for hours every day after he came home from the office. We went over and over the lines. There were only two people who knew how important that time spent was. Me and him. It certainly wasn't Philip Gittelman!

The series involved Carlin riding on her bicycle along a pathway next to a long row of trees. She represented a vibrant mother who took care of her family and used good advice that my husband offered. The series ran for about thirteen weeks.

I was invited to a gathering after the production was completed for a photo shoot. There was a picture taken of all of us and my husband placed it in his study along with the *Playboy* covers. When he took his belongings from the house during our separation before divorce, he left that photo behind along with Babe Shapiro's painting. I was surprised because he always seemed to value both of those friendships.

Carlin and her husband, Peter Masterson, were well connected in the arts and Washington, DC circles. I got involved with them in a fundraiser for CAN and convinced all of our friends (including my therapist) to fork over two hundred fifty dollars apiece for a table of ten. I can't remember much because I drank too much. Afterwards, Carlin kept asking me what was wrong. She didn't realize I had a problem.

Shortly after that evening, Carlin invited us to their home. I think it was close to New Year's. Robert Redford and his wife, Lola, Dustin Hoffman, and Tommy Tune were among the guests. Their way of entertaining was low key and family oriented. I went overdressed in my designer clothing while the women for the most part wore nondescript outfits. Robert Redford and the other men were in jeans. Tommy Tune, who is about six foot eight, avoided me while I was drinking due to my personality change. My flowing gown and leg placement at a flattering angle didn't cut it with this group. They were above superficiality. I came home and knew my world was crumbling. The truth — I was in the middle of the ocean all by myself, without an oar. I needed someone to tell me where I was going. I didn't know where I'd been and didn't know who I'd become.

Interesting though, I did know when my husband was out of sight that he led a secret life. I never questioned it. I also had incredible denial about my own behavior. I saw myself as holier than thou, some version of an impregnated virgin compared to him even though in time, I had affairs.

I had recurring dreams of flying. It was never outside, always inside my house. I would fly to the ceiling by spreading my arms out and using them like birds do. I would feel the air resistance as I tried to get higher and higher, experiencing the overview. These dreams were always wisdom-filled, happy. They were contrasted with recurring nightmares of my husband leaving me. I saw what he did with other people when he no longer needed them.

I became aware that my husband didn't support his mother and was resentful that she ran the household. Early on in our marriage they lost their daughter on Christmas Day. My husband lost his sister. She was the middle child and someone had slammed into her car. His mother would cry a lot and his father would just sit there, stoic.

My husband had such compassion for his father saying, "That was so hard on him. That was his little girl."

But there never seemed to be any sympathy for his mother and there was always a distance between them. The funny thing was, when she was with other people she couldn't stop talking about him and his achievements.

Looking back, I loved both his mother and father for different reasons. His father was the one with broken English; hers was perfect. He was an artist with a sweet humility about him, painting murals on walls. He made a living as a taxidermist. She ran the family, was highly organized and religious. Both of his parents had a mutual love of nature and their flowers won every award in the tri-state area for the largest blooms. Some of their dahlias were ten inches wide and featured in Sunday newspapers. During the summer, they would always have a beautiful bouquet for their church.

The time they spent with us involved long hours in the hot sun perfecting our rose garden, explaining how to properly cut, water and fertilize the flowers. His father would repair our stone walls and together they would prepare massive amounts of spaghetti and meatballs to place in our freezer. I was truly happy when they were around. Who wouldn't be? Later on I realized I was married to them, not my husband. With him there was always underlying tension. Our intimacy and quiet time involved a huge bowl of homemade caramel corn with lots of butter, fresh apples and nuts, and watching the New York Yankees … special attention paid to Reggie Jackson. Then there was *Saturday Night Live*. I remember enjoying that.

Every spring I would get homesick to be in Gardner with Grandma. Everyone who knew me well knew about her independent, pioneer lifestyle. That included my husband. He packed his camera. We flew off to Colorado to be with her.

She greeted us at the top of the steps. I cried. I couldn't quite believe that I was there again after all this time, and that she was real. She and her surroundings were still my security and heaven. It didn't get more real than Grandma's homestead at the end of the long narrow red road.

We entered the kitchen to the smell of fresh cherry pie baking in the oven. Grandma was fidgety, playing around with her apron strings.

"Hear you're a doctor from New York City? Nothin' like you has come to visit me in these here parts." I watched her shy grin. "Hear you're a throat doctor. I have somethin' wrong with my swallerin' rig."

My husband was very down to earth with her and fascinated. About fifteen minutes after he arrived she had him looking down her throat. He had become an OTORHINOSWALLERINRIG'NOLOGIST!

Things went well at first. He was truly captivated with her and the property. We took photos capturing the magic of the land. My husband also took pictures of me that I later used as headshots for modeling.

We had planned on staying three days but were gone after two. No electricity to puff his hair. Not to mention the second morning when all hell broke loose. Grandma placed warm water from the stove into the trough for my husband to bathe. He started washing up. She walked through. Nothing got in the way of her daily routine and getting out early to feed the cattle.

"You ain't got nothin' I ain't seen before."

That was the wrong thing to say to Mr. Italian Stallion. Within the blink of an eye we were packing.

I felt awful leaving Grandma so soon after not visiting for so long, but he was impossible and I knew it would be better for all of us if I just went along and got him out of there.

We returned home to an invitation from Dr. Roger, who was organizing an international symposium for facial plastic surgeons. He asked both my husband and I to contribute to the sessions involving inner and outer beauty. This would combine plastic surgery, exercise, makeup, and emotional well-being. I wrote a story using only slide-film images and music that would bring everything together. It was titled *Passages*.

I called Bill King, the photographer who had done almost all of the covers for *Cosmopolitan*, and asked if he would contribute his knowledge of what beauty consists of. Elizabeth Arden was also involved. We worked with a man by the name of Pablo Manzoni. Pablo would bring new trends in makeup to accentuate the success of surgery or to use as an alternative if someone wasn't ready for a procedure.

The entire production took about five months to put together. I set the slide film to music with my husband's help on the technical part. He had developed into a very good photographer over the years and did the photography. We all met in the hotel where the convention was held, and an hour before we were to get together for a meeting, my husband decided he didn't want to use the film I had orchestrated because he thought it was too corny. I was stunned and convinced him to show it to Bill King beforehand. We agreed that if Bill didn't like it, it wouldn't be used. Bill King loved it, its simplicity and tasteful beauty.

The program was talked about for years afterward and used as an example of innovative excellence. We were the IT couple everyone wanted to be with. There was an article written in the *New York Times* but no mention of my name. When I decorated his office, there was a large photo spread of my work in the newspaper, but no mention of my name. My husband finally admitted after we had a joint therapy session that he was jealous of me. I hadn't gone to school but I was looked up to without having to pay my dues. His patterns didn't change after counseling. I placed a state-of-the-art sound-and-lighting system in our home; he took credit for it. Equality between men and women had not yet evolved, at least not for us.

I accompanied him to almost all of his meetings held in places like Las Vegas, LA, and the Bahamas. I met a very good-looking doctor who was going through a divorce. He would introduce me as his wife when my husband wasn't around and we would laugh. He was exciting and handsome with a deep cleft in his chin, and he drove a Rolls-Royce. We ended up having an affair. He came to visit me in New York and stayed at the Plaza Hotel. We filled our noses with cocaine from rolled up hundred-dollar bills while drinking ninety-proof Stolichnaya and eating blinis with caviar from the Russian Tea Room in our luxurious hotel suite. It was an intensely vacant relationship filled with romantic agony, everything that one thinks is important when in the throes of addiction. We both later ended up in 12-step programs. It was the first meaningful experience we had together.

Victor's friend Fred resurfaced again a little later. He wanted my husband and I to meet him at Doris Duke's house, the New York socialite affiliated with the highly acclaimed Duke University. Fred was her hairdresser. She needed some cosmetic work done and Fred thought she would be pleased with my husband's artistry. I had never been in a space as dramatic and fastidiously decorated as her living room. Her walls were high-gloss black lacquer, smooth as glass with lighting strategically placed for flattering effects. The darkness contrasted with light, regal molding, and the clean, elegant Deco furniture. We waited for her for about ten minutes. She came from her kitchen with someone who I presumed was her butler. She appeared tall, had a seasoned, no-nonsense appearance, and provided a matter-of-fact description of what she wanted done.

I left there with a feeling of dread. *Oh my God, I'm going to be just like her in a few years!* In my mind, I was the girl still getting away with looking freshly young but almost at the crest of the hill, and she was the one over the hill trying to claw her way back up. I had just read a short story that revealed what a man was thinking when he looked across the table at his older date. In the morning light he saw clearly the traces of age on her face and throat — the little scars left by time. He presumed her promiscuity...

What a living nightmare of words for two people like us!

Chapter 11
Plastic Perfection

I wonder what happens to plastic surgeons when words are only words of what needs to be fixed. Do they get warped? I would think a steady diet of that kind of conversation would bring on insanity.

My husband was addicted to sunbathing and on weekends we were always at Jones Beach. We'd get up early before the traffic was bad and make the trip with the top down. My face would be as red as a beet and his face would look like dark-brown varnish. I would tell him it was dangerous for me to be out in the sun so much because I was fair. He paid no attention. However, he did place zinc oxide on his own nose. Nothing concerned him much during these trips except when people would spread their blanket too close to ours when he was drinking his wine and eating. We would have to pack up to a new location.

I later got cancer on my nose and needed extensive reconstructive surgery.

My husband built an impressive wine cellar in our cool basement after taking a wine-tasting course at a Four Seasons restaurant. He brought home a book weighing at least ten pounds titled *The Joys of Wine*. It covered the complete history of vineyards throughout the world and included proper etiquette procedures when ordering fine wines at restaurants like the Four Seasons. He had a handwritten list on the cellar door with his beautiful architectural penmanship. I got into his prized vintages when my drinking progressed out of control. He came home once to find three empty bottles.

1970 RED BORDEAUX: Honor of being among the very best vintages since World War II — fully developed merlot grapes add soft, round elegance.

WHITE BORDEAUX: A bounteous vintage in grapes, medium dry with charming fruit — wine of velvet smoothness, luscious fruit, and long life.

The third bottle's description read:

Very firm wine with strong spirit, character, depth, and balance — slow maturing — worth waiting for. Will last for twenty years.

His words: "You aren't a Class-A person anymore. If you don't stop drinking my wine I'm going to send you off somewhere."

He compared me to liquid royalty that didn't measure up. *I don't care because I don't care about anything but drinking.*

During Nixon's Watergate scandal, my sister Shanda came to visit and we all went out with a colleague of my husband's. We were talking about Nixon, but toward the end of the night after drinking, I developed a personality change, talking loud and getting argumentative. The next morning I was up early, making Shanda breakfast.

"How can you look so good and have energy after drinking so much?" At this point I didn't realize I had been abrasive the night before. "Penny, you were not yourself after dinner last night. I've never seen you like that." Her eyes were filled with pain, shock, and worry.

The drinking problem didn't seem real. Her look was. That day I started wanting to stop drinking, not for me but for her, because I could see it was hurting her to be around me. Shanda was the beginning of my wake-up call. I had to learn to trust the small voice inside that said listen to her, even though the progressive disease had distorted my thinking process, behavior, and natural instincts to care for myself in a healthy way. Addiction is called the disease of denial. My focus was on my husband's behavior, blaming him for my circumstances.

The decadent seventies and sobriety were like oil and water. They just didn't mix. I started taking trips to escape from reality. The first one was to LA, where I called my friend, photographer Larry Gordon. He met me at the Beverly Wilshire Hotel and took me to his home in the hills. He had just received some upsetting news, so he was not in a partying mood. He suggested I go visit Hugh Hefner's mansion. He called so that I could get in. The day was cloudless as I arrived into a titillating space filled with different varieties of tall trees. There were cascading waterfall pools and drinks to be shared in the sparkling champagne setting. The massive property with exotic animals on lush, landscaped grounds complemented Hugh Hefner and his mansion. I was in heaven.

After returning from LA, I found out my Uncle Buss had been hospitalized for surgery on his neck and he became partially paralyzed. I flew to Colorado Springs to be with him. I was so proud of the changes he had made in his life. He was loved and admired by everyone he came in contact with at The Broadmoor in Colorado Springs, where he was the resident golf pro under Dow Finsterwald.

On the way back, I ran into Bruce Cooper, Wilhelmina's husband, and we arranged to sit together in first class. He told me the bad news that Wilhelmina was dying of cancer. I thought about the long string of pearls she had gotten me from Majorca, Spain. I suddenly wanted to hold onto them like Catholics hold their rosary beads. I began feeling guilty for changing my agency to Eileen Ford. Wilhelmina became a treasure in death. Her elegant behavior had been consistent, down to earth, unemotional, and supportive. I began to realize she had treated me with respect I had not yet known how to give to myself, her, or others. Wilhelmina passed at forty years of age.

I kept hearing through small talk with family members that Grandma was getting too old to run the ranch by herself. My Aunt Mildred had gone to live with her, but it wasn't going well. Shanda and I took a trip to find Grandma was being treated badly when she didn't have control of her bladder or remember to take her pills. There was talk between my father, aunt and uncle about selling the ranch. After hearing about it I called my father.

"If it's put up for sale, please promise me that you will call because I would like to buy it." "I have a brother and sister and what I say could be voted against," he told me.

My plan was to find a caretaker for my grandmother so she could still live there. I knew it would break her spirit to move her from her surroundings, but it was more than that. It would break mine too. I had to prepare for the worst.

Shanda and I planned a trip to Cerrillos, New Mexico, to visit a man named Frank Fabin who lived not too far from Grandma's. I had met him in New York City through a stylist I used to work with in Chicago. He worked for Tressard Fabrics in the 979 Decorators building on Lexington Avenue. He was among the many artists fleeing New York City for an alternative lifestyle during that time. He had moved to New Mexico, built and lived in a cave house and changed his name to Sky. His home looked out onto a sea of red rocks and salmon sunsets. "Sky" fit right in with the atmosphere and was the one I was planning on asking to be with my grandmother. I knew he would love her and the Gardner area. I also imagined him making friends with Peter Rabbit and perhaps falling in love with the ranch enough that he would not want to move. This was probably wishful thinking because of his gypsy hippie soul.

Shanda called with small talk, then slid in that she found out the ranch had been sold to a man from Texas who worked for the Atlantic Richfield Company — they did hard-rock mining for underground pipelines. My father, aunt and uncle had convinced my grandmother to sell, and then sold her down Orphan River. She would be taken care of in a home for the elderly in Walsenburg.

I began living in darkness. One day I woke up with no sun left in me, yet I was still "really good" because of falsely boosted spirits from drugs and alcohol. My mother called during that time saying she had a bad dream about me being out in the ocean drowning and that she couldn't get to me. I remember not knowing how to respond to her.

I could still space out in the middle of the ocean with drugs. It allowed me to have hope, to be loved in songs ... songs like: "When a Man Loves a Woman," "You Light Up My Life," "Me and Mrs. Jones,"

"I've Got Love on My Mind," "Let's Get It On" ... on and on! I was insatiable. I needed it. I needed music *bad*. Vinyl records. There was something about the needle going into the groove and turning around in a circle of sound.

When at parties or discos, it was the Bee Gees' *Saturday Night Fever*. We could escape and forget everything but dancing. At home we'd always be sharing a new, exciting album like *Oxygène*. There were artists like Chuck Mangione, Morgana King, Tom Waits, Blossom Dearie, and Kenny Rankin who most people didn't know about. Then of course there was Billy Joel with "New York State of Mind" ... great pop music that you couldn't stop listening to. People like Elton John and the Jackson 5, James Taylor and Carol King ... "So Far Away" ... Carly Simon, "You're So Vain."

Music marks the time frames of our lives and connects love's many forms. Is the beating heart always secretly searching for another sexual partner to find expression, a new rhythm?

Why is it that when many of us find our first love we aren't satisfied for long? Why is the heart a lonely hunter? I would find the answer many years later.

My husband's days would be spent performing surgeries with his new nurse by his side. For evenings, she would make dinner plans for us all. She would show up knocking on our door with her husband and we would make our way to 85th Street, to a restaurant right around the corner on Columbus Avenue. As I walked behind them, I watched. She had a sundress on that showed her slim figure and pretty legs. An arrow of pain shot through me. That evening in the restaurant she commanded all of the attention. He had given her an adorable new nose and she was now more beautiful than I was. He would later marry that nose and remove our history. That night I drank around the clock.

In the early eighties, sobering events took place while we watched Michael Jackson moonwalk across the stage. John Lennon was gunned down thirteen blocks away from me on Central Park West, and the first case of AIDS was in the news the same year. By 1997, sixteen thousand were infected daily by the disease and over half a million had died. Nothing to write home about … "Strawberry Fields Forever." John Lennon had stated the Beatles were more influential than Jesus Christ...

In 1981 IBM's first personal computer was developed and within a short period of time, pushed hard on us as a necessity. Like gophers, geeks started rising from out of the earth to decipher the problematic complexities. I ignored them. In 1983, the beginning of the global internet started and by 1985, ".com," ".edu" and ".gov" came into being. For me all of the gadgetry hook-ups were too involved; it complicated life. I was better off without them.

Meanwhile, movies like *Star Wars* started using computer graphics. Would this new revolution, even though seemingly ignored, enhance my life — our lives?

I met a producer named Jason who hired me to do an ad for Kodak that took place inside Penn Station. I remember wondering how such an insecure guy from a small town had such a good clientele. Jason used his position to talk my husband into giving ten thousand dollars as an investor for a film. Jason started calling every day to tell me about the script and the director, Gary, who had written the material. He shared funny stories about Gary's friendship with Orson Welles, how big he was and how small Gary was and how he got entangled in his eating habits while working on projects together.

"Orson would buy them hamburgers for lunch and would gobble his down immediately. When Gary would start eating his, Orson would say, 'Why are you eating on my hamburger?'" I would laugh hysterically.

Later on he sent the screenplay and asked me to work on it as a creative consultant. The timing was great. My husband wanted me gone. Off to LA I went. I knew that Jason would pursue me. What he didn't know was how bad of a drinking problem I had.

There's a period of time in addiction that until it turns on you, the creative process can be quite good. I remember the Beatles talking about acid trips taking them into other worlds and using the visuals later. There were times working on the film that I would have bursts of creativity. I also had my first blackouts. While in one of them, I told the crew I had hepatitis B. Jason called my husband, worried about himself and the rest of the crew. I can't remember words like that coming out of my mouth, what led up to them or why I would say something so untrue. I was somehow able to smooth things over, stopped drinking, temporarily, and with shaking hands completed the job.

Most memories of being on the West Coast are blurry ... being placed in the back of Jason's vehicle ... going on location in a Winnebago every morning with a nice, pretty girl picking me up for the commute. We scouted for houses to shoot a family scene in the desert. I remember spending the night with Gary at his house in Venice and making love with him at night on the beach. After having a bottle of wine, I didn't care about anything but him. He had the essence of and looked like Keith Urban. When I was getting ready to leave, he asked me if I needed a ride to the airport. I said no but longed to be with him again.

After returning to New York City, I vaguely remember some of the crew visiting for a few days at my apartment on Central Park West. I think it included Maureen McCormick. I do remember a woman had my piano tuned as a thank-you for letting her stay in New York City. She was a conscientious worker credited for keeping the film together.

Jason called a few months after the film was edited and wanted to meet in Manhattan. I met him at his hotel but wouldn't go to his room.

"Are you afraid of me?"

"Yes."

I never saw or heard from him again. My husband declared a ten-thousand-dollar loss on the movie. I was to blame. He called my therapist upset that he hadn't picked up on my drinking problem and then added before he hung up that I had an abnormal relationship with my cat! I would dance around with her in my arms like she was a baby.

Our lives defied logic. When his mother found out about our marital woes, she would tell me that he spent hours trying to find me just the right present. She also told me to keep all the potted plants beautiful … that healthy plants would be helpful in mending our relationship.

My husband bought me a Yamaha piano for my birthday and my husband's old partner introduced me to a young woman named JoAnn who had just graduated from Juilliard who became my piano teacher. I stayed up all night with my friends, Cocaine and Alcohol, playing the piano while my husband was trying to sleep. I was obsessed with learning to play professionally and would record while practicing Debussy, Bach, and Schumann to see if I had developed sufficient muscle control in my hands (after doing loud exercises). I did excel quickly to the amazement of my teacher and also neighbors who could hear me all night. Who wouldn't improve, practicing sixteen hours a day over a two-year period?

My husband paid three thousand dollars so I could learn to speak French but it never came to fruition. This was at the time of the savings-and-loan debacle. Heating oil and interest rates were sky high. A tremendous amount of money went down the drain because I didn't follow through on things. We had money while many others were hurting. Division between rich and poor was looming. Ronald Reagan had taken care of the wealthy, lowering taxes for them while interest-rate inflation soared to 12 percent in the nation. It sparked the mini-series Rich Man, Poor Man.

I had plans in the works with my new "friend," my husband's nurse. We were to design clothing together. Her father owned a large bridal and fabric business and it seemed logical that together we had what it took to be successful. I visited his large facility with her. If all of this wasn't enough to fill my spare time after modeling, I started developing a small film of vignettes titled *Kisses* and got everyone I knew in on the filming. There was a vignette showing the love we as humans have for animals. I had taken Miso, had her tranquilized so she looked dead and placed fake blood on her. It ended with a kiss as she was "dying." The morbidity and drama of it all! I also photographed my "friend" in her beautiful wedding gown outside in a Larchmont park, underneath a weeping willow tree, an appropriate setting. It ended with a kiss and the vignette symbolized sacred marriage. I had earlier shown the film outline to my therapist and he thought it was quite good. I included the kiss of betrayal of Jesus by Judas after he suggested it. I just couldn't keep myself together long enough to finish projects.

Once again, I spent all night on cocaine and alcohol practicing on the piano. Morning came. My husband was upstairs shaving, getting ready to go to the office. After getting off the piano bench, I looked in the mirror and my eyes were blazing. I clearly saw Jesus's eyes reflecting back at me. I knew something profound had happened. I ran upstairs and told my husband. He didn't respond. How could he? He hadn't experienced the phenomenon and I had kept him from having any sleep.

It's hard to explain a spiritual experience with words. It contains supernatural energy that goes through your body, yet is much bigger. It contains an eternal component and melts negativity away — compartmentalization between your heart, mind and soul. It is weightless, filled with ecstasy, light and peace. Although it is drug- and alcohol-free, it can happen when you're on them. It is always unexpected and when it occurs you know without doubt that it is real. The memory doesn't fade and there is no way to erase it or bring it on. It's God's call. It was a touch of Heaven's healing that marked my future path.

I would later understand I had two spirits inside, battling it out. The One that was bigger than I would win. I didn't experience withdrawal symptoms when drugging and drinking eventually stopped. In God's time, I would be able to soar with eagles into high places.

Our favorite neighbors next door to us in Larchmont had a huge stone home built like a castle twice as big as ours. It was on an impressive plot of land up on a hill, with sloping terrain and magnificent landscaping. It made all of the other houses seem unimportant. The owner, Ralph Bolton, then in his eighties, had been an executive for Standard Oil and spoke seven languages. Josephine, his wife, had been an opera singer until her career was cut short with a vocal-cord problem (her operation left a poor result). They had a full-time live-in caretaker they had brought with them from England. They were members of Westchester Country Club in Rye and we became members through them. They would have us over for lunch on their three-tiered terrace or during the winter months, in their massive dining room filled with expensive antiques and large round vases that looked like they had been discovered after being under water for thousands of years.

My husband took care of Ralph's ear-nose-and-throat problems even though he had stopped that part of his practice for everyone else. They were the most loving neighbors and we both valued their friendship. Ralph later took me to his church in Larchmont when he knew things had gotten bad for me and was instrumental in getting me to All Angels Church in Manhattan.

Ralph had to have a procedure done at the local hospital. My husband and his nurse (or "girlfriend" as I called her) looked after him. Josephine told me when I was visiting her one day that Miss It Girl was making herself indispensable to my husband, and that they were often seen together at Westchester Country Club. At this point in my marriage, I had no control. Whatever I tried to do had no effect. I went off on yet another tangent to block the living nightmare.

My next adventure was taking classes at New York University. This decision was a good one, even through progressive, crippling alcoholism. Professor Nick Tanis taught the film class I attended with about thirty students. Tanis was tall and thin with dark hair. I was impressed with him because he focused on teaching us writing, storyboarding, setting up locations and editing. He did all of this after receiving news that he had cancer. He liked my work immediately. In my first film, which dealt with healing from nature, I told a story with a close-up of a caterpillar crawling up a tree in Central Park and Tanis ended up using that piece as an example of an advanced concept.

Because I had modeled, a lot of students wanted to use me in their films. I was also photographed for NYU's Summer 1982 catalog. I was having trouble keeping up with everything and ended up taking my own footage to an editor, telling him how I wanted it spliced. Because of my drinking, I couldn't thread the machines used in those days and still leave time for other students to access the equipment. I remember being so happy when I received an A- from Nick Tanis. It was my first college credit. I then said goodbye to my friends at NYU.

My husband and I, along with his lover / office manager / nurse and her husband, were on our way to Greece to do a rhinoplasty on one of Aristotle Onassis's relatives and also to celebrate my birthday on August 6. Miss Thing was already his private nurse and was needed on the trip. I hadn't discouraged the arrangement. Unconsciously, I wanted the truth to come out.

We all met Mrs. Onassis at her home for dinner. I remember she thought my husband's nurse was his wife and seated them together. I vaguely remember him taking along many of his own instruments and with his nurse's help, laying them on the bed in our room the night before surgery. There are snippets of clarity. By this time in my drinking, I didn't know if I was dreaming when thinking about the day before or if it had actually happened — except for the severely painful things. They are forever memories collected, part of who I am ... selective memories not to be dwelled upon. I remember going to dinner in our hotel and sitting on a piano bench next to the player late at night, then later wandering around the hotel grounds by myself ... being in the bathroom suite of the hotel, my husband washing down my legs with water from the bidet ... I must have fallen down ... crying, saying I wanted to go home. Later everyone said I was ruining their vacation. For my birthday I got a bottle of champagne from my replacement and her husband, then a short fur coat from my husband that he bought at the hotel. *She* was upset with my husband after I received it.

We all flew somewhere a few days after the surgery was completed. It must have been Skorpios, the private island that Onassis owned, which had been barren before he surrounded it with sand, making it a family compound. I had no idea where I was at the time, except being in the water, next to a big white ship in the noonday sun with a floating device around my neck. I didn't trust that it would totally keep me afloat. Water kept going into my mouth and entering my nose. Everyone was laughing at me when I panicked as some of my face would sink into the water. As we left on our way back to the United States, I remember the fading Greek ruins against the blue sky, their marble Doric and Corinthian columns gleaming like a movie set backdrop.

Once I got home, I got on my knees at the side of the bed. "God, please help me."

Help came quickly. I went to my therapist and told him I wanted to stop drinking and couldn't. He suggested I go on Antabuse, a drug people take that will make them sick if they drink. I then made an appointment with a psychiatrist for a one-session analysis in order to fill the prescription. I remember asking her if I was stupid. She assured me I wasn't because I was able to comprehend complex issues. I carefully took in her elegant office on Manhattan's Upper East Side.

"I'll write out the prescription, but have you ever thought of attending a 12-step program? There are some wonderful meetings at a church near here, at 55th and 5th. It's called Fog Lifters."

I went straight from her office to a meeting. It was August 13, 1983. I haven't had a drink since.

Chapter 12
Welcome to the Real World

The one-hour meeting was on the fifth floor. There were about forty people present, some on their lunch break from businesses they worked for in the area. That particular meeting was full of artists — mostly writers, singers, and actors. During the first six months I remember living in a pink cloud, convinced I was being brainwashed. I started going to another meeting across the hall leaving the beginners behind, thinking they were much sicker than I was. I chose as my sponsor a former model-turned-actress in the "more sober" room. It turned out that she was a member of Actors Studio and ten years older. She lovingly taught me the twelve steps and passed on the promises that I would receive in life if I just kept attending meetings.

I lived in those rooms almost every day through the eighties. The more I went, the more I knew I needed to go, realizing I didn't know how to care for myself. At that time I didn't even realize that as a member of the Screen Actors Guild and the American Federation of Television and Radio Artists union I could re-enter work at some point, take acting classes and have a new career. I had no connection with the work I had accomplished. In my mind, I was convinced I had only been successful through the help of drugging and drinking since it relaxed me into being more creative. The reality was that the disease had robbed ten years of my life.

The very nature of alcoholism strips away emotional growth and, once one stops drinking, it all has to be made up. It takes a long time before brain distortion is normalized. Years. I truly believed that my artistry was gone. My sponsor helped me start getting self-esteem back. I was hired to do props and wardrobe for a production of *Suddenly Last Summer* by Tennessee Williams, directed by Madeleine Sherwood, through the Actors Studio.

At our meetings, there was always spiritual material set up along with 12-step information. A young man volunteered to present and maintain all of the books and pamphlets. He had been going to meetings regularly, sharing about his ongoing struggle with AIDS. I walked up to him as he stood behind the long table of literature. Our eyes met. We studied one another. It was a forever moment.

"I'm looking for a really good spiritual book. Which one do you recommend?"

Without hesitation, he picked up *God Calling* and handed it to me. It had changed his life, helped him to live with grace while dealing with a disease that had none. The book changed my life as well, it led me to the Bible; and the memory of that young man is still with me every morning as my eyes catch the living words that pop off the page.

After a while I started attending meetings for adult children of alcoholics (ACOA). I believe it was this program which helped me the most, even though my parents weren't alcoholics. The meetings were a protected environment where everyone was free to talk about their childhoods, to become aware of lingering pockets of fear and how these could compromise the body. At ACOA, I was given tools to start on a new path. I didn't know what sweetness in life really was, how to relax in order to receive the many gifts that fear had crowded out and stolen from me. I remember this being the first time in my life I felt I could be myself with other people. I was later blessed to pass all of these lessons on to women incarcerated at Rikers Island, opening a new pathway for others with the same tools I had been given.

My sponsor was instrumental in getting me involved in acting classes with Warren Robertson. He was highly regarded in New York City as a teacher and chose whom he wanted to work with. Jessica Lange had been with him and young students like Christopher Plummer's daughter, Amanda, who already had blooming careers and wanted to hone their craft.

I was concerned about not being able to memorize quickly enough to keep up with the class. Warren laughed and said it was just a matter of developing new muscles and within a short time I would overcome the problem. There were about thirty students in his class and we always started with loosening up exercises. He only played pop music that was the very best to dance to. He would have us gather in small groups to dance, sometimes with calisthenics so our bodies were on the floor intermingling. The goal was to "free our instruments," releasing sexual inhibitions before doing the scenes he would give us each week.

While I had a tough time with memorization, I was naturally creative in music choreography. A student by the name of Stuart Williams asked me what dance company I was with! He had developed a crush on me and the fingers of his hands would lock up when he was around me. I never noticed this. Warren did and mentioned it to Stuart in class. He placed us together to work on a scene between an older woman and a young boy. The play was *Tea and Sympathy*. Stuart was about eighteen years younger than I was.

I drove my Porsche to his home in Connecticut where his father presided over the church which was located next to their home. I remember the wide, curving driveway with towering Norway spruce and European birch making their presence felt as I approached. I had enjoyed the drive past Victorian houses in the historical district lined with granite walls and a cemetery. I knocked on Stuart's door with the *Tea and Sympathy* script in my hand. His father answered and came out with his son behind him. He was cold and stiff, with dark hair with rather pointed features, and didn't look at all like Stuart, who was blonde with an angelic face.

He stared at me and then at the Porsche. "You look like something out of Central Casting."

His sharp words and demeanor shocked me, but I kept my composure. There was some small talk about class, with his father asking questions. I remember looking at Stuart. His body language looked as if he had just been whipped.

"How is Stuart doing in class?"

"You'll have to ask Stuart that."

His father went back into the house after failing to get information from me.

I followed Stuart into the magnificent church. We sat down in the pew together and stared at all the stained-glass windows surrounding us. We were two rebellious children against an authority figure, with the thrill of wanting to act out the romance of *Tea and Sympathy* in a chambered, gothic tower of prohibition. I was only about one year sober. I had a lot to learn about light and reflection coming through those sacred windows.

Because of the unscripted scene with Stuart's father, the pastor, we got little done that day except to read our parts out loud and decided to meet in Larchmont after the next class. I didn't drive to class, so we took the train from Grand Central Station together. We reached the Pelham stop on the way to Larchmont. I was looking out with my hand resting on the glass pane of the window. He must have been watching me. He took my hand as though, if he didn't act then, his life would end. He kissed it, sucking my index finger quickly before the moment vanished. He had never touched me before. I melted. His boyish sweetness blew me away. He held my hand in his lap like he wanted it to be there forever.

My husband and I struggled with our marriage in my newfound sobriety. We went to one more therapy session together and were told our relationship was father-daughter rather than two equals, and how it would have to change to make it work. It had gotten to the point that I would ask him if I could go to the store. I remembered his mom and dad coming to visit in the early days of our marriage. His mother was strong and independent; his father sweet and caring. The apple fell far from the tree.

They showed me attention and affection that never existed in my own childhood, and it meant the world to me. It was sunny as he and I worked on our hands and knees caring for the rose garden during one of their visits and my husband's breath was riding a happy whistle.

Through all of the highs and lows, through the fog of my drinking and pain of recovery, I still clung to the hope that we would someday be old, walking down a path together, holding hands.

One day, and I don't know which one it was … the music died. There are things that happen in life that defy explanation. As drugged as I was during the seventies and early eighties, there was a clean, clear energy that allowed me to take in certain information. *The Family of Man*, photographed and illustrated by Edward Steichen, fell into my hands. Reading material was of no interest to me at that time. His name meant nothing, but his work never left me. Reliving and writing about this time has been difficult because I was scattered, shattered in so many pieces. Broken. There were no quick fixes. There was nothing sexy about getting sober. One doesn't stop drugging and drinking and then everything gets normal. It took years to unscramble my brain before I was comfortable enough with myself to build a new life. It took listening to other people's stories, learning from them and then slowly putting mine back together. The good news for anyone reading this book who thinks they might have a drinking problem: You can get the best therapy and help that money can buy in AA, and it won't cost a penny. It's a fact. I've lived it. And if you can accept this free gift, life will eventually blossom beyond your wildest dreams.

The AA programs gave me stability and strength to face things head-on that I hadn't been able to before. I learned that alcoholism is a disease that enjoys isolation. I had support from many people to address the complexities within the illness. The healing process started only when I stopped hiding. I shared secrets. My process started helping others in the same open way that others had helped me.

Bill Wilson is one of the co-founders of AA. He too had a spiritual experience after crying out to God. His description included a great bright light, a feeling of finally being a free man, followed by God's wonderful Presence. He never drank again after that and continued working in the New York Stock Exchange. In 1938, he wrote the book *Alcoholics Anonymous* and is responsible for meetings branching out all over the world. Most of them are held in churches. They are free from politics. *TIME* listed him as one of the most important people in the twentieth century and wanted him on the cover, but he refused. He also refused an honorary degree from Yale University. Why? He considered the ego a hindrance, an interference to direct communication with God.

I remember having one final face lift from my husband after returning from Greece. He didn't resist this. It's not realistic that old patterns suddenly disappear. I was still trying to relieve anxiety with external quick fixes when the inside was in need of slow, steady repair.

Negative energy extended to the entire office after my husband's nurse had been hired, and this was felt on the day of my surgery. My friend Helen, who worked as his office manager for years, had become vulnerable, afraid of being fired. I reassured her that everything was okay. I even kept up my "friendship" with my husband's nurse but I insisted she not be present for this final face lift, and she wasn't. I remembered things she had said only a few months earlier, behind my husband's back. "His only interest is to become famous."

We laughed about it together.

I passed this information on to Helen. "Help him keep that goal and everything will work out fine." Helen was a vulnerable, struggling single mother who had just moved into a new home with her two children. She was stressed out. I helped pickle all her floors with the same toxic material I had used in the office. It was my crazy way of saying that I was on top of things, had it together, still had power.

A few days after surgery, Helen's body language told me that not only was she on her way out but so was I. She knew something I didn't.

I spoke with my psychologist, who said, "Be strong. Insist that woman be fired." I remembered a conversation with my husband about "that woman" getting into modeling after she'd expressed an interest in it. He said, "She's too intelligent for that."

Despite all this, I wasn't ready to sever the sacred bond. For me it really came down to "for better or worse." My parents had stayed together under terrible circumstances; so would I.

That woman told the office staff and my husband that I had been having affairs. His handsome ENT associate on the West Coast was mentioned. She also made the accusation that I was a lesbian, which she knew would be completely unacceptable to him.

My husband came home from the office, went upstairs, and lay on the bed in a fetal position. I knew something terrible had happened. I asked him what was wrong. He was broken.

After a couple of days he recovered and said that if I didn't do the cooking and the shopping he was going to divorce me. "You're trying to keep me down."

I became frozen for a period of time. Again, I called my therapist, who was upset with me. "Why didn't you call me immediately? We could have straightened this out. Sometimes I feel like shaking you!" He then revealed that Miss It had placed a call to him and his reaction was, "I wiped the telephone off and hung up."

I continued attending 12-step meetings every day but kept waiting for the next shoe to drop. I was still hoping that time could heal the marriage and the nightmare would go away. At this point we were in counseling together and the therapist was trying to help us make it.

My husband's birthday rolled around and my therapist said it would be a good idea to have a party for him. I thought the idea was ludicrous but did it anyway, inviting all our friends plus my new friends from AA. I hired an opera singer to sing "Happy Birthday" to him. The party was held in New York City at a doctor's house. I had Ellen help me plan the details. His nurse/girlfriend was of course there, and I mentioned what had been going on to Babe Shapiro, our close friend whom I spoke with almost daily. Babe knew I had been suspicious for some time and had tried to assure me it was nonsense. I knew Babe cared for me and only wanted me to be happy. He simply couldn't believe it was anything serious.

By the end of the evening there was a clear division between drinkers and non-drinkers. After the party my husband dropped me off at our pied-à-terre, thanked me and left.

He began disappearing without explanation. A week later we planned to meet for lunch. He never showed up. I remember feeling sick to my stomach as I left alone. I had planned on catching a ride back to Larchmont with him.

A few days later, he again said he would pick me up at our New York apartment for lunch and was four hours late which was very out of character for him. I thought he was just playing games, being ugly, but was it more than that? His study in Larchmont had become a mess and so was he. Was learning about my affairs the trigger?

138   How Nature Healed a Broken Soul

Then Helen called to tell me that she had never seen anyone treat my husband as badly as his nurse/girlfriend did. A few weeks later, Helen was fired.

I wasn't able to tell my therapist how bad things were; I felt guilty. In my mind, everything was my fault. These emotionally crippling thoughts would slowly become unveiled and then changed through my regular ACOA meetings.

My therapist said that what had unfolded in that office with Helen's firing was nothing short of a lynching. "Why are you not doing anything?"

"Helen was my friend. We had a lot of fun together."

He looked at me with an exasperated expression.

Deep down I knew I needed to move on to a new life. My husband and I were not a perfect fit; I no longer had the passion to stay.

I sat down at the kitchen table across from my husband. "You are not a class-A person anymore!"

Even in his pain I knew he'd heard me and gotten it.

I'd been sober for over a year and it would be more than two years before the divorce became final. During this time, my husband and I had separate, clandestine lives. I continued acting classes in New York City. One weekend, I changed my usual pattern and took an early train back to Larchmont. It's a day I'll never forget. The roses needed watering. My husband was leaning over our bedroom terrace. He had been in Paris for six weeks, a trip I found out about from my own detective work. His shirt was off and his skin was bronze tan. He wore dark glasses and kept a Sony Walkman plugged into his ears. I thought about my vows to this man and ran inside. I saw he had placed our wedding photos and all pictures of us together face down. I started crying and tried to hug him.

"I understand what you're trying to do, but this marriage is over. With the way my pension is set up it would be better for you to file right now rather than for me to do it."

He took off his dark glasses. I hadn't seen his eyes for weeks. He looked at me in a pleading way.

"I'll take care of you. You'll get more than Johnny Carson's wife." They were also going through a divorce at the time.

I looked deep into his eyes the same way I did when I was studying Katsu's. My cat's eyes were mysterious and seemed to go on forever. His were vacant, like marbles. I remember thinking he must be insane to think I would believe something like that.

My husband's "everything" started ringing the house, saying she needed to speak to him about office matters. I started hanging up on her. She was persistent in calling back and said if I kept interrupting office procedures, her husband would look into taking legal measures against me.

His new "savior" was not the only one calling our home. There was also an odd woman by the name of Nancy who lived a few blocks away, wore too much makeup and knew there were problems in our marriage. She started fishing for information, sympathizing with me, saying that there was a woman sending my husband flowers in the office. She used his first name, which indicated she was more than just a neighbor or patient. How did she know that someone was sending him flowers? When had she been in his office? It was a crazy conversation. She asked me questions that I would have been the last to know answers to.

I also received a call from Colombia, his rosemary-and-thyme love from the past. Her voice sounded a million miles away, hurt and vulnerable. She also had many prying questions. I didn't tell her that I knew her... that her name had been etched into my brain.

While I was still in New York City, my husband removed a fifty-year-old holly plant. It had framed our front steps and he replaced it with rhododendrons. We bought one hundred narcissus and tulip bulbs to plant in a rock-filled area by the windows in our dining room. When I started to help by handing them to him he said he wanted to do it by himself. We had always made beautiful flower designs together inside our home, often with his parents' help. Even when I had moments of nostalgia for what had been, he resisted. It was nothing but a cruel game.

My husband's new obsession was Dr. Ruth. He talked about her sexual openness and expertise. Throughout this, unbelievably, we were still involved sexually once in a while. I felt it was time to end this connection and I never shared a bed with him again ... but emotional separation is never final. Even after marriage ends, it stays a part of who you are.

I found out that he was leaving the country to share some operating procedures; he'd be gone for about a week and the girlfriend was going with him. I remember wondering what her husband thought about that.

My husband packed the slide film *Passages* I had worked on, but I removed it from his luggage and hid it at a neighbor's house. He and his new mate were booked on a Concorde flight to Paris before traveling to England.

At this point, I was in recovery and not working. Money was tight for me, even though he had plenty. The next morning while he showered and shaved before going to the office, I went down to the Mercedes and found a large stash of cash in the trunk. We both knew it was *his* money, even though we were married. And I had "stolen" money from his bedroom drawer when drinking and he had complained about it to some friends of ours. Now he was keeping his cash in the car! *Should I take it all at once or only a little so he doesn't know?*

I had been paralyzed out of guilt when he made me feel like a thief, but desperation is powerful. In the end, I lacked the courage to take the money from the trunk and ended up fourteen thousand dollars in debt by the time the divorce was final. He and his girlfriend seemed to always be three steps ahead of me. Now I know why my therapist wanted to shake me.

In time I became friends with a woman named Claire who, like me, attended AA meetings regularly. She was interesting to be around because unlike me, she read Charles Dickens religiously while working on a new book she started writing in sobriety. I admired her passion and commitment to the written word.

I shared with Claire my plan to get into my husband's office in the middle of the night to copy all of his financial records. I needed to establish what procedures were off the books and done for cash. I found out that one of the regulars on *Saturday Night Live*, who was married at the time, had brought his girlfriend in for a rhinoplasty and paid cash. Was that the money I had found stashed in the trunk of the Mercedes? By this point I was basking in almost three years of sobriety, and knew I had to act fast.

I was able to talk a young locksmith into meeting at my home at midnight. We went to my husband's office and I watched him slither up to the door hidden by shadows from the street. He wore dark clothing and looked like a thief. I could see he was both scared and excited about the well-planned caper. He easily maneuvered the lock to get in.

Mission accomplished. I paid and thanked my locksmith for his beautiful black-cat agility.

I turned the lights on and got to work. The file cabinets were locked in the rear consultation room. I had my tools in hand, bending aluminum to pry drawers open. My husband would see what I had done when he flew back from Paris. I found more than I was looking for. A diaphragm was mixed in with the office records. It was contained in a small tin case, otherwise it might have sprung out at me. It looked dangerous but I took it home along with all of the records I (we) copied until five o'clock in the morning. Reality from that night still burns in my mind.

Yellow pages were used to hire a private detective. I was fortunate enough to get a good team. We met at my apartment in New York City. The woman was quiet and young, the man middle-aged and confident. Their combined intelligence was just what I needed. I knew their work was not going to be easy. It turned out that my husband changed planes at the last minute. Eventually, my detectives had caught up with my husband and his girlfriend, photographed them and retrieved records from the hotel they were staying in, including room service dinners for two served with wine. The Class-A wine added up to an astronomical bill. Another detective task accomplished.

One afternoon, as I was backing out of the driveway to go to a piano lesson, my husband pulled up behind my car in his Mercedes. I hadn't seen him since he returned from his trip. I knew he wouldn't cause a scene outside because of the neighbors. He went inside and sat down at the kitchen table. His voice was low, even, and deadly.

"I decapitated you in my mind."

I called my sister and told her what he had said.

A few days later, Stuart from acting classes called and invited me to his parents' home for the weekend while they were away on a summer vacation. He played chef, preparing sole with fresh basil. We made love in his parents' bed that night. Afterwards he followed my every turn, keeping my back protected and warm with his body. It was a sleep dance, a beautiful ballet. He said my shape reminded him of embracing a cello. I couldn't quite return the same unguarded, open innocence. I didn't know what that kind of love was.

It wasn't long before Stuart got enmeshed in the bad energy of my personal life. I told him my husband was having an affair and I needed to catch him living with his girlfriend. I would put on a disguise wearing a short black wig and we would go to the parking lot behind my husband's office. She would always accompany him to place things in the back of his precious Mercedes. We tried to follow him but Stuart's clunker couldn't keep up. It ended up being a dangerous task and we finally had to give up.

I was sober enough to know I wasn't good for Stuart. My life was out of control, so I sadly ended the relationship. In the future, Stuart would become a man of the cloth, like his father, presiding over a church not far from me in Pennsylvania.

I was no longer my husband's property and was not allowed to touch *his* property. His new black Mercedes was the first car that I hadn't contributed to monetarily. I remember looking down from the guest bedroom of our home as he would leave for work every morning. His ritual was wiping it down with a cloth until there wasn't a speck of dust. He was now at the top of his career after working diligently for almost twenty years.

Why did I keep watching him through the window long after dark heaviness had settled around my heart? What was I feeling? Now I know it didn't have much to do with him. It came from a much earlier time in childhood when I had cried out for help feeling so ill. Sleep finally came … help also came but I felt isolated and alone in my pain. Destiny. I had chosen the perfect partner.

At this point I had been excised, like a tumor. The scalpel blade was sharp, cutting through all the layers of time we had spent together. It wouldn't be long before I watched him drive away one final morning. Our life together was over.

Two things happened in one day. I was walking from the train station on Chadsworth Avenue going home and saw my husband with his girlfriend in the Mercedes. Her eyes darted all over the place. She couldn't look at me. His eyes stayed straight ahead, waiting for the traffic light to change.

When I got to our Larchmont home, there was a letter in the mail addressed to my husband. Inside was a statement that included his new address, precisely the information Stuart and I had been looking for. It had been sent to the Larchmont address by mistake, and now with no effort on my part, I had what I needed.

My husband's office was now old enough to collect a diverse history. It's where I had a facelift and also where I found someone else's diaphragm. It was a place I had been on my hands and knees making the oak floor he walked on during surgery look peaceful and ethereal. The thin, translucent layer of pickling on top of the wood added a three-dimensional glow. I imagine my husband must have taken full advantage of the ambiance and used his prestige to entice his female entourage. Soon he would be free. Which woman would fulfill her dream of marrying a doctor? What would happen to the marble, the desk, the residue of me, the first wife?

I picked up the phone to call my husband's favorite Ms. Everything's husband. We hadn't spoken since my meltdown in Greece. I had no credibility but told him about his wife continually calling my home. I told him about catching her with my husband at the airport.

His reply, "They were working together, and my wife went over to visit her relatives in England."

"She told me that you were going to contact a lawyer in White Plains if I didn't stop disrupting office procedures by hanging up on her when she calls my home."

"She said what?"

I didn't tell him about finding what I had to assume was his wife's diaphragm with my husband's office records. I had planned on returning it so he could give it back to her, but my husband found where I had hidden it. It took off on yet another blazing journey — so elusive, so hot, that thin ring of rubber in a tin case.

Ms. Everything's husband agreed to meet in a cheap Japanese restaurant. It was almost two years since meeting on the trip to Greece, now our eyes met across the table. I couldn't believe he had been in so much denial.

"You were such a mess in Greece, Penny." "What are you going to do?"

"I'll find somebody else and move on … allow revenge to have its place at the proper time."

I never saw him again.

Chapter 13
The Nature of Separation and Fusion

I started going back to our apartment in the city on Wednesdays and Thursdays. When I returned to Larchmont on a Friday, my husband had moved out, taking half the furniture and all the antiques we had purchased from Lillian Nassau. He took a Lalique vase and our Italian designed Atelier sofa and chairs. The house that I had taken so much pride in was destroyed … everything stripped from its special place. The stability of the home's careful arrangement helped me to stay together. It was now gone … no money, no comfortable place to live. He and his new fiancée had executed a well-orchestrated plan to break me. What they didn't realize was that I was already broken.

The following day, while sitting on the floor in the living room, the doorbell rang. I was served with divorce papers. Anyone who has experienced this knows the effect.

During this turbulent time, my husband appeared on *Live with Regis and Kathie Lee*. There was a scheduling problem that day, and he was placed last with little time to talk about rhinoplasties. I watched him from the television he had left behind. He had managed to keep himself together, come full circle right in front of me. And I was jealous of his success, frightened by the change of being alone.

Alcoholism can cause psychosis with side effects long after the drinking has stopped. For a while I became frozen. People in the AA program were watchful, helping to lift me up, get me to a better place without judgment. My world began to slowly widen. Acting classes loosened me up. It was good to be around so many different people.

I met a woman named Diane Warner. We both started studying with Larry Moss who was known as one of the top teachers in New York City. Larry was dating Twyla Tharp at the time, and he had a group of well-seasoned actors, like Kate Capshaw, who later married Steven Spielberg. Diane's husband, Jan, was with William Morris Agency and had written the score around a story for a Broadway musical where a woman falls deeply in love with a soap-opera star and starts writing him letters. I was invited to the backers' audition. The work in progress was introduced to raise money for production. Larry was familiar with some of Jan's work and wanted Twyla to meet him. The project never took off, but sitting right next to me was a lithe, wired flirt with a face a little like Vincent van Gogh's, and a lot of money. His name was Conner Barlowe, and it turned out we were both going through divorces, both getting beat up.

Conner was charismatic with a great sense of humor. On our first date we went to the romantic restaurant One if by Land, Two if by Sea, then to his business address on the Upper East Side. I had driven my Porsche into the city and was lucky to get a parking space on the street. We talked until the wee hours of the morning and then I took the elevator down to the street.

My Porsche's battery was dead; I must have left my parking lights on. There was a cab driver next to me who had jumper cables and offered to help, but in the end, I had to call the Porsche dealership. I remember the car slowly being raised up on a flatbed. A strong beam of sunlight was on it and seemed to rise up and fade away. I felt that something extraordinary was happening ... a haunting separation, like I would never see my car again.

Two days later, the dealership called with bad news. The electrical system was burned out. The jumper cables had been placed backward. And worse, the rest of the car was totally rusted out. "I removed the floor mats in the front seat and there's a big section of your car completely gone next to the accelerator. The entire back end is rusted out underneath. Have you been driving on the expressway?" There was anger in his voice. "You're lucky the car didn't fly apart and you weren't killed. You put other lives in danger."

My husband had taken care of all of the mechanical tune-ups on all of our vehicles. Now I knew what he knew. He had taken the new well-kept black Mercedes and left me with the falling-apart Porsche.

Conner owned an impressive fleet of automobiles and insisted that I take his Jaguar. He was generous, exciting, full of energy and oddly unsettling. I would soon find out that he embodied two personas that made him unpredictable.

He read Edgar Cayce books. I started reading one beside him in bed. Edgar Cayce had read the Bible seven times by the age of twelve and could work in supernatural energy until three o'clock in the morning. He was called the sleeping prophet.

My new bedlam partner was also inspired by Donald Trump's book, *The Art of the Deal*. Conner's success during that time depended on doing deals. The alluring bad-boy lifestyle was layered with inner demons, periodic drugging, and womanizing. The only constant was chaos. When we met, he had three lawsuits going on and no driver's license, and during the separation from his wife, he had been so distraught, he hadn't filed income taxes.

Even though I had been drug-and-alcohol free for over three years, I still wasn't sober enough to know that being with him was perilous. As crazy as it sounds, I believe Conner was placed into my life by God. I remember one time being in a trendy disco, an old converted church. It had transformed into an S&M club, with scantily clad men and women behind bars. Conner ended up buying cocaine for everyone. I was the only one who took a pass. When off drugs he was loving, always encouraging my artistic endeavors. I wrote my first screenplay and poetry while with him, and through Conner was able to start seeing things as they really were. I would see him and his friends sober and then on drugs and see how it diminished them. My process of breaking away was beginning. I no longer had any desire for drugs and alcohol that had been a primary focus in the past.

He and his chauffeur would pick me up at Carnegie Hall after acting class. I was mesmerized sitting inside the Daimler, sinking into soft, cushy leather that never lost its fresh smell, intoxicated by the cloud-like surroundings framed in exotic swirls of burled wood. Soon

I would be sharing the sensual interior with an impressive fleet of Conner's other women. Like me, few of them could resist the seduction of the regal vintage Daimler.

One evening, Conner picked me up at 85th and Central Park West. We were on our way to an event at the Morgan Library. I had on a long black velvet Yves Saint Laurent gown that flowed into the back seat. He lifted the soft fabric to view my legs. It was a habit of his. It brought excitement and undergarment drama. Titillating sexual conversation always ensued. Any sense of privacy from the glass enclosure separating us from the chauffeur would quickly evaporate. The man in the front seat hung on every word. Conner was entertaining him, enjoying him as a third party! It was a game that probably had gone on for years.

"I'm going to be dancing with another woman a couple of times tonight."

"Why are you telling me this now?"

"She just flew in from California and I need to talk with her."

"You're trying to start a fight and I'm not going to be part of it."

This kind of behavior always preceded a binge, separating us for a couple of months. He would eventually get back to his best behavior, give me a call and we would resume our relationship like nothing had happened.

One night, we were in my basement discussing some ideas for a film Conner would be producing — the French Normandy architecture of my home in Larchmont had inspired him — and came upon a big box on the floor next to the empty wine cellar. Conner picked it up to clear the space and saw it was filled with canceled checks from old income tax returns. I had written them to my husband many years prior to the eighties.

"Give these to your lawyer. They'll help your case."

During this time I was in trouble financially. My husband had canceled all the credit cards (only available to men until the early seventies) and without employment I couldn't apply for my own. If it hadn't been for Conner, I also would have been without a car. I filed a court order for temporary alimony before our scheduled court date. There was a six-week period when I had no money. I had to call my parents. Their "power of example" daughter had turned into an alcoholic, would soon no longer have a husband and was now begging for money. They reluctantly sent three hundred dollars.

John Herget, the landlord of my New York apartment, surprised me with one thousand dollars and placed stuffed animals, windmills and balloons on my terrace to cheer me up. Babe Shapiro was at my side, offering to take care of me monetarily if I needed it. My therapist suspended his fee until I could pay him. My Larchmont neighbor Ralph Bolton took me to church, and Conner gave me six hundred dollars. I learned who my friends were outside of AA, and at that time except for my longtime friend, Enid, they were men.

Conner had been around the block many times — divorced more than once. I was a stunned deer in the headlights. We served as one another's Band-Aids through the proceedings. John Vassallo was representing me. This was after I had already gone through three bad lawyers. John had the essence of the actor Anthony LaPaglia in the television series *Without a Trace*. (Vassallo would later become Peter Jennings's lawyer when he divorced yet another wife.)

Were Conner and I good for one another during that time? I was beside him while he took his driver's license test. Tears in his eyes told me the answer; I had become his stability. We both built a bridge for one another to move forward separately, later on.

The time came for my husband's deposition. My lawyer said it wouldn't be necessary for me to be present since I became ill for the first time in twenty years. But I needed to be there. I went.

During the proceedings my husband was asked, "Did your wife contribute in any way monetarily during your marriage?"

"Absolutely not."

John Vassallo then reached down to the floor under the table and brought up a dramatic oversized box filled with nothing but canceled checks I had written to my husband. He handed one check at a time across the table. He had to read the amounts and what they were for into a microphone:

"Forty thousand, down payment for house in Larchmont; nine thousand six hundred for Mercedes Benz; eleven thousand five hundred for Porsche Targa."

The automobiles were all registered under *his* name. Then John read out money given to my ex for setting up his practice. It trickled all the way down to checks written even before we married. What's amazing is that my husband's composure never wavered during the entire testimony; he remained confident and aloof. His lawyer's shoulders started drooping more and more with every check, until he was like a spineless jellyfish. He had been caught totally off guard.

John Vassallo studied my husband carefully, like he was an entomologist discovering some fascinating insect he'd never seen before. "What do you have to say about this?"

"I forgot."

I couldn't see beyond the fog around me. Shiny stars had lost their luster, fell to earth, and got washed away down the river with a twenty-year marriage. I no longer saw magic in the sky. I got hurt bad. But I had hope. I had gotten hit hard, but I hit back harder.

My husband must have gone home after that deposition and told his fiancée about the bad day he had. My lawyer finally told me that my husband's girlfriend was with him right before I signed the papers ending our marriage. "Legs is next door with your husband. I made sure to keep you separated until this is over." We both laughed.

What I ended up getting wasn't as much as the approximately $24,000,000 Johnny Carson's wife got, but looking back, it was just the right amount. I had to learn once again to make my own money and experience my own freedom.

My friends said, "Fight hard for what you deserve, then leave the past behind and never look back."

They hadn't told me that the big D is evil's finest tool of subterfuge trickery. Marriage ends; divorce lasts forever — a stalker, following you wherever you go. It comes with a prenup. "Till death do us part, in sickness and in health." The bellicose division weaves into all relationships.

In Greek mythology, the first mortal woman was sent by Zeus to punish mankind for the theft of fire. Zeus gave her a box to open, letting all human ills out into the world, and in a later version, letting all human blessings escape.

Years have passed. Chronometry is revisiting the dark ark of testimony. I am now clear headed. Why was I never asked to do a deposition?? Was my husband's deposition part of the public record or was it removed? Why was there so much energy around my husband requesting to file the papers that would become public? Why aren't justice and truth essential points in all legal documents? We seek truth because we need it badly in everything we do. Life depends on it. In 1986, I didn't question the legal system. I only questioned why I wasn't able to save our marriage.

Three weeks after my divorce I was at a 12-step meeting. A woman around my age was talking about the difficulty she was having because of stress due to her husband's drinking and how it was affecting her scleroderma and ability to get her work out as a writer. She had been on a deadline. As she was talking, I looked at her hands. They looked like mine. Her face was flushed. She had tiny red dots on her lips, just like mine. A chill went through me.

I invited her to lunch at my apartment. She had trouble climbing the stairs. She was out of breath. We spent the entire afternoon talking about life. I learned about scleroderma. We compared symptoms of the disease and she gave me the name of her rheumatologist. I was diagnosed with scleroderma three weeks after my divorce.

I felt a trip to Colorado was needed. I told Conner about Grandma Esther's pioneer life. He wanted to meet her, look at the property she once loved, lived on and cared for, and possibly purchase it from the current owner. We flew to Colorado.

Our first stop was the nursing home to see Grandma. She was lying on the bed in a small room with a television set. The atmosphere was shrouded in gray. There were no windows, no natural light. Her mouth was partly open and the thin, translucent skin covering her high cheekbones revealed frail features. She seemed to be soothing herself by moving her tongue back and forth over a wart on the inside edge of her lips. I picked up one of her weathered hands and squeezed it for a long time, looking into her eyes, hoping we would connect. I had been told she had Alzheimer's. It was hard to know if she recognized me and I knew I couldn't accept it if she didn't, so I didn't allow the deep breath or the pause for the silent moment of truth to take place.

"Hello, Grandma!" My eyes longed for her love. "The time I spent with you growing up meant more to me than anything. I talk about you all the time to everyone. And a friend of mine has insisted on coming all the way from New York City to meet you."

Conner was front and center, observing.

"You always took such good care of me. Now I want to do something for you. Would you like for us to help you up, take you out for a ride? We can get some fresh air. The Indian paintbrush and honeysuckles are blooming!"

No matter what I said, I felt no energy in her body. I didn't give up after trying small talk.

Finally, I came up with words she connected to.

"If you had only one wish, what would it be?"

There was a long pause, and then, "I have no wishes."

I remember a conversation from much earlier in her life when she had been feeding her little calf milk from a bottle. *"When I die I want my ashes spread over this here meadow."*

Mom and Dad had come with us that day and we all stayed with Grandma Esther for a few more minutes before getting into the car. Conner found out that the nursing home was being paid from money saved after the sale of the ranch.

"You can fix that so the state pays for her care." He had no idea how far removed that was from my family, how thankful my grandmother was that she didn't need to live on public assistance subsidized by taxpayer money.

I had been with her when ARCO was trying to make a deal with her for mineral drilling rights. Grandma Esther couldn't be bought. She didn't even allow them to finish the sentence.

"Git off my land."

Quiescence was looking up into her blue sky. There were no telephone or electricity wires, no cell phone towers, television, VCRs or computers. There was nothing to interrupt the direct line of communication to God.

Grandpa Jesse came for a visit. He had found out the sold ranch had tripled in value and hired a lawyer to try to get some of it back. It had been in his name. Esther knew his patterns but he no longer knew hers. She had tended the soil and was intensely married to the land they had staked out for homesteading. He hadn't been the one working the land. She was the one caring for the pasture and mending barbed-wire fences. Yet he had given her one priceless gift. Independence. In the past he had been able to hurt her by coloring his hair and carousing around with their oldest son, passing as his brother, using their hard-earned money to pay ladies of the night to take baths in champagne. I remember her sharing "this nonsense" as she called it while peeling vegetables she had taken from the root cellar. As children we would hang on every word. It was our soap opera before television came into our lives and we loved tuning in every day to listen to a new story. No more. Grandpa Jesse wouldn't be getting any land or money back from Grandma Esther's homestead.

The Methodist Church in Gardner was filled to capacity after Grandma Esther Flora died on November 13, 1989. There was no shortage of pallbearers from the boys' orphanage offering to carry Grandma Esther home. Her pioneer spirit was their inspiration. To them, she was a rainbow-arched umbrella of protection from life's bad storms. She was the engine. We were her caboose — cars and trucks of many colors linked closely behind, huffing and puffing in the climb up Big Mountain. "I Think I Can ... I Think I Can ... I Think I Can."

YES! I know I can, through God who strengthens me.

What none of us knew that day as we closed the final chapter of Grandma's story, was the truth of what had taken place in the same Gardner church we were sitting in. It wasn't until years later, doing research for this book, that I was informed of a secret that had been kept from everyone in my family.

The Ku Klux Klan had stormed into that church during an evening poetry and tithe gathering where everyone was asked to publicly pledge what they were giving to the church. A tall man led the procession of long white uniforms with torches, but his gown didn't quite hide Grandpa Jesse's signature green alligator boots … This was stunning news to digest and I was grateful Grandma Esther had passed before it came out. It was best that his darkness hadn't tainted the light guiding her long journey home.

After Grandma died, I had dreams about her still being alive. I remember asking in the dream if it was real. It answered, yes. In one, we were connected as one body while walking upstairs. The recurring dreams stopped when I started writing about her.

I leaned on my seal point Siamese, Katsu, for love during this time in my life. At home in Larchmont with her was the only place I truly felt comfortable … to love and be loved back, unconditionally. Katsu would always be at the door to greet me when I came home, waiting to be picked up, waiting to play games, and waiting to sleep next to me on my pillow. The feel of soft purring fur next to my ear was a form of meditation before going to sleep. I was in my own little peaceful world with her. This was around the time the *Challenger* exploded, all seven of its crew members killed. Tim Berners-Lee, inventor of the World Wide Web, made his first successful communication via the internet. No one knew then how this new exchange of information would alter our lives. At that time, for me, all that mattered was Katsu.

She got locked in my next-door neighbor's basement when they were away on vacation for eight days. I had a posse of people out looking for her and got the newspaper involved. A neighbor taking care of the house next door found her when she made a noise. Had she survived eating mice and drinking from the dehumidifier? I realized when she was gone that I would have done anything to have her with me again. She was thin and hungry, but snapped back to health in a few weeks.

The biggest mistake I made in raising her was to have her declawed. It took away her natural defenses. I didn't know any better at the time. In her life, it meant no more climbing trees. After all, I had to save my furniture. She could no longer be Queen of the High Places and part of her spirit seemed broken. I also didn't understand when she killed a bird, brought it into the house and dropped it at my feet, that it was her present to me. Can the very nature of both a two- and four-legged animal be changed by training them? I had seen a cat that was taught not to kill and actually released his birds. I had been fascinated when witnessing this. That cat clearly knew birds were off-limits, not playthings.

Katsu was seventeen years old when she suffered a stroke. I nursed her for about six weeks until her kidneys started to fail. She would stagger and lose her footing, but still loved going outside. I spent her last day with her in the grass. She slowly made it to the backyard and I saw her look up to the mimosa tree I had planted years before. She then looked up into the sky for a long time and died in my arms. I had a ceremonial burial for her underneath Babe's mimosa tree.

Losing a husband, Wilhelmina, Katsu, Uncle Buss and Grandma within a three-year period at the end of the eighties left me stunned. I coped by putting one foot in front of the other, doing what I had to. This was around the time of Chernobyl. Then the Berlin wall came down. The worldwide order of things seemed to be crumbling and then rebuilding. The fifties' brain file, "The Russians are coming! The Russians are coming!" could finally be removed. They lost the cold war. I watched the process on television, the long lines, how the citizens had suffered with very little food or goods before the downfall. The end of that war was very soothing to me. We won! The world was a safer place...

I was still taking acting classes with Warren Robertson, who later ended up leaving the United States. He was a highly sensitive man and had great insight as a teacher. I remember him saying to the class before he left that I sometimes reminded him of the painting *Christina's World* by Andrew Wyeth. Painful. It was of a disabled girl in a field, looking longingly at a house. I was shocked. I'd had a dream about the painting a few months before and written out the following words combining the dream with poetry:

It was a white summer house, somewhere far away, isolated, maybe in Connecticut, Pennsylvania or Vermont ... with lots of long, gentle wind and waving grass. A tenacious purple hollyhock bush stood tall growing up the side of the house to the right of the front door. Sitting in the middle of the steps was a turquoise-green-and-white ceramic cat ... divinely protecting the entrance. Inside was a happy man who used to be Vincent van Gogh. He had come back to life with many colorful strokes, without brushes. Both his ears were proudly pink and healthy. At a distance outside was a fragile, disabled girl lying in the grass, locked in a painting. She had been there for some time, looking longingly at the hollyhock house. All of a sudden a miracle happened — the longing stopped because she could see inside, feel love inside for the first time. Then joy! She stood, breaking free of her crutches, from the fragmented fantasy of canvas meadows and the frozen frame around her, and began walking an unfamiliar path to the horizon of the bountiful. It is where sky and earth meet with a new destiny. There was a message. God's joy in you will keep you strong.

Not long after returning from Colorado, Conner and I took a trip to northeastern Pennsylvania. We were looking for property to invest in. Together we bought the home I am now living in, and Conner bought a house for himself.

Conner also purchased several hundred acres of land sprinkled with several cabins and a large stream that ran year-round. We both loved the laid-back country feel and had fun exploring the wetlands. There were trees with exposed unique root formations as far as the eye could see. Several varieties of spongy moss made a protective blanket for different specimens at the water's edge. Nature's soothing medicine had been waiting to greet us ... the soft ground cover welcomed the hard, unforgiving, bedeviled ground I had buried myself in.

We walked alongside immaculately high-stacked wood walls to a stream free of branches, framed with a soft, moss pathway ... except for one beautiful, upturned tree root in the water. The caretaker must have left it there as a sculpture. To me, it was a vision of art that I would later transform.

One day, there was a terrible summer storm and Conner's house flooded out in the basement. The weather forced me into our smaller Shohola property for the night. It's a white one-hundred-year-old farmhouse almost the same size and layout as Grandma's cabin. I woke up to the sun shining through a seemingly ancient, leaded sash window with many stories to tell. There were two deer outside on the crest of a hill. After staying this one night, I didn't want to leave.

The house is surrounded with cattail wetlands, adorned with different varieties of moss. It's peaceful and private except for an army of wildlife wandering in and out of the yard. I was in heaven until Black Monday in 1987, when the stock market came crashing down. The movie *Wall Street* had just been released. We were living with a "greed is good" mentality in America. I called my financial adviser after losing over forty thousand dollars, on paper, in one day. He wasn't at all concerned. "It'll pop back up."

I had just taken out a home-equity loan on my Larchmont residence to invest in the Pennsylvania real estate, and my adviser placed all of the money from the divorce settlement into a portfolio of stocks. Comparing it to today's market, it would be equivalent to something like a three-thousand-point loss in one day. Needless to say, Black Monday carried a "red memory" going forward. CNBC became a daily ritual so I could learn about how money is put to work — I became my own adviser.

Luckily, the real estate investment was fruitful. I sold off some of the property, splitting the proceeds with Conner and bought him out on the remainder of his share in the property. I then enclosed the remaining four acres as a sanctuary for animals. I experienced the joy of redneck hummingbirds and the chagrin of redneck locals hunting animals and dumping their beer cans in the stream across the road from me. My new friend Leona, who lived next door, told me the original owner of my property drank too much and finally lost the home and his young son. He left seven refrigerators behind, washing machines and enough broken glass to play hopscotch into eternity.

Never mind, I was the perfect person to be in this spot, free to find the beautiful earth under it. This included a hillside filled with jagged fieldstone and mountainous groves of oak, maple, pine, blue spruce, and dogwood. My longing for the flowering dogwoods left behind in Larchmont and the frozen mounds from winter's freeze at Grandma's melted in the Pennsylvania summer air. All of it was right here. Plus the animals!

I reluctantly went back to the city to be with friends in my Adult Children of Alcoholics group. I met a beautiful woman there, an actress who had turned down an opportunity to be in the soap opera *All My Children*. She was hurting. Her father was a minister and there had been a lot of trouble within her family concerning alcohol. A group of us got together for lunch. During the conversation it was recommended that I go to Video Associates where a woman by the name of Kim taught soap-opera technique. They felt I had the perfect face for the new part.

During this time I wanted to try everything so I started the class, commuting back and forth from Pennsylvania by bus.

Kim took an interest in me because I was a "country soul with outside sophistication." She gave me a monolog to memorize, taken from Truman Capote's *Breakfast at Tiffany's*. It was the section in the movie adaptation where Audrey Hepburn is sitting at the bar talking with her old friend. He comments on her always rescuing "wild things," injured animals with broken wings and legs … I would, like her, become a shepherd of the woods, except I am real and live in Shohola.

Truman Capote's early writing was endearing and inspiring. It created a need in me to write. I started a screenplay in the country with few distractions. Al-Anon friends were encouraging. My new sponsor in Manhattan wrote for *Saturday Night Live* and I ended up being an AA sponsor for a medical doctor who wrote poetry. It's amazing, the combinations of people brought together by metaphysical forces.

My teacher, Larry Moss, eventually went to the West Coast and I started taking acting classes from his first wife, Susan Slavin. She taught at Carnegie Hall and quickly found out how scattered I was. She took me aside, told me my spirituality was highly developed, but soon got to her real motive. The class had been given an exercise to open an imaginary curtain and see what was inside for us twenty years down the road. My curtain opened into pure light.

"You need grounding, and I am recommending one of the best psychiatrists in New York City. You are just spinning wheels right now."

I followed her advice. Dr. Disalvo's diagnosis was general anxiety disorder, and at the end of each session he would ask me what we had accomplished for that day, trying to keep me focused. He steered me away from fantasy.

I brought him my screenplay titled, *And as Promised, Kisses*. I explained the story line. The protagonist has a house in Larchmont and makes a living as an artist, making beds from nature. As she is drinking and smoking, her bed catches on fire. The moss hanging down from the canopy is ignited, looking like sparklers.

Dr. Disalvo read the entire body of work and said it was good. His words gave me enough confidence to contact a workshop in Maine where there was a teacher named William Kelley who had won the Academy Award for his screenplay *Witness* starring Harrison Ford, about the Amish in Pennsylvania. His class attracted people from all over the world who came to perfect their screenplays. Prior to attending, everyone had to send their work in for review.

I took my sister Shanda to the workshop with me because I knew it would be over my head. I had never written a screenplay, never read a book teaching me how and hadn't read much of anything since the bookmobile in childhood. There were about thirty-five actors in the class, including people who had worked on major movies doing production and sound.

We all fell in love with William Kelley. He was funny, loved to drink, looked like Santa Claus and was a great storyteller. What we didn't like was what he dropped in mid-sentence while we were holding onto his every word:

"There is a 99 percent chance that not one of your screenplays will ever be made into a movie." We all had high hopes before going to him that with his refining we had a good chance of getting on the big screen. After a few days, he began mulling through sections of screenplays he had selected and announced to the class, "Penny James is one hell of a writer. I compare her to Carson McCullers."

I had no idea who she was and seriously questioned his sanity. I asked a few people about her after class. I truly thought that William Kelley had had a few too many beers while reading my work.

Weekends in Maine were filled with liquor and cocaine, so I stayed in my room and didn't mingle except to dance at parties in the early evenings. The Saturday before I was planning to leave, there was a party right outside my room. I was trying to sleep. People were banging on my door at four o'clock in the morning. I remember thinking I couldn't stand it any longer.

Sunday, I took a walk by myself and saw William Kelley and his wife, Nina, off in the distance coming down a hill. They had just come from a chapel, and church was written all over them. I found out later that earlier in life, he had planned on becoming a priest. I walked back to my room with a sense of peace.

The telephone rang. It was the Maine workshop office: "We would like to invite you to stay for an extra week. We want to set you up in one of the teacher's cottages. The only thing you would have to do is assist the teachers during the day if some emergency should arise." I humbly accepted.

Before leaving, William Kelley asked me to stop by. I took my sister Shanda along, not knowing what to expect. He and Nina were staying in a sweet cottage right out of *Hansel & Gretel*. His wife answered the door and took us to William's study, where he sat me down. My screenplay was in front of him. He started a detailed critique. By the time he finished, all hope was gone.

"If it needs all of these corrections, why did you tell the class it was so good?" "The Prose. If this were ever to be made into a movie, it would probably get good reviews, but I think only 1 percent of the population would even understand it. I suggest you place it into a drawer for twenty years then make a novel out of it."

He saw the hurt in my eyes. He is gone now, my friend in a higher place ... but his words are still with me.

I met a woman from Amsterdam while in Kelley's class. We had a lot in common. She wasn't into drinking parties either and had recently gotten a divorce. She had just been nominated for an Academy Award for a short documentary she produced about the New York City Ballet Company and was working on another documentary about desperate women needing a man. She came to visit me in Shohola after class ended and spent the night during one of the worst lightning and thunderstorms I can remember. Lightning struck so close that the entire house shook. The next morning, she was relieved when I got her back to the city.

Four months after my screenplay was written, I received a telephone call from Ralph Bolton, my next-door neighbor in Larchmont.

"I'm sorry to have to make this call. Lightning struck your house and there's a big fire. Josephine and I saw a utility line catch fire like a sparkler and snake over onto the roof over your bedroom. There was a loud boom and crackling sound. It's been out of control for about three and a half hours. Your renters got out safely. How much insurance do you have?"

I later found out from one of the firemen that it was one of the worst fires in Larchmont history. The fire got inside the walls and because the house was constructed so well with metal mesh support, they couldn't get to it.

Approximately four months after that, I received a call from 249 Central Park West in New York City. It was my friend, Enid: "I'm calling to tell you that there's been a big fire in the townhouse next door to our building. The firemen had to break through your apartment to get to your terrace to put it out. There's fire damage in several units on your end."

I told her about the fire in my home in Larchmont. She had been a guest there many times. There was silence on both ends of the line. Life changes in a flash. Enid was stunned. So was I.

Forget the term general anxiety disorder. I was in high-gear stress. There were problems with insurance agents, renters, and the bank. Larchmont Savings & Loan recommended that I tear the house down and sell the lot because there was so much water damage. Decisions had to be made. My whole life was a whirlwind. I had to ride it, direct it, and learn to stay calm in order to make sound decisions. I decided to rebuild.

Slate roofers came in to repair the sky-filled hole over the bedroom where I had mirrors on each wall to create a sense of infinity and a custom mirror on the ceiling over the bed I had designed to give the effect of a reflecting canopy. The bolt of lightning had struck directly over the bed. That ceiling mirror had fallen onto the mattress and all the wall mirrors came crashing down with it ... shards of narcissism shattered ... in the bedroom of broken dreams.

Before rebuilding, the entire house had to be bleached to rid it of mold that grew in the water-saturated walls. I ended up being my own contractor after having so many problems with hired help not showing up. I had porta potties for my new crew placed where the rose garden once was in the front yard.

During the restoration process, I received a phone call from Video Associates. I had been booked for my first soap-opera job on *All My Children*. I remember being angry with God because of the timing.

What kind of game from far-out left field was He playing on me? Two fires in four months seemed unbelievable, and then booking me on what could have been the beginning of a new career, when I most likely wouldn't be able to follow through. Why were these out-of-control fireballs being tossed my way — a curve and then a slider, when all I wanted was to reach home base, win and have peace. I was running all over to position myself in the healthiest location on life's playing field, so I wouldn't get burned again.

All of this was happening on my way into m-m-middle age and m-m-middle class. I didn't like either one. Neither was alluring or magical. I didn't like real life. It wasn't softball. There were too many hard knuckle balls ... too unpredictable. The only thing I could do was change my attitude, which I did, but with a lingering, bitter aftertaste.

The fire burned everything in the section of the attic where the lightning struck, but the thick walls separating the maid's quarters remained intact. My husband had placed a closet full of his winter

Ralph Lauren suits in that area. (But) my wedding dress and all of my other clothing over the master bedroom had turned to ashes. I also lost the large portfolio of photos and tear sheets that I had used to get work for almost ten years. My wedding album, wigs, trophies for Miss Colorado, Football Queen, Homecoming Queen, and the jewelry given to me surrounding these events were all gone, along with my coveted National Honor Society pin and yearbook.

Replacing them would be future treasures I knew nothing of. I was slowly becoming connected to the rhythm of something much bigger than I was, headed for a place where eagles dwell with their young, to teach them to fly. I would begin to know the heart is designed for loving people, places, and experiences, not things. Following the death of old materials, new plantings rose from the ashes, bringing resurrection.

"To appoint unto them that mourn in Zion, to give unto them beauty for ashes, the oil of joy for mourning, the garment of praise for the spirit of heaviness; that they might be called trees of righteousness, the planting of the LORD, that he might be glorified. And they shall build the old wastes, they shall raise up the former desolations, and they shall repair the waste cities, the desolations of many generations." (Isaiah 61:3-4, KJV)

I pounded several long nails into a big oak tree in the backyard and strung up Ralph Lauren's tweedy fabric suits to air them out in the fresh breeze, then placed them into my newly purchased 1987 brown-and-gold Toyota truck, adorned with a Harley Davidson logo in the back window. I had told the used car dealer that I wanted a truck that was so ugly, it wouldn't bother me if it was stolen or got hit, but it had to be in very good condition under the hood.

It was a no-brainer. The dealer took me directly to the one with a Hell's Angels' attitude. It was truly one of the ugliest trucks I'd ever seen. I parked it out in front of the porta potties now adorning my once beautiful home. The garments hung in the rear of the cab as I drove out of Larchmont facing frowns from all the neighbors. I took the expressway to get down to Manhattan to search for just the right "tweedy" men to keep warm. It was fall and getting cold.

Homeless people are always around until you're searching for them and then they can't be found anywhere. It took days of wandering to find eight men. Forget the grumbling under my breath … *This is ridiculous, I must be nuts. I'm freezing!* The spiritual compass was being exercised and would reach holy perfection in its own time.

I got through the renovation with a newfound friend by the name of Peter Perciasepe. He was a volunteer fireman the night my house caught fire, the one telling me how bad it was. He was employed by Tishman Management Services, so he knew how I should deal with my insurance company; and after living in Larchmont all of his life, including once working for the town of Mamaroneck, he knew how to help me. Along with this kind man who entered my life, a fresh green maple leaf made its way through the gaping hole in the roof of the house, falling on the stairway going up to the third floor. It was from a living tree, planting the idea for what was to become a meditation room. I hired a man who specialized in pickling to make the new wooden floor look three dimensional. I bought paint in every color of the rainbow, added white to each one and slowly adjusted shades between dark and light with each step to a seemingly flawless blend of all the colors leading to the top.

My hard work paid off. Renting the newly renovated house happened quickly. I returned to the lazy serenity of the country, leaving the maple leaf behind — or so I thought.

Chapter 14
Bed of Trees and Pillow Scrolls

The thought of the magnificent tree roots lying in the water on Conner's property would not leave me alone. It was the driving force needed to fulfill a mission. During the same time, my sister Bobbie sent a book with photos of churches in Paris. One window had what looked like wooden branches separating a series of religious scenes. The framing structure typically used to keep stained glass together was replaced with tree branches. I remember thinking how cool it would be to wake up and see the sky through a stained-glass branch canopy, reflecting rainbow colors where I once had only a mirror. It wasn't long before this became reality.

My neighbor, Leona Lee, and I became close friends through a mutual love of nature. She was living in what would eventually become her home. Her companion had breast cancer, and Leona was caring for her. I was told that right before she died, Jesus appeared on their property. Leona pointed to the ground where the sighting occurred, near the line between our two properties. It was close to where I had planted a weeping willow tree in honor of my grandmother. The tree hadn't done well even though I nursed it with tender loving care, going as far as protecting it with a wooden structure I built and covered in burlap. Without realizing it, it had shaped into a cross. I couldn't believe my eyes as I stared at this "sighting." I began to feel billions of water droplets coming down around me, hearing a sound like a roaring waterfall, then a sound like the thunder of hands clapping in a huge arena, coming from exactly where the cross structure was. I ran over to the spot. I was about two hundred fifty yards away, and it was while I was running that I was told to build a bed out of trees for Jesus. The design, trees, location, and headboard had already been selected.

I heard a story once about three trees on a hill in the woods.

The Tale of Three Trees

The first tree hoped to be a treasure chest, the second tree wished to be a mighty ship, and the third tree wanted to stay on the hill, grow tall and make people think of God.

After a few years, some woodsmen came and cut down the trees.

The first tree was made into a feed box for animals.

The second tree was made into a small fishing boat.

But the third tree wasn't made into anything. Instead, a man was nailed to the tree.

The tree realized that it was strong enough to stand at the top of the hill and be as close to God as possible because Jesus had been crucified on it.

With God, it's the heart that produces the wood that bears truth … He had been preparing yet another messenger of the cross.

It wasn't long before I collected everything needed to make the first Bed of Trees. The caretaker and I spent long hours together, examining majestic tree roots. He had a heart as big as Miss Pinkerton, and just as kind. There wasn't a job he wouldn't help me with — digging, nipping, sawing, and carrying what I wasn't able to. He also recommended Heather and Jeff to help with carpentry and glass designs. I ended up using four hardrock maples that complemented one another as bedposts. And I couldn't have done it without him.

Charles and Allison Moore lived in the area and helped me out in every way they could with artistic work, which included planting, heavy lifting and also blessing me with Thanksgiving dinner at their home. They insisted on working without pay. I couldn't have done it without them, either.

My truck with the Harley Davidson sticker was long since gone along with the Larchmont house. I'd gotten new transportation, a new truck — white and beautiful, the first Toyota Tundra made in Japan. It had all the comforts of a car with an unusually smooth ride. I took my time driving, enjoying a shortcut on a country road. Fresh, budding green was in the air. The energy was hard to describe. Luminous light, bright, free-from-thought, elevated mindfulness that brings defined clarity. Whenever my thoughts surfaced, they muddied clear water.

This is too good to be true. When is the ax going to fall?

It didn't. We all worked together creating this Bed of Trees with a sense of wonder. We had minor challenges as we reconstructed a portion of the tree root that was compromised from being in the stream. Also, the lead carpenter disagreed with me on how high the bed should be and designed it shorter while I was away. The majestic quality had to be restored, with planters raising the height of the bedposts that had been cut. It worked out perfectly because the clay section that shaped and topped the posts would be filled with earth as art. Building was taking place before us, almost on its own.

I kept trying to talk to Jesus. He was the carpenter, yet he wasn't there. I was untroubled but didn't know what was taking place. "I was told to make this bed for you."

Silence.

Then God answered, *I am the artistry in you. Glorify my name. You will be making two beds. The second bed is for Jesus.*

We ended up displaying our first bed, *God Calling*, to four locations within one year of its creation. Looking back, I realize every location had a purpose that I was totally unaware of at the time.

Heather and I worked most every day on the roots, softening some of the sharp cuts from the caretaker's clippers. Sanding would get difficult. Hardrock maple is just as it sounds: it is like stone and seems nonporous compared to other wood. Those roots were hardy, intended to last many lifetimes.

Heather and I became inseparable because there was so much fine-tuning to do. After the canopy branch design was complete, we began working with the glass that would fill in the spaces as a mosaic. Working in water patterns within the iridescent glass, so that one shape seemed to flow into another, the infinite, colorful canopy was created.

Heather's children, eight-year-old Susan and ten-year-old Jordan were always laughing and playing around us. Jeff, her husband, got up every day and drove into Manhattan. His job was to build the sets on a popular tv show. He became enamored with the Hollywood crowd when they came to visit the set and would tell me about meeting people like Mia Farrow. He had "made it" with the big boys and shared Cuban cigars after tapings. He came home late, got up early and was not usually around until the weekends.

One Saturday, we all played a game of softball together as the sun was going down. It had been a beautiful summer day and I remember wanting to share the song "Wind Beneath My Wings" that I had been practicing to sing in church. It was not well known until Bette Midler made it a forever song in the movie *Beaches*. While in the middle of the ball field I was drawn to Jordan, ending the song with him. I remember looking into his eyes, so innocent, blue and beautiful. After that, whenever I spoke to him his eyes would sparkle.

During the evening at home, I made a scroll the shape of a pillow from parchment paper and copied word for word the messages God had given me to share. After it was complete, I asked Heather what she thought of the spiritual material.

"I am a meat-and-potatoes sort of person and don't know much about religious things like that."

"I don't either. I just scribbled it down when it came to me. I feel so strongly that you are meant to write this, to do the calligraphy."

She did, and the words took on a form resembling branches. It was perfect.

I traveled to All Angels' Church in New York City, the one on the Upper West Side that my neighbor Ralph from Larchmont had suggested. It's located around the corner from a high-end food store on 80th Street called Zabar's. I remember kneeling in prayer on the padded bench, looking up to three men who were participating in the Sunday service. I felt anxious and strangely uncomfortable because their body language was stiff, not open to one another. It turned out there was a power struggle going on. Which man of the cloth would be leading the congregation?

The next Sunday there was an announcement that one of the men had committed suicide. How telling body language is. It never lies.

I ended up staying in the church even with the upheaval because so many talented artists attended. One member was directing the play *Gideon* by Paddy Chayefsky and asked me to be in it. It was from that experience I volunteered to prepare Thanksgiving dinner for the homeless. I did it out of guilt after learning a few cast members had signed up selflessly while I had only focused on my acting career.

Most of the people in that particular church really studied and knew the Bible. They would gather at one another's apartments on the Upper West Side. I avoided getting involved because they knew so much more than I did. Some spoke in tongues. It was embarrassing when we were asked to turn to a passage and I didn't know where it was. When I tried to read the King James version, it wasn't clear to me, and I was truly not that interested.

Thanksgiving came. I prepared turkey, kale, and spaghetti and meatballs with the volunteers, set the long tables with silverware and napkins, and helped carry large, heavy cauldrons that had to be constantly refilled and moved. I left at the end of the day so exhausted I couldn't walk all the way home and finally took a cab back to 85th Street. When I was back in the comfort of my apartment, I thought about the experiences I had had throughout the day. I really enjoyed sitting down at the long table, sharing stories of my drinking days with the homeless, tales that had taken place before getting sober, and planting seeds of hope. I bonded with them even though I was once married to a doctor and lived in a French Tudor castle in Larchmont.

The Sunday after Thanksgiving, I returned to church. A crowd of hungry people were again waiting to be fed, curving all the way to Zabar's halfway down the block. There was a severe recession at the time making the gap between rich and poor more noticeable.

I started working my way up toward the entrance and saw many faces from Thanksgiving. When they saw me, they began to move aside. So did all the others I didn't know, making a clear path for me to go up the steps of the church, like the Red Sea parting for me. I will never forget the blessing given to me that day. It felt way better than being fed at the head table of the most prestigious restaurant in Manhattan. The week before, on Thanksgiving, I had been seated at God's table.

As winter settled in, nature stilled. Most of my animal friends disappeared for a time beneath the white shimmering landscape. Then, slowly, the ground thawed and spring came bursting forth with new life: daffodils sprouting throughout the grounds, baby birds hatching in the nearby maple tree and fawns prancing right outside my door.

I reflected on Mother's Day, which was quickly approaching, and that I hadn't been home to see my parents since I had gotten sober. I remember my therapist telling me how important it was to return the three hundred dollars they had lent me in hard times. He was right. That debt kept me in an unhealthy, compromised position. I gained freedom when I returned it.

My experience with them in Pueblo was different than it had ever been. They were so happy to see me and did everything in their power to make me happy. We took long drives up to the mountains and went to Pass Key restaurant where we had all gone as children. It was a favorite of ours because they had an incredible sausage sandwich with hot peppers that everybody in Pueblo loved. The downer was watching my parents as they tried so hard to be happy, seeing how over the years they were still beating one another up verbally.

It wasn't long before old patterns surfaced, both of them trying to get me involved in their arguments. When I was alone with my father he would say how hard it was being with Mother because of her mood swings and crying spells. When I was alone with Mother she was quick to inform me that my father was running around with other women. In Al-Anon that passive aggressive behavior is called dumping. I was able to tell both of them separately.

"What is happening is between the two of you. I can't help you. It's hurtful. I came home because I love both of you and I'm not taking sides."

I no longer needed to correct my father's grammar; it sounded just fine the way it was. And I listened carefully to Mom until she got her words out. In her depressed state, she struggled with that, but after a while she started opening up and telling some secrets from her early childhood that had bothered her for many years. I felt privileged that she trusted me enough, knowing I would not judge what she had been ashamed of … how she had to redo one year in school. I wish I could have told her something I did not know then — Winston Churchill failed the sixth grade. Sophie was not alone! I knew my mother had seeds of fear regarding intelligence, and that paralyzing thoughts had robbed her learning process; and yes, mental illness robbed her of a healthy life. I realized how hard it must have been to be a parent under those circumstances. My mother and father had done the best they could. I wonder if I could have been as good of a parent under the same conditions. Probably not.

It had taken almost ten years to develop a new way of life with and away from them. Adulthood is a process, an invitation to be fed all the things childhood doesn't offer. It took approximately eight years of sitting in 12-step rooms listening to stories before I received my "doctorate." My relationship with my mom and dad now had healthy boundaries, and I remembered all the good things they had done for me. When drinking, I blamed them for all of my problems. That was my reality at the time. I remember calling my mother, crying, telling her I could never be happy unless she was. I felt that very deeply as a child. But through Al-Anon I learned to separate from her depression and try to find my own joy.

I had gone to see my parents at just the right time. Shortly after returning home, my mother's health started failing. When she wrote letters, her penmanship was different, words were scrambled. She started losing weight. Shanda and her husband, Patrick, went out to care for Mother for several days. It had become too difficult for my father to be with her at home. He placed her in a newly-built, upbeat facility that focused on senior socializing along with proper healthcare. She refused to speak with my father when he came to visit and kept to herself. I called her after hearing about a craft class they were holding where women created gifts for others. I thought it might help her. It was a day that she was very clear headed when I spoke with her:

"Mom, I've been thinking about you so much since I started working on screenplays and creative design projects. I remember you winning a contest when you wrote about the loving kindness of our neighbors in the country. Do you remember the neighbors' name and yours being read over the radio? I sure do. You inspired me to do some writing of my own. I think I'm tapping into writing skills that come from your side of the family."

There was silence and then I heard a sound — a low, guttural wailing that told me everything … I was hearing an exorcism with no priest. The sound from Mother's entire body resonated in my ear.

"Mom, do you want me to come out and be with you?"

"No, I want you to remember me like I used to be."

I honored her wishes. She died six months later in March 1991.

Bobbie and I shared a room at Best Western in Colorado. I heard wailing outside the hotel window, echoes of unfinished dreams in the wind carrying mom's voice. An angel was flying in the strong wind with the mission to strip away the ragdoll of Sophie's soul until the last trace of her mental illness had vanished. She had tumbled downstairs from her attic, away from the tiny precious music box of love she'd held onto. She twisted around, then with a trembling rattle, made her way to the hotel door banging next to my bed. The small, strawberry-stained ghost of a girl not wanting to be here was finally gone … She was now clothed in fine white linen. God had taken her home.

As hard as it was to say goodbye, I knew I had to play the high notes in her life's eulogy. The funeral was not held in church but in a funeral home on the same block where my parents lived. I mentioned her sense of humor and the shy, mischievous smile she would share when she sometimes heard a funny, slightly off-color joke. She was unique. She was one of God's most beautiful flowers. The words continued. I could see a gradual softening of muscles around the eyes of Mom's friends, a communal grief facelift. I gathered momentum:

"Mom and Dad were married for forty-one years, in sickness and in health, till death parted them. No easy feat in this day and age."

The entire atmosphere turned stone cold. There was no more eye contact. Her friends' bodies stiffened as they looked down to the floor. "The last secret Mom shared with me was that she dreamed of becoming a singer. I can hear you right now, Mom, you and God performing Heaven's music in perfect harmony."

That day, I held on tight to my sisters. We were her babies. The sediment of depression had seeped into our blood when she carried us as a young mother. We were now huddled together, trying to find the illusive joy we all needed.

"And of the angels he saith, Who maketh his angels spirits, and his ministers a flame of fire." (Hebrews 1:7, KJV)

I started reading the *Good News Bible* shortly after I arrived home in Pennsylvania. Bobbie sent it to me in 1989, with the following inscription inside on the first page: "Penny, you've come a long way in this life. I'm very proud of you. May the good in life be your strength and the beauty your joy! This is the edition we use in my church at St. John's. With the greatest of love, Bobbie."

I began to read simple, understandable words with clear explanations preceding them. I ended up reading every word, start to finish. The Old Testament at that time was difficult to swallow, but when I started reading the New Testament and saw some of the documentation from Paul, I was truly shocked. God had passed on to me some of the same things that he told Paul two thousand years ago.

From that time on, there hasn't been a shadow of a doubt for me that God and Jesus are real. I now believe that through quiet communion with Jesus, one can naturally know the living words even without the Bible. They slowly filter into the brain through the Holy Spirit and travel to their all-knowing home in the soul. I believe we are born with this information way down deep inside of us, but it doesn't surface until the spirit is fully exercised. This requires discipline. One can't expect to know the spirit's trigonometry before learning basic algebra. It's a slow, steady transition into being reborn. The Bible eliminates confusion and the living words must be read. It simply happened for me in reverse.

My interests changed almost overnight, and during the course of the nineties I lost the desire to act, especially in soap operas. Even though I could make an income comparable to modeling, the thought of planting unproductive seeds in women sitting, watching a fantasy drama on television made me nauseous. I couldn't bring myself to memorize words that paralleled the rat's nest of what I was striving to forget. I ended up not going to a single movie for nearly ten years; I stopped listening to popular music on the radio and lived in a rural area. I was once again a child in the woods, discovering an outdoor fireplace that nature had made on my property. It was waiting for me, ready to enjoy. Soft carpets of different varieties of lichen also welcomed me.

Peat moss, prolific in wetland areas, was used by the Vikings on their ships to preserve fish and provide fuel. Mummies were found thousands of years later, encircled in this particular form of moss, preserved for science.

Outside in my swamp boots, I lived among wild iris with tough leaves that looked like swords. Most of all, I got to hear home sounds of tree frogs and crickets at night, creating new jazz and saw how a dragonfly among fireflies can transform into a helicopter. We were all wading together, immersed in nature's spongy bog, waiting patiently for God to reveal our history, a new story to be told. I began to learn a little about what family life consists of among chipmunks, a walking stick bug on the endangered-species list, praying mantises, ants, bumblebees, wasps, and tree frogs.

Inside this private space, the wetlands gave me an opportunity to observe the comings and goings of wild turkey, bear, and deer. I started to recognize the patterns within their family units, a chance to witness their in-the-moment, simple pleasures. Most of the time it was without turmoil and conflict; chipmunks don't care what the other chipmunks are wearing when they venture out from their moss-and-twig palace doorways. Bears aren't worried about an uneven playing field in the stock market. They don't give the silent treatment when flowers don't arrive on Valentine's Day or go into a rage when someone gives them the finger traveling over our country roads. I wanted what they had — these animals, my new neighbors — to join their inner circle.

In the seventh century BC, the poet and prophet Habakkuk said, "The LORD God is my strength, and he will make my feet like hinds' feet, and he will make me to walk upon mine high places..." (Habakkuk 3:19, KJV). Reliving fresh words from almost three thousand years ago melted the distance from past family roots.

Deer have been around for over three million years, sharing a percentage of our DNA. They live with four-chambered stomachs similar to cows and, like people, have their own distinct personalities. When in danger, they disappear instantly. The deer around my property here in Pennsylvania have white underneath their tails that point straight up showing as a warning flag, resembling a feather duster zigzagging back and forth as they sure-footedly leap and fly through the air. Before fleeing, the female deer warns the rest of the herd with what sounds like a combination of a sneeze and a snort, exhaling a build-up of pressured air. That was Whisprina's job. There was something especially gentle and loving about her. There is a pecking order with all animals that she didn't participate in. Once in a while, adult female deer can be vicious; rearing up, batting at one another with their front hooves when proper territory and food-related protocols are not followed. What's interesting is that wild turkey and other animals are never bothered while gobbling up food right next to them.

Turkey and deer seem to enjoy one another's presence in the woods. The bucks hang out together spring and summer, except for the new fathers. They take an active part in playing with and protecting the baby fawns along with the mothers. If it's a boy, they dance around, playing gentle head-butting games with their budding horns, well into winter, hooking and disengaging, careful to not poke the eyes of their little ones. Do they know, without knowing, that the eye mirrors love and preservation?

Whisprina, different from the herd, would stare at me a lot. When not feeding on grain she seemed to want to hang around near me, becoming tame in about six months. After a while, I started noticing that at times she was drooling at the mouth and had a noticeable thickness in the throat area under her jaw. Every now and then I would see a few deer like her. Other than having these somewhat worrisome traits, they all seemed quite healthy.

Whisprina mostly hung out with an older deer I called Grandma, who had eyes that were once wise, but were growing childlike. You could tell the two of them had been companions for a long time, unusual in that deer tend to die around age four because of hunting, but Grandma appeared to be at least fifteen years of age when we met. Over the course of six years, I fell deeply in love with Whisprina, Whisprina's baby (that I named Daystar), and Grandma.

Concentrating on life amid nature calmed and restored my scattered mind. It was the perfect medicine. I was finally focused on a higher calling. When Heaven's sun went down each day, Whisprina, Daystar, Grandma and I comfortably lay down and went to sleep.

A spiritual awakening was given to me on a "serving tray" along with a message: "Give away what you receive."

While recently watching a Sunday episode of *In Touch with Dr. Charles Stanley,* I took in a big, thirsty drink of gratitude; it reminded me of the meaningful process. The Baptist minister had photographed a bird resting on a tree branch and then shared the joyful experience of capturing the image. He had just gotten a new camera and placed it on his tripod, carefully positioning his equipment to get closer to it. He couldn't make eye contact or the bird would fly away before he could get the shot. After taking the first photo, he got a surprise second shot of the bird rising from the branch with wings colorfully spread, in perfect focus. Like the bird, I was no longer on the tree branch waiting for who knows what to happen. I was free, flying high above acres of forest with the eyes of an eagle, selecting trees to make bedposts.

Two beds, *God Calling* and *Infinite Stillness,* were born symbolizing where we give birth, create our fondest hopes and dreams, hide with our secret fears, love with fierce passions and perhaps, experience closure. The most important intimate events of our lives happen in and around a bed. Trees were used as witnesses to proclaim God's message in Revelation 11:3-4, KJV.

Being out in the open air I examined roots, gathered moss, and dug up wild bell flowers and twigs to be part of the bed's design. I used hardrock maple with their roots intact as the bedposts. The process taught me how to appreciate all of the free gifts received every day that at one time I had taken for granted. They were catalysts to living a productive life. Integration of the entire design took approximately two years.

During this time, Matthew Korn, my architect from the Larchmont house fire, sent me the original blueprints of my home, along with a photo he had found of it, right after it was built. He was thrilled because his first memory of the house was an architectural meltdown, covered with ashes. I called him to say thank you and told him about the beds.

"I know the perfect gallery to show them in. It's part of the National Park Service not too far from you, in the Delaware Water Gap. It's called Peter's Valley."

That is where the first bed, *God Calling*, eventually ended up ... I had finally settled down enough to listen to the clarifying whisper instead of falling victim to the confusing, superficial noise of my own mind. The late singer/songwriter Portia Nelson described the transition in "An Autobiography in Five Short Chapters":

I.

I walk down the street.
There is a deep hole in the sidewalk.
I fall in.
I am lost. I am helpless.
It isn't my fault. It takes forever to find my way out.

II.

I walk down the same street.
There is a deep hole in the sidewalk. I pretend I don't see it. I fall in again.
I can't believe I am in the same place. But, it isn't my fault.
It still takes a long time to get out.

III.

I walk down the same street.
There is a deep hole in the sidewalk. I see it is there. I still fall in ...
it's a habit.

My eyes are open.
I know where I am. It is my fault. I get out immediately.

IV.

I walk down the same street.
There is a deep hole in the sidewalk. I walk around it.

V.

I walk down another street.

I will no longer depend on the wrong people, places and things that once moved me into emotional, dead-end madness! I choose to never again wait for a telephone call that will never come. I choose to never be stuck counting on someone and then being let down, whether in love or in business.

Meanwhile, *God Calling* became known as *Bed Spring* and was introduced at Peter's Valley Gallery in Layton, NJ, located within the Delaware National Recreation Park Area. The exhibit location was only a few miles from the stream it grew beside.

The display was a challenge to assemble but looked magnificent when completed. Forest flora and vines climbed to a trellis-framed canopy surrounded by four bed posts created by maple trees with root segments attached. Sections of iridescent water glass reflected rainbow colors onto the mattress, a living collage of moss and delicate flowers within the rectangular frame. The maple headboard has a space to insert a bronze twig, a flowering branch or a hummingbird nest.

We brainstormed, made plans to include as many artists as possible, flowing as one mind, from one medium to another, relying on the omnipotence of the Master's roots. As bed visitation began, guests increased regularly. Families gathered and revisited, poets shared their own bed poetry leaving writings behind for all to view with the bed. Photographs of construction of the beds in progress were displayed, vignettes from my screenplay shared and experimental video clips planned.

Back on my property in Shohola, I saw Whisprina's friend, Grandma, have what looked like an epileptic seizure, something that would recur about twice a week for over five years. Old-timers called the chronic disease of the deer's nervous system "falling sickness." I could tell a seizure was coming when she started scratching her ears and shaking her head, like an overload of electricity was exploding in her brain before she collapsed to the ground. She would kick her legs in the air until the storm passed, lie still for about twenty seconds, then rise, dazed, and quickly get back to normal.

I saw one of her episodes right after studying Vincent van Gogh's painting *The Starry Night*. He had created it in a mental institution at Saint-Rémy-de-Provence during an intensely troubled time in his life. It looked to me like a brainstorm. Much, I thought, like the inside of Grandma's head just before her seizures occurred; only he had used the electrical current to connect all of the energy fields of Heaven onto canvas.

I continued to focus on God and the important work He was doing in my life to counter the unsettling events in society. Like dropping new life on the fertile wetlands of my property. Whisprina gave birth and hid her spotted twins among a backdrop of cattails for about three weeks before bringing them up to see me. She spent a lot of time licking their entire bodies. While watching her, I thought Whisprina didn't need Dr. Spock to be taught how to raise her babies. Nature has its own way of caring for and soothing one another.

During the winter months, I spent time alone communicating with the roots of God under the snow, to more clearly understand the relationship between Father and Son. God chose to have His son's birth take place in the comforting home of animals. God used a wooden trough as a cradle, filling it with soft straw for His baby son who was lovingly called His Lamb. Jesus's life ended on the cross. The Father had to experience taking His own child's breath away.

I had also taken an innocent life, only I had stopped my baby's heartbeat in a panicked, confused state with a very different motivation. I had not been able to honor how precious and valuable life is and, most of all, I did not know in my frightened youth how much I loved that which I thought I cared nothing about. My aborted child was a messenger who taught me to understand the properties of unconditional love. I did this with Jesus, who in his short life never traveled more than ninety miles from where he was born, yet arched his words over every nation: "Then said Jesus, Father, forgive them; for they know not what they do. And they parted his raiment, and cast lots." (Luke 23:34, KJV)

It is love that held Jesus to the cross for so long. He is in my heart and breathes the same air I do. There are two rainbows reflecting from the irises of his eyes. I carry them with me at all times. The bottom, an upside-down rainbow arch, represents the earth, and the top arch represents Heaven. You may have noticed that when there is a double rainbow, each arch's colors are in reverse sequence.

I didn't know that my Heavenly Father would have me back in Colorado to take care of my upside-down rainbow father. He had developed sudden health problems and was diagnosed with an aneurysm. I hoped that doctors at St. Mary Corwin Hospital, where I had been sick as a child, would be successful with the surgery.

I was surprised that Father actually seemed to be enjoying himself in the hospital. There were a lot of young nurses for him to flirt with and they did pay a lot of attention to him. He now had silver hair that brought out his eyes. When the intense yellow sun hit them through the hospital window, they were aquamarine, kind of like the color limestone makes the water look like in parts of Europe. The only thing his beautiful eyes didn't settle kindly on was the patient next to him. He was Black, around sixty-five years old, close to my father's age. Father stayed three days, and each time I visited, he became more comfortable with his roommate. It turned out they had a lot in common and were eventually talking nonstop about their crazy younger years with women and gambling in Las Vegas, which they both occasionally still did.

My father recovered in about a week, and by caring for him at home, we had quality time to talk. It was such a different experience from knowing him in my youth. He was fully present, not the faraway, unreachable man I knew as a child. I was able to revisit some things that had been bothering me. One, that he had missed my wedding. Two, he hadn't honored his own mother's sacred life. From my point of view, he had prematurely taken from her the land that had kept her joyfully alive — her ranch. He listened and didn't become defensive or angry when I brought up these raw subjects, especially concerning Grandma.

As we were talking, the doorbell rang. It was Mr. Jones, Father's hospital roommate. Mr. Jones had gotten home from the hospital, and after resting, had prepared for my father fresh-off-the-grill barbecue ribs. The delicious smell filled the entire house. We spent about an hour chatting nonstop, laughing about childhood memories of wading in creeks, catching minnows and feeling velvet sand squishing through our toes. The only difference was that Mr. Jones had spent his childhood in Alabama, and my father and I in Colorado.

After Mr. Jones left: "I usually don't like niggers."

I looked up at him and saw tears well up in his eyes. I allowed moments to pass before speaking. "Daddy, I need to tell you something. That word is offensive. Times have changed; you can't use that word anymore. It makes a Black person feel like you're looking down on them. It violates their dignity."

As I was talking, the phone rang. I answered and there was a long silence on the other end of the line. Then, "Is Joe there?"

It was the hesitation, the way the woman on the other end said "Joe" that I knew I didn't need to ask, still didn't want to know.

The phone was in the kitchen, far enough from the living room where I could block out sound I didn't want to hear. My father finished the conversation and sat back in his comfortable, corduroy La-Z-Boy chair. When he was seated I looked at him, sadly.

"I could tell that the woman who called you was surprised to hear another woman answer the phone. You must not have told her that one of us kids was coming home. The way she said Joe … I can tell she's been around a long time."

My father's head dropped. There was no reason to say another word, because our eyes both met with the truth. I now knew that he had led two different lives for many years, one with Mom and us, and one with her. The telephone call had come at exactly the right time. I had gotten my grievances out, and my father had listened. It was all I could do to hold back from running to him and hugging him. He had graced me with the truth, truth I had been yearning for since I was a little girl.

Especially if you are a girl, the love you have for your father can be the strongest love of all, no matter what has taken place. In that moment, I knew without a doubt how much he loved me too. When it's real, you just know.

A few weeks later, after I got home to Pennsylvania, the telephone rang. "I'm going to take your grandmother's casket out of the Gardner Cemetery and have her cremated." Our time together during his recovery had clearly left an impact on both of us.

He went to her gravesite with hired help to carry out Esther Flora's wishes. Finally, the closed-off, narrow-minded Ku Klux Klan mentality that my grandfather had taught my dad didn't have its way. My father's mind had opened. He and his sister and brother, who had thought they could be happy with some of grandmother's wealth, didn't end up enjoying it much after all.

Ashes flew from the airplane window and floated down on the meadow. The mission was complete with the generous help of Jerry Smith, a wealthy farmer who owns his own plane *and* my grandmother's property. As we were flying, I looked down to see cows peacefully grazing. I could almost see some of Grandma's stardust filtering down, landing on their eyelashes.

Family members close to my father's sister, Mildred, and brother, Cutis, were incensed by what we had done, digging out Grandma's body from the dirt and spreading it about. My father didn't seem to care. He stood taller, began new dialogue, even started talking to me about personal things that were bothering him.

"My neighbor next door treats me like a second-class citizen because I smoke a cigar."

"No, Daddy, you treat yourself like a second-class citizen because you smoke a cigar. I'll let you in on a secret, and it's the truth. You'll have a lot more girlfriends following you around if you quit."

He did. And he did!

I had finally taken on an adult role, placed in a position to give him love that his father had deprived him of before departing early in life.

Chapter 15
Lust and Dreams

Love lust. Money lust. Fame lust.

"(I Can't Get No) Satisfaction." Mick Jagger struts to a primal riff, followed by the sound of trumpets. He carries a Covenant Box of stone tablets. It's hard to leap up and over into Heaven's Gate with such heaviness … with a band of Hell's Angels following while seducing *Angie* and the Rolling … I wake up.

Where do dreams come from?

I had a dream about making love with Richard Chamberlain after seeing *The Thorn Birds*. I longed to be with a man like him. Forget that it's fantasy; it's what my imagination was drawn to, rather than a real person. I was addicted to secret, romantic, passionate love.

Excitement. It was stirring inside the gypsy soul of my past, fluttering like a pair of wings to the ground. I desired a forbidden man of the cloth to lust for me. He is poetic with holy words, but doesn't follow through with them. Bad boys, especially if they are priests, are irresistible.

I remember getting on my knees and asking God to send a soul mate for me. His answer was quick: *I am who I am. Be with Me.*

No, No, NO!

I dug deeper. It was *The Thorn Birds* symbolism that I was attracted to. From birth, the birds would search for the perfect thorn tree to impale themselves on so they could sing the most beautiful song ever heard while dying. There were similarities with Jesus's Crown of Thorns. He had collected in them all our infidelity, torture and punishment … waiting for the thorns to be removed before the crown could become the sweetest song ever heard in Heaven.

After getting in touch with my fiery fantasy, I shifted focus to God's fresh pine trees and floral aftershave. This brought about a double-edged sword of results. I was still harboring conflicting emotions swirling around in my head, thoughts and feelings locked up that needed sorting out.

The dreams continued … I was staying in a country cottage space over a weekend. There was produce in the kitchen and a bottle of wine. My former boyfriend, Conner, owned the building and came over with his wife. Another former girlfriend of his was also staying there. The place had a long wicker couch with an interesting, contemporary shape. It was stained green and where the joints came together, it looked uneven and faded — like the wicker weave was green but had no unity to the parts.

Conner was sitting in a matching chair, and I wondered if he would start playing provocative Machiavellian sexual games, pitting one of us against the other, the two of us past girlfriends with his wife there. He didn't. I thought once his wife left he might reappear to resume his mind-play with us, but again, he didn't. I was relieved, but the house felt lonely and empty without him. I re-stained the couch to bring all the defining elements together, but it wouldn't take. I then used a thicker paint to sketch in the design, but it still was uneven.

There was what appeared to be an expensive bottle of wine, and I drank it. Was it left there for guests or not? His wife reappeared. I explained what I had tried to accomplish, to finish off the designer wicker. Like a magician, she flipped over a hidden tag. It contained a famous designer label with a price of only fifty dollars. "Where did you buy this?" I asked.

Suddenly she was showing me real estate in the city, telling me she thought this was the perfect place for me. It was small, dark, and box-like with no enticing details. I told her that the timing was wrong for me to move. While saying this, I felt guilty for drinking the wine from her and Conner's cupboard. I felt sick, and then I woke up.

After analyzing the dream, what I got from it was the ripple effects of creating a real and fake design. We get up each morning and present ourselves to the world, covering our flaws.

We offer ourselves as a splendid design. We can also become enablers for others' splendid designs, knowing it's partly fake, yet never challenging it. Instead, we cover up for them, continuing the charismatic inauthenticity.

Very few of us have the courage to go deep enough to accept who we really are and come back up with our authentic self. In the dream, when I drank the wine of the past, it was a sign that I was still unable to resist alcohol, using it to bury those deep places I was not yet ready to visit and work through. My dream was a red flag reminder to achieve and retain authenticity.

It takes two or more to play a game. We all have a black-and-white checkerboard. When we explore and find what's hidden underneath, we have the freedom to not act from negative feelings and insecurities. Making this choice goes against our lower nature, feels illogical, terrifying, not of sound mind. And yet, if we make our way through the dark tunnel we eventually emerge into a steady, uninterrupted flow of pure love that is infinite and stronger than evil. It is then that our adversaries are caught off guard. The gaming has vanished, and we enter into the supernatural where we have no control and no longer need it, where miracles happen in moments when we least expect them.

When I first started writing, I was an emotional cripple. Without awareness of the value in my dreams, all I felt was discomfort when I woke if the dream had been dark, or happiness if it had been light. Or sometimes I questioned if it even was a dream, like the perception of my birth. My mother had named me Betty. I had not been her choice. She already had one child she didn't want but delivered me anyway. I had a full head of copper-red hair. The nurses at the hospital fell in love with my brightness, carried me around, showing me to everyone. They nicknamed me Penny. That became my new name and their affection toward me influenced my becoming Mother's favorite child. I learned early on, way before I was supposed to, not to sound my voice or cry like my sister. I avoided causing my mother trouble. I felt guilty for being alive, I thought I didn't deserve to be alive because my birth had made my mother unhappy. The ridiculousness of those thoughts were revisited in my mind when the telephone rang. It was John Dorney, a neighbor. His first words were a song that he sang with such joy!

"You must have been a beautiful baby."

John had become a vessel, a spark of love from my Heavenly Father. He wasn't aware of the gift he was giving. As a child, I unconsciously had given up my right to be happy. Was this why I was always running so fast as a child? Was I trying to chase and catch all the magical fireflies in the darkness that were always so elusive?

This time a knock at the door, another unexpected interruption to my thoughts. "Excuse me for interrupting your day."

He was a young man, around thirty years of age, with dark hair and troubled, tired eyes. "I used to live here when I was a baby, and I was wondering if you would mind if I just look around."

He was anxious. "I was taken away from my father when he lived here because he had a drinking problem." He told me his father's name.

"It would be my pleasure to show you around. My next-door neighbor, Leona, knew your family and told me about how good your grandfather was with stone. He built this smoked-eel house."

I didn't tell him about the garbage, beer cans and glass I had cleaned up. He hadn't come to hear that. I showed him all of the beautiful bedrock, the birdbath, the mailbox, all lovingly constructed by his family in blue stone from the property. I invited him into the house with the stone foundation that perhaps his great-grandfather had built. We later sat in the kitchen as I shared all the photographs I had taken of the animals. It was by no accident they stood up tall staring at him, up close and personal through the window! He left relaxed, with shining eyes, saying, "I'm adopted, and have a good mother and father."

Not being from the area, I had no idea how much this "hot spot" of land was attractive to local hunters. Through Whisprina, I was beginning to learn about the pain inflicted on animals by hunters. She had nursed one wounded buck back to health; he had a big hole in the middle of his back. I also observed a broken arrow through one of the legs of her babies less than a year old. Her therapy for both of them was massaging around the wounds with her tongue.

Word had spread about the collection of "trophy twelve-point bucks" on my property from the supply of wildlife grain. One Sunday afternoon I noticed three trucks parked on the road right outside my driveway. I started walking toward them with an uncomfortable feeling. Before words were spoken, four men approached me. Were they harassing me, knowing I was a woman alone? I could smell that they were hunters. My grandmother's grit took over my body, and my voice was as cold as the steel on the double-barrel shotgun she once rested on her windowsill.

"Can I help you with something?"

Their pastel-pasted smiles insinuated that they were just out enjoying the day and I had misread their visit. The small talk wasn't out of line. The aggressive behavior making their way up my driveway was. They left, but I knew trouble was ahead.

When life is good and true, evil's darkness, with equal energy, always comes to meet it.

The battle begins. Its goal? To make good and true appear to be too good to be true.

The decade of the nineties would bless me with off-the-chart joyful moments countered by a few sad storybook endings. The children's books I read from bookmobiles are partly responsible for instilling my unbridled passion for creatures and the wilderness. That child still inside me from so long ago cannot fathom that there is separation between humans and wildlife. After spending intimate time with my deer, Grandma and Whisprina and her family, I became even more convinced that I could get forever close to them and they would be a treasured part of my own family.

Whisprina's last baby, Daystar, had a little friend from another mother, and they were around most of the time. After they both had their milk, their favorite game was chasing one another with the energy of two Ferrari engines. That's what made watching Daystar knock over Whisprina while she was feeding him so painful. The area around her throat became so thick that her tongue started protruding from her mouth. She had become thin and weak and had trouble swallowing. She ended up staying right up against the house next to the porch. She was drooling at the mouth, but by lifting up her head high enough, she could somehow get the grain to drop down her throat. What I had noticed about her early on was a slow, progressive disease. Luckily, Daystar got old enough to start eating grass and grain on his own before he lost his mother. Whisprina always loved hydrangea leaves and it got to the point that she wasn't even able to wander out far enough to reach them. I would feed them to her until she could no longer swallow.

I called a friend, Bob Phillips, and asked that he put her down when she could no longer eat. I learned later that deer, before dying, always make their way up into the woods. He was able to find her and end her life.

"It was hard to shoot her with her baby around."

I learned from that painful mistake, realizing my motivation was partly from not wanting to see Whisprina in the state she was in. I hadn't allowed nature to have its way into the great depth of suffering. Having said that, she was mine. Animals belong to people who take care of them. I had done everything I could for her for seven years, except allow her to suffer until the end. Tough call.

Daystar was my first baby from the woods. I became his godmother and catered to his every need. Because he was small and hadn't yet earned his privileged position within the deer pecking order, all of the others would pound on him with their hooves when I would give him privileges that they didn't receive. When this happened, I would run out and chase them away from him with a pointed finger and menacing growl. "No, no, no!" Much to my surprise, with persistence, I was able to change their pecking order.

They became comfortable waiting until "King Daystar" was full before going to finish their grain. I believe he was the first fat deer that ever lived because I catered to every irresistible Bambi expression he tossed my way. I gradually had the privilege of seeing his features mature into antlers of majesty over a period of three years. At night, I watched him sleep under the stars in the exact same spot under the same tree where his mom had rested when she was alive. It was his comfort zone. Grandma, like me, enjoyed Daystar's presence. She was with him most of the time.

I was staring out at a few leaves still on the trees behind the house. The ones on the ground were covered with snow. All of a sudden I heard a loud blast and saw Daystar rising up in the air, on the crest of the hill. I knew he had been shot. I raised my window and screamed, "Whoever you are, I'm going to get you!"

I put on a bright-orange insulated down jacket. I was shaking because I know how bad reality is. I went up the hill and followed the drops of blood on the white snow that led me to a man with a rifle.

"Who are you and what are you doing on my land shooting a deer?"

"I was with a companion. He shot the animal from my nephew's property and it ran into your yard."

"That's not true. I saw the deer fly into the air right outside my window when it was hit."

I contacted his nephew who owns property adjacent to mine. He was at my home within thirty minutes after contacting him. We were talking beside his bright-red pickup truck with a gun mount inside holding two rifles.

"I don't know how many times I've told him to stop hunting on my property, and he just won't listen," my neighbor explained.

And then, Divine Intervention! A volunteer who helped the game commissioner heard the story, and from there, word spread quickly. The game commissioner and his friend with good ears eventually had the hunter convicted. He paid a fine and his gun was taken away for two years.

It wasn't long before Daystar's Grandma started failing. At times it looked like she had developed Alzheimer's; she often hid among a grove of milkweeds. One morning she came to greet me in her favorite spot behind the gallery window. She left her nose print on the window as a goodbye present. I watched her struggle up the hill into the trees, her final resting place. I would guess she was around twenty years old when she made her journey. Deer generally don't live that long. What was even more unusual was that she and an older bear would sit in the sun, not far from one another, shortly before she died.

Death comes with nature's constant resurrection. New life and joy would soon be greeting me after losing my three favorite companions. Periodically I would travel into New York City and meet with John Vassallo. We had developed a friendship over the extended time I had been hobbling around with the arrow of divorce through my leg.

John was a great storyteller. He had a tremendous sense of humor mixed with courtroom drama. Over an olive martini and escargot, he would organize his unique comedic rhythm — subtle nuances would build on one another until I was choking with laughter. We were much too loud for the poor people sitting next to us, and by the time our main course arrived, it's a miracle we weren't asked to leave. After one of our outbursts, John started talking about the Gennifer Flowers debacle.

"I hope he makes it. He's a smart guy and I think he'd make a great President." "I disagree, only because of the patterns he has in his personal life. That kind of destructive behavior tends to repeat itself." "That can be kept separate."

"How? He's one man and the pattern would affect all areas of his life." I couldn't accept that a politician could separate dishonest compartments of behavior to be an effective leader.

We always said goodnight early. John was a perfect gentleman, kissing me on the cheek before going to his home near Central Park. When I arrived at my apartment, the phone was ringing. I was informed by my neighbor that my home in Pennsylvania had been broken into.

Back to the country I went.

Chapter 16
Wake-Up Calls

Once I returned from New York City, the state police came and sprinkled gray dust on furniture that had been tampered with, trying to get fingerprints. All of my kitchen cabinets were left open at the same angle and upstairs in the bedroom my lingerie was taken out of the drawers and spread on the floor. Even with unbiased, determined state police, no telling fingerprints surfaced. No one was arrested.

In my life I was being tested. I was placed in a position to find and eliminate disputations, jealousies, and a lot more in order to become one with creative forces. When good and evil were aligned, life situations became so intense, I would just space out. I was very good at it. We all have different ways of working through our challenges. In my darker moments, I was a cross between a valley girl and an Alzheimer's lady, and sometimes I didn't know anything!

I started watching a new cable station called the Weather Channel, which first aired in 1987 and was well established by the nineties. I would zone out on it all day. Weather from all over the world was now in my living room. I gradually became fascinated not only with tornadoes but with forecasters like Jim Cantore. I also watched some of the female forecasters' stomachs grow and wondered about, you know, their personal lives … like who had gotten them pregnant? This was my spaced-out pastime since I was not going to the movies or listening to the radio. I believed I was the only weather freak who found bipolar weather both soothing and riveting. This was until Bill Cosby mentioned during a television interview that his favorite hobby was listening to rambling weather reporting. (We found out later that he also had another diversion.) It became part of our at-home culture to be up close and personal with Katrina, Andrew, Sandy, *and* Cosby. Life-and-death survival of the elements! I was riding on the whirlwind of it.

My next adventure was another trip to Colorado for a family vacation in Vail. My sisters and I met up to see Michael Martin Murphey, the country songwriter and singer. He was performing with, of all things, the Pueblo Symphony, which I had once played with. Now they were at the Betty Ford Performing Arts Center. The outside auditorium had the most perfect sound system and made the crossover union between country and classical magical. Michael Martin Murphey performed one of my favorite songs from the seventies, "Wildfire." It's about a horse. He had written it from a dream. The audience was spellbound from the collaboration. Afterward Judy Collins, whom I know through spiritual work, also performed a small, intimate inside concert.

The entire three days I spent in Colorado didn't seem real because of a series of ups and downs, including one supernatural happening. I went to a clothing store to buy suitable attire for a trail ride I was planning to take. I found both comfortable cowboy boots and a western blouse from the same place. The man helping me was slim, around five foot nine inches tall, and had blonde hair with kind, light-blue, vulnerable eyes he listened with, making him soothing to be around. He was helpful but not pushy. I thanked him as I was leaving the store.

Suddenly a strong lightning and thunderstorm came up and I was forced back inside. I resumed a conversation with him and told him about the Bed of Trees I had made. He then started telling me about a woman who had never left her bed, who was being considered for sainthood in the Catholic Church, that she had written many books about her experiences with Jesus and Mary visiting her, and that he would send them to me. I remember taking one last look into his eyes. They were misty, the area surrounding his eyelashes a little red, like he had been crying.

The storm passed and I left. The next day I was dressed in my new blouse and boots, mounting the horse given to me for the trail ride, but my body was not strong enough to swing my leg over and place my feet into the stirrups. My muscles had stretched out, but had turned into what felt like Jell-O. I had to be helped and felt embarrassed that my body had lost so much strength. I had gone horseback riding a couple of years before with no problems.

A few weeks after arriving home in Pennsylvania, I received a package from the Divine Will Center, located in Jacksonville, Florida. Inside were three books: *The Kingdom of the Divine Will* (for beginners), *When the Divine Will Reigns in Souls* (intermediate) and *The Book of Heaven* (advanced). They were written by Luisa Piccarreta, who lived in Corato, Italy, from 1865–1947. She is now on the road to canonization as a saint of the Catholic Church. Ms. Piccarreta had a mystical experience when she was seventeen and started writing out conversations with Jesus from that time on, without leaving her bed. It is believed she was given grace known as living in the Divine Will directly with Him, and that she didn't eat enough to sustain her while bedridden, but spiritual energy through Jesus kept her alive for sixty-four years, until her dictation was complete. She had been ordered to write down all of her experiences by the priest who visited her every day ... now, those experiences were in my hands.

Along with the books was a notation: "These books are sent at the request of Michael Letourneau, who has given us a donation to cover their cost. May God bless you."

I read each book slowly, cover to cover, and sat with them thinking about the intimacy we both shared with Jesus. Our experiences mirrored one another's, except she had spent much more time with Him, therefore knew Him better, had given more testimony and took responsibility for writing everything down. I was grateful she had done this. I couldn't wait to contact Michael to thank him and tell him how much I had learned. I grabbed my sales receipt to get the address of the store and wrote a long letter thanking him. The letter was returned, saying there was no one with that name. I then called the store in disbelief and was told the same thing. How could this be true?

I've since tried numerous times to locate Mr. Letourneau, but to no avail. It's like he never existed, except I know he was real. He graced me with the gift of the books.

In early spring, there were new members added to my nature family. Muffin's future mother, Sophia, wandered into the backyard with two cubs bouncing close behind. Around eleven o'clock in the morning I heard them over the noise of the television, which hadn't interrupted bear life. Sophia was mowing through, flattening a grove of flowering milkweed I had nurtured for butterflies to lay their eggs. Watching the stakes holding the plants fall to the ground was not what I had in mind, but hey, they were irresistible! She was big compared to the cubs, over two hundred pounds. The little ones looked like they were about one pound a piece, like tiny, rusted cotton balls with legs attached.

I got my camera to get a shot, outside and away from the reflective glass window. I was careful not to move suddenly, acting like I didn't know she was there. Sophia was about forty feet away and turned to study me, sizing me up with body language like, "Cut the crap, I know what you're doing. This is my home and I've been around here much longer than you. You are the newcomer. Welcome."

The next day, just like clockwork, she was back again at eleven o'clock, and this time tapped on the window like she had done it a million times before. The tap seemed to say, *I'm placing a fast-food order after sleeping all winter. It's like this — from the Den to Denny's, get it? I'm ready for a waffle with honey on it.*

What became clear was that this was a pattern of hers. Had Dottie, the woman who lived here for a long time before me, been feeding her? If so, why hadn't I seen Sophia before now? She seemed to be a tame bear with no fear of me. It went both ways. When she peered at me through the glass, her eyes were clouded and I could tell she couldn't see me well. Because I had never seen a live bear up close, I just thought that bears in general didn't have good eyesight. The eyes seemed too small for her broad forehead, yet appeared ancient, sacred, and wise.

It was an amazing thing, looking into them and slowly getting to know Sophia. She was consistent with her patterns, gracing me again with her presence around five o'clock in the evening with another tap on the window. It was thrilling, getting to have her around twice a day for a few years. I began to realize that human beings, generally speaking, don't know bears at all. We know that they are strong, fast and can kill instantly, but their personalities are as individual as ours are.

During this time I received an invitation to do volunteer work for women at Pike County Correctional Facility and took the opportunity to share my bear family photo and story with the inmates who were locked away from nature. That was the fun part. After a while I began to see the tears behind their faces. You know, the bad ones who were locked up that never get attended to. My challenge was to get them to trust again so the healing process could begin.

Much to my surprise, the facility was modern and immaculately clean. It had just completed being built, in 1995, but needed to be filled with love.

Sharing my intimacy with the animals changed the atmosphere at the prison. It was no surprise that approximately 90 percent of the incarcerations were drug and alcohol related. How different our lives would be if we had some of the same patterns as bears — living in the moment, enjoying the environment we are in without needing to place drugs and alcohol in our bodies. It is truly crazy that we don't stop doing this.

It was early April when I got on the bus on my way to do spiritual work in New York City. As I had learned from early childhood, life on the bus is never boring. Listening to conversations and studying body language can be more entertaining than watching the Academy Awards. One of the passengers seemed to have enough talent to wrap his hands around a trophy.

That day I met up with the strong smell of urine. There was a young man in the center of the bus attracting attention and I wound up sitting behind him. He kept grumbling under his breath. His New Jersey accent had textured sounds and he had many voices, like characters from the *Godfather* or *Sopranos*.

"It smells like sour piss in here." Then in a higher tone, "The bus smells like rotten rubber tires."

He continued his one-way conversation between himself and his many voices. "It's pissy in here and the smell is coming from a hole below this window. They should call this bus Shitline instead of Shortline."

He whipped out a small bottle of men's aftershave from the middle of nowhere and began patting it all over his face, but didn't stop there. He poured a bunch on his hands and started sliding them down over the length of the seat in front of him, like slicking down a racehorse before an event. I was careful not to make eye contact.

When we got off the bus at the Port Authority, I was too curious not to start a conversation with the man of multiple voices. I mentioned that the smell was unacceptable and that I would be making a complaint to Shortline. I thanked him for making the bus smell a little better and mentioned he seemed to have been grooming the seat like a horse. He looked at me, surprised, and said that his business involved racehorses. He asked for my telephone number. I declined.

On another of many bus rides from New York to Pennsylvania, I became fascinated with a woman around fifty-five years old as she took beautiful jewelry from a small suitcase to view it. There were some period pieces from the twenties, thirties, and forties, but mostly she studied a colorful, wire-woven crystal that looked new to me. I finally introduced myself and we started a friendship. She had come to the United States from the Black Forest in Germany, had once owned a house along the Blue Danube and was a jewelry designer selling her wares in New York City. She had been born in Russia and revealed to me that she was a communist. I don't think I'd ever met a real live communist, except in my childhood imagination. She didn't believe in God.

This woman and I spent many hours over several bus rides asking one another questions. She shared that over the course of a few years, other countries across the globe had developed an intense dislike for the United States and there was a united front underground to take steps to harm our country. She informed me that our country was no longer respected for its leadership. I was a little shocked as she spoke of Europeans' impressions of American gum chewing and arrogant stupidity. Her biting words were describing my homeland and cultural behaviors. It hurt, and yet she didn't have the presence of an angry person, just a knowing one.

I remember mentioning the conversation with the Russian woman to my brother-in-law, who was working at the Pentagon at the time, and he said little. About six months later, I took my pillow-scroll documentation to a copy place located in NYC. The owners looked like they were from the Middle East and spoke a foreign language between themselves when not conversing with customers. I had been frequenting another copy store that seemed to be owned by the same people. I went there often to have copies of my Bed of Trees projects printed. They had taken extra time to get important photographs right for me. I ended up dropping by their business a couple of times a month to have them help me.

In the summer months, I would always wear a bright-red scarf to cover my head because my long, naturally curly hair is unruly with humidity. It's easier to cover it. Was that the reason why the owner became comfortable enough to ask me to dinner? Had he become attracted to me because, like many women from Middle Eastern countries, I covered my hair? I never went out on a date with him, but a while later I received a letter through the mail written partially in Arabic. Inside the envelope was a check for a thousand dollars made payable to my married name.

Since my divorce, I had returned to using my maiden name, but hadn't legally changed it back. New people I met didn't know me by any name but Penny James. Along with the check was a note thanking me for my hospitality. The entire correspondence was bizarre because on the outside of the envelope it said, "To be opened and handled by P. P. only." Why would someone be sending me a check for hospitality when I hadn't given it? How had they gotten my legal last name? I thought it was possible that my landlord was playing games, trying to get me out by saying I was subletting illegally. Needless to say, I didn't cash the check.

About two months later, another check came, along with a note saying the first check must not have reached me. A lot of strange things had been going on at the time. I now had two thousand dollars in checks, and to add to the mystery, a young man bought the building from John Herget, the man who had owned the property for so long and had been so generous to me. The new owner became wealthy almost overnight, after selling a dot-com company right before the dot-com crash. He wanted everyone out, but many tenants fought to stay in the building.

I had given my keys to several people over the years to water my plants while I was in Pennsylvania. When an expensive necklace with a Coptic cross disappeared from my bedroom bureau drawer, I suspected one woman who had a drinking problem over the rest, so I wrote her a letter saying that I had a piece of jewelry missing, described what it looked like and asked her to keep an eye out for it. The note ended with, "P.S. I go to AA meetings regularly and would like for you to attend one with me. Would this be possible?" There was no response, so I went to the police station three blocks away and filled out a form for larceny. Within a few days, they came to see if they could lift fingerprints from the bureau. I called my insurance company and sent them photographs of the piece. They were going to pay for its duplication by a jeweler of my choice.

The next time I came to the city, I opened the drawer, and to my surprise, the piece of jewelry was returned.

The world outside would get even more bizarre. A few days later, someone was buzzing me from downstairs at eight thirty in the morning: "It's law enforcement. We need to speak with you."

"I'm in my nightgown. Why are you buzzing me this early? What do you want? I don't believe you're the police."

"Come down and we'll show you identification."

I went down to the vestibule. Separating me from law enforcement was a thick piece of Plexiglas that had been placed over the doorway window because of a shooting incident several years earlier. The glass had become foggy and it was like trying to look through a scummy bathroom shower door.

The officer flashed his badge. "We're investigating the Banjar Terror Squad. Open up." "I don't believe you."

"Open up or we're coming in."

I looked past the officer and saw what looked like a SWAT team outside starting to surround the building. I opened the door. By this time another tenant, Marsha Blue, was coming down the stairs on her way to work. The officer showed me a photograph of a man who looked Middle Eastern. "Do you know this man?"

"No, I've never seen him."

"We have information that he's living in your apartment."

Marsha spoke up. "We've both been living here for many years, and there's never been anyone who looks like that in this building."

The officers left shortly after. I went back upstairs and called the police I'd been working with regarding the jewelry theft incident.

"We've never heard of the Banjar Terror Squad. That information didn't come from this precinct."

I hung up, shaking. What had happened? Was it somehow connected with the letter containing the checks that were sent to me? What if I had cashed them? Was I somehow being used as a decoy to throw police off from their real location in the city? Was I picked from the street because I covered my hair and looked like a Middle Eastern man would live with me?

I made copies of the two checks, sent them to the FBI and asked them to call me, but they never did.

A few months passed and I again went to the copy store to have more copies made of my pillow scroll. It was a beautiful, crisp blue morning. There was a young man already there getting copies of what also looked like a scrollwork testament, written in Arabic. It stood out because areas were highlighted with different bright colors of ink. I studied it as I stood next to him. He was small-boned, not much taller than I am, and was speaking in a foreign language. I wanted to show him my writing because I thought an amazing thing was taking place. Two people from such different cultures, side by side, sharing spiritual messages that were so meaningful. I placed my hand lightly on his shoulder and leaned in toward him.

"I have scrollwork here shaped like a pillow."

But he never said a word as he turned away to leave.

I couldn't have imagined that soon, on another clear, crisp morning, three American planes would be used as weapons of mass destruction and the Twin Towers would crumble killing almost three thousand people from many different countries.

Life isn't a neat and pretty little package where all the ribbons are tied. Before that day, I had never heard of the word *Banjar*. The word initially sounded like *Banjeer* to me. The closest I could come up with was sketchy Banjar history. I found out there is a Banjar language, and in 1526, there was a Banjar Kingdom and war that accompanied an Arabic script. Did I just hear it wrong? Maybe it was Bandar?

A few weeks later, there was an article in the *New York Times* about Arabs funding terrorism through organizations funneling drug money. There was apparently an extensive network of money flowing to support the underground movement to destroy the United States. It was later reported in *Newsweek* that checks written to associates of two 9/11 hijackers for approximately one hundred thirty thousand dollars were traced back to the wife of the Saudi ambassador, Prince Bandar bin Sultan. The ambassador did not respond to *Newsweek* at that time, but told the *New York Times* that he was outraged that he and his wife had been in any way connected to terrorists, insisting that they had simply been responding to a letter from a destitute Saudi student in the States, pleading for help to cover medical expenses for his wife.

Inside the Bush administration there were dividing opinions about how hard to press the investigation. There were a handful of people at Justice and Treasury who believed we should be putting the screws on the Saudis, but that did not happen. In a meeting between Prince Bandar and Condoleezza Rice, the issue was barely mentioned, given the United States' interest in Saudi bases and its appetite for the country's oil.

Chapter 17
Post 9/11 — A Decade of Numbers & Reckoning

Through the open convertible roof of our Porsche 911 Targa, my husband and I first arrived in New York from Chicago back in the seventies, and saw a Manhattan skyline that took our breath away. Then, the famous view — and our whole world — changed on 9/11. I realized the skyline once again looked as it had that first time.

Living a simple life hadn't stopped chaos and it was progressing too fast to keep up.

How could I choose to incorporate all the new happenings, cope with the many changes? The debate between progress and preservation rolled on both inside me and in the world at large. From about 1880, the Machine Age made a tremendous impact on peoples' lives. In less than thirty years, the light bulb, phonograph, telephone, radio, automobile, and airplane became part of our existence. Was life in America more satisfying when we bought into all of these new things, which resulted in seismic cultural shifts?

More recent innovations that have invaded our daily lives are the internet, social media, and an around-the-clock ticking news cycle. Information can be relayed over the World Wide Web in real time. Businesses develop almost overnight with venture capital funding. We are living witnesses to the internet gold rush, with only a few Americans getting rich and doing it faster than ever before.

The dot-com stock market crash began with a slow rumble in March 2000, culminating in October 2002 at a loss of five trillion dollars. In September of 2001, almost seven hundred employees from Cantor Fitzgerald would tragically lose their lives in the World Trade Center while crunching numbers for the New York Stock Exchange. They had been part of building the greatest wealth in our nation, operating from the tallest buildings, and yet it all came crashing down.

The 9/11 attacks exploded with precision in a series of meticulously planned, falling dominoes. Planes went down in a field in Pennsylvania and at the Pentagon in Washington, DC. Communication as we knew it halted to an eerie silence; all air traffic was commanded to the ground; the usual nonstop hum of American life was replaced by unforetold fear of using planes as missiles again.

I suddenly had feelings about the unpredictability of war … sensing a touch of what others have lived before me and still do in many places today. It was strange to accept that it could happen here, on home turf. I couldn't reach anyone outside of Manhattan and no one could reach me for three days. My family was worried sick, and on the opposite end, I was worried about Patrick, my brother-in-law. He still spent a lot of time at the Pentagon.

Ironically, toward the close of his naval career, he was involved with a strategic defense initiative called Star Wars under President Reagan. He is an aeronautical engineer—an actual rocket scientist— and his job was to build anti-ballistic missiles. I couldn't get out of the city for several days during the aftermath and felt trapped. The only person near me that I was able to get real comfort from was Johnny Holliday. We had been up most of the previous night before the planes struck, composing music for lyrics I had written, titled, "I Promise I Will Listen." We were finally able to speak by phone, and Johnny's voice was calming.

This was at the time the well-known country singer Alan Jackson was writing his song "Where Were You (When the World Stopped Turning.)" We all identified — frozen, in a state of shock. We held Mr. Jackson's uniting words in our hearts. They were now history inside the crystal ball none of us had looked into.

Johnny said, "It feels like we're in a war."

"Johnny, we are in a war."

I was finally able to get to the Port Authority on 42nd and 8th Ave and made it back home to Pennsylvania. I was scheduled to do volunteer work at Pike County Correctional Facility and glad I was able to make it over there without canceling. I was surprised that the inmates knew so much about what had happened. They were focused on numerology, the way the numbers 911 went down. 9-11-2001. Ground 0. I learned from them. For me nothing made sense except for the most important number left out — 666 Antichrist. I was in a daze, but put one foot in front of the other and realized soon after that I had to go back to New York City because I was scheduled for jury duty. I can't remember how many days that was after the buildings came down.

I took the subway from 86th Street and remember getting off near Chinatown. The air near my apartment in upper Manhattan was still a little smoky, but taking a subway ride for ten minutes and seeing what the street was like near Ground Zero was overwhelming. I walked into lavender, gray, green, swirling cultures of smoke. It was raining. Droplets of water were trying to squelch it. It wasn't working. It just got heavier.

The street was empty except for a small thin Chinese woman approaching me. I could see through the thick air that she had an umbrella over her head and a white mask covering her nose and mouth. There was an eerie silence, then an occasional clanking in the distance with the soft sound of barking dogs in the background ... and the smell of death. Burned wings of different religions and races. I couldn't see the street signs and got lost, but somehow made it to court on time. I remember going up an elevator and checking in and seeing several people sitting in chairs. I rested my arms and shoulders on the counter next to them. A middle-aged woman with piercing eyes looked at me: "Are you okay?"

I started explaining to her that I had scleroderma which affects my lungs and hadn't realized that the air quality was still so bad:

"EPA said it was safe after three days." The words coming out of her tightly drawn lips revealed she didn't believe them. "I'm going to send you down the hall to someone else who can release you from jury duty."

She knew my body shouldn't have made the trip.

The New York Stock Exchange ended up being closed for over a week ... a colossal blow. Were we, the supposed infidels, being taught a lesson? I remember Sue Herera, an anchor in financial journalism who was presiding over the new opening on CNBC, saying something like, "we can show our strength by not selling our stock." I was moved by the comment and believed that collectively we would hold her sentiment in good faith.

Most days, the New York Stock Exchange symbolizes the Oz behind the curtain of what makes business move, the bull of power that drives our economy. On that day, when Sue Herera made her plea to sit tight in the wake of 9/11, it seemed to me that we needed the NYSE to represent the early days of American growth and development, human to human, the intense cohesive glue of handshakes and honorable contracts, values from my childhood that kept our great nation together.

But at nine thirty when the market opened, there was a massive sell-off. Nothing is more important on Wall Street than money. I learned from that; I changed. Those values from our early days, the work ethic and honesty that made us proud Americans, have faded. Greed has seeped in and taken over. The core of humanity has been weakened. That day we betrayed ourselves in the market as an emotional reaction to 9/11.

"For I know the thoughts that I think toward you, said the LORD, thoughts of peace, and not of evil, to give you an expected end." (Jeremiah 29:11, KJV)

A year later, *American Idol* with Simon Cowell was televised. Fresh, unknown faces from grassroots America had an opportunity to express themselves and become famous, singing.

Life seemed to settle down a bit. We were recovering with our dreams still intact.

God's purpose for me was bigger than I could ever imagine. If only I could let go of the limitations I perceived as containing my purpose ... but the one small compartment I thought was my portion of His work was only one tiny drawer in the mix of His many. Inside, there were still spurts of *Alfie*, a movie that made Michael Caine famous in the sixties.

Also embedded in my partly fractured brain was the doubt of my future, finding the strength to release the past damage and move forward. The thing I held onto hardest was the art. The Bed of Trees. I was commissioned by God to do them, yet my mind kept me in fear, the lowly place. What if the beds got destroyed in yet another fire? I wouldn't have the energy to build them again.

The brain's bedeviled wandering and wasteful worrying is relentless. Our positive and negative thoughts use fired-up neurotransmitters that travel to separate areas of our minds. I learned why dreams had me sitting on the edge of tall fences and almost falling off cliffs. How did I finally get beyond the anxieties of fight-versus-flight instincts?

It's so simple — being in conversation with God's living words. They fire every healthy transmitter, target the inner pathway to wholeness and give bold courage that launches the spirit into high life, soaring. High life takes on a whole new meaning, raising us above the base level of survival on Maslow's hierarchy-of-needs pyramid. Living in faith is freedom preservation, maintaining a healthy path to become our best for the world we all share.

Making grounded decisions took me to the other side, learning to relieve stress the world brings on. Being in the new existence revealed magic, truth and peace, things I was looking for on the outside but couldn't get. I was still holding on to old thought patterns, but the Higher Power slowly began to reprogram my brain. I worked to stay focused because each day brought new opportunities for wholeness as the world changed around me.

Country life is a community experience. My home in Shohola sits right in the heart of the rustic belt. Looking back to the creation of the Bed of Tree beds, when we suddenly needed to change location, my neighbors, Heather and Jeff, opened their giant barn to me on short notice, so I could continue the artwork. Needless to say, this reinforced the bond between us.

Several years later, my dear companions, Heather and Jeff lost Jordan, their son with the clear blue eyes. He was killed in an automobile accident in a car full of teenagers. Heather couldn't adjust to the loss and turned to drinking to fill the void. I tried planting seeds of faith when she asked me questions after her drinking got really bad. She and her family had not been raised in a spiritual atmosphere, so words from the Bible were not comforting to her. Instead, she went to clairvoyants so she could continue speaking with Jordan through them. When that didn't ease her pain, she came back to me.

"I look so ugly now. Jordan will hardly recognize me. I'll be so embarrassed for him to see me."

"In Heaven you and your body will be restored to perfection."

Although Heather is no longer with us, she is very much alive in the pillow scroll, the rainbow glass canopy, and roots of the bed. I see her in the eyes of the rainbow.

Muffin came shortly after Heather's passing and filled my life with joy. I had a lot to learn in the moment-to-moment relationship that developed. I woke up in the middle of the night to what sounded like a baby crying right outside my window. I got a flashlight and pointed it to the ground, searching everywhere. Nothing. But I couldn't go back to sleep because of the haunting sound.

When dawn broke, I looked out and saw what appeared to be a curled-up ball in the branches, just out of arm's reach. The fear in her eyes was heartbreaking. I ran downstairs and warmed some milk before going outside. I left it at the base of the beechnut tree and called out to her. She climbed even higher. I finally went back upstairs and opened my window and started talking to her in soft, loving tones. It wasn't working, but I didn't give up ... cooing sounds, then singing.

She may very well have gotten sick of my voice, because she finally started inching her way down. I went back outside, careful to give her distance, but continued talking in soft tones while she got closer and closer to the milk sitting under the tree. Finally, Muffin began drinking it.

I named that moment *pragma* (the name ancient Greeks assigned to long-term, mature love). It is when I knew I had become the cub's mother. It wasn't long before I called another moment *ludus*, meaning playful love. I was so thankful I had gotten close enough to know Sophia's parental side and had been allowed to touch Muffin, or the bonding wouldn't have happened. Sophia must have died from natural causes. I had just seen her the day before when she brought Muffin for me to touch and play with. It wasn't hunting season and I hadn't heard any gunshots anywhere. It was part of The Grand Plan. I realize now I wasn't prepared to lose Sophia and find her helpless cub crying next to my window.

I learned that before Muffin would accept grass and other natural foods to eat available from the woods, I would have to breathe on and touch it. I wore black Ugg boots for her to start the climb up onto my shoulder. I was her tree. She liked to tuck her head under my chin and feel my breath on her face accompanied by my usual cooing and kissing sounds. I realize you might be gagging, but life with her seemed perfectly normal and natural to me and would last almost thirteen years. She adjusted quickly without a bear mother and, interestingly, the only thing that seemed to make her fearful were other bears. When they wandered through, she was just plain scared and would take off at about forty miles an hour until she reached her favorite tree nearest to me to hide.

I later learned that adult male bears have been known to kill cubs. That's why the females (called sows) are so protective of their young and the fathers are never around after mating season. Hunters and mature male bears are their predators.

I kept my relationship with Muffin private except with my immediate family, a few close friends, and inmates at the prison. I found it burdensome to hear others warning me about how dangerous bears are, or telling me to check out the story about the photographer who lost his life in Alaska while trying to be friends with a polar bear. The truth is, people without awareness are more threatening than any black bear I have known. The life we're living, through negligence, includes children smaller than I am with guns. It boils down to getting to know what exists around you, being realistically aware of its nature and your own.

Man is the most dangerous animal on the planet. People kill one another at an alarming rate. A bear killing a person is extremely rare.

How do we protect Mother Nature when it's always been Mother Nature protecting us? It was just three years after 9/11 that a tsunami in the Indian Ocean, with the energy of twenty-three thousand Hiroshima-type bombs, killed thousands of people. Shortly after, in 2005, Hurricane Katrina hit Louisiana. The first decade of the new millennium was shocking, with barely time to breathe between man-made and natural disasters, a series of wake-up calls.

Nature doesn't like deals done at her expense, taking advantage of her generosity, slicing off a melting iceberg as sparkling water, bottling it and placing it on supermarket shelves to make money, only to find it floating in an oil spill.

Good-faith, no-fault monetary settlements within the *Art of the Deal* manipulate legal loopholes that allow negligence with no criminal jail time to muddy names; it only takes enough money to stop the process before justice can prevail. We all want justice to prevail. We must unite and know what's going on in order to have corrupt parts of laws thrown out before adding others in.

Are you aware that oil companies drill into our earth with only minimal rules protecting our environment? Disrespecting nature through lack of ethics, truth and moral character causes chaos and results in disintegration. The violation of nature's resources, placing money first, and the dirty power that goes along with the addiction to oil is one causal factor in our breakdown.

We have power through networking. We have collectively become aware that bullying governments can be brought down, and so can corporations and precincts with special interests that control government through money, power, and lobbying. A vast majority of the lawyers who enter government offices are placed there carefully by a machine that designs and moves players like pieces on a chess board. Once they are in, payback comes in the form of appropriations — sliding money in at the end of some legislation that is actually intended for an unrelated purpose, hidden from the public until after the fact. A cleaner government based on understanding why "In God We Trust" is written on our currency, has got to register and hold meaning.

On the first anniversary after 9/11, it was no accident that I was able to get the Bed of Trees named *Infinite Stillness* into Riverside Park as an art installation. It was placed in the People's Garden between 90th and 91st Streets, which is part of New York City Parks and Recreation. My sister Shanda came from Virginia to help. I also hired artists Linda Davis and Woodrow Blagg to place the bed for viewing without bruising any of the beautiful flowers surrounding it. The plan was that the crew would meet me at the park with everything loaded on my truck early in the morning. It turned out to be an arduous day. When they didn't arrive on time, I grew concerned but figured that packing the bed's many parts had taken more time than anticipated.

It was a beautiful, sunny morning. I sat among the flowers waiting for them to arrive and met a young Black photographer with short braids adorning his head. He had heard about the Bed of Trees and came by to photograph it. Steve Hopkins ended up hanging around most of the day and we got to know one another.

While I was waiting for the crew, I saw psychologist and talk show host, Dr. Phil McGraw, being interviewed a short distance away. After his success on the Oprah Winfrey show, Dr. Phil and his wife, Robin, would become household names and part of our new culture. They co-developed a well-thought-out program curbing domestic violence using cutting-edge brain therapy combined with emotional analysis and treatment. I was delightfully surprised to see him in the park.

A few planes flew overhead. We had come a long way in one year. I looked up at them without fear. Around eleven o'clock, my sister and the crew arrived. They had somehow locked themselves out of my apartment. While the bed was being set up, groomed, and protected with the healing power of eucalyptus and Spanish moss, many people gathered around, including some of the gardeners who had been tending to their favorite plants within their individual plots of ground. In one area, I saw some blue-eyed grass that I had fallen in love with on my property in Pennsylvania. It was such an honor to get to know some of the people who were digging around in the earth that day, sharing their tips on gardening.

Steve, whom I quite naturally became friends with, photographed a woman with a small baby. She became very upset when he took the picture and demanded the footage. When he explained to her that he wasn't taking the photo for professional reasons, she wouldn't accept the explanation and called the Park Service to complain. Did she think he was using it for Bed of Trees publicity? The next thing we knew, a medium-height, thin, white man arrived in a strung-out rage, pacing back and forth on the grass along the garden's edge as if he had jurisdiction over it.

"This is the ugliest bed I've ever seen. I'm going to have it removed."

This was right after a young Latina woman said, "This is the most beautiful bed I've ever seen!"

What happened next was truly amazing. The group of people that had gathered around started yelling at the angry man. A verbal brawl started in Riverside Park over a spontaneous photograph that captured a tender moment between mother and child. Perhaps the photographer should have asked first. Perhaps the two of them could have settled the problem without involving others, but it ended up being one of the most turbulent, then peaceful, frustrating then satisfying, experiences of my life.

As the sun went down, time came to dismantle *Infinite Stillness*. Many people lingered and a few asked if they could help and have a copy of what was written on the pillow scrollwork. It was the sweetest thing! *Infinite Stillness* and communication art had prevailed. A new chapter in the bed story was created and yet another had already happened.

One day not long after this, I was switching channels on television and saw the tail end of the movie, *You've Got Mail*, starring Meg Ryan and Tom Hanks. I had missed seeing it when it first came out because in 1998 I was still isolated in nature. The film is based on the 1937 play, *Parfumerie*, and was updated for modern viewers, using Instant Messenger rather than traditional correspondence. The love story ends by the flower garden in the exact spot in Riverside Park where my bed was.

Looking down from a window of the past, a man cleaning a black Mercedes in 1984 is behind me now. Life is so different from what I imagined it would be, but it turned out well. I know what love is.

It wouldn't be long before Olivia Goldsmith, author of *The First Wives Club*, would no longer be with us. Her book was made into another movie I haven't seen, and it became a cult classic for women of a certain age. It starred Diane Keaton, Bette Midler, and Goldie Hawn, with several cameos including Ivana Trump and Kathie Lee Gifford. I didn't recognize the Goldsmith name until it became national news that she had died during a plastic-surgery procedure.

Olivia Goldsmith, age fifty-five, had checked in to look more youthful, more beautiful — but never checked out. Her death recalled and spoke to first-wife memories of desperation, insecurity, and ugliness that plastic surgery can't cure. The author's life story had many similarities with mine, except she used her experiences to write revenge fantasies about mistreated women turning tables on the men they love. The women in her stories came out winners in the end, and made it onto the big screen.

Looking back at the seventies and eighties, I have the raw privilege of viewing who I was, what I've learned and who I have become after re-experiencing division … divorce in its many forms of darkness. My former husband had been chosen by God, part of His Plan for my severance and resulting growth. Through him I was given sewing salvation, sutures for closure and recovery and fresh air for planting healing seeds.

Back in Pennsylvania, I always left my swamp boots outside the kitchen door. Muffin developed the habit of taking them up into the woods when I'd leave for New York. I'd return home to find them missing. She didn't like me gone one bit. There would inevitably be a few things torn up around the yard. After bear hugs and food, we'd make up. She was still tiny, nevertheless the property got walloped. Her mischievous paws loved having boxing matches with daisies, enjoyed knocking over potted plants and stomping on carefully planted irises at the sides of the porch. She also delighted in breaking branches on my lilac bush, eating the fragrant blooms I loved to smell because they reminded me so much of my mother and childhood. All of us were together in spirit having a fun day! Until...

Daddy died on Father's Day. Shanda became concerned when he didn't answer his phone for three days. Sheila, who lived closest to him, made the trip from Gardner to his home. "We're going to get you to the hospital. Everything is going to be okay." He made it through to the morning, but a little after five o'clock he stopped breathing, and the phone call came that no one wants to make or receive.

After hearing the news, I felt my feet no longer had grounding beneath them. Now, both my mother and father were no longer connected to the world we once all shared as a family.

The negative energy had gone all the way through to my vehicle. The battery in my truck was dead. Days before I had bought a leather covering for the steering wheel of my truck and the only thing I could do was sit there, stitching the leather of the cover around the wheel that controls several thousand pounds of metal. Before long, the needle became dull and my hands went numb. The shock and pain kept the tears from coming. I silently wished my dad a Happy Father's Day.

My memory went back to the time we were a young family driving from Colorado Springs to Pueblo, after visiting my aunt. It was early evening and we were crossing railroad tracks when suddenly there was a strong rush of wind that moved our car forward. That train missed crashing into the tail end of our vehicle by an inch. There had been no warning and none of us heard any noise beforehand. We all knew something bigger than any of us had protected us.

I thought back on my father's driving record. He was eighty-four when he died and had never been involved in any accident during his lifetime that I knew about. He taught all of his daughters to drive and made it seem so easy. Feeling the stick shift manually the old way was fun and natural, until technology ruined it by making things automatic. New cars can even park themselves. Why? There is so much satisfaction in knowing how close and how much in front of a vehicle you must be, to curve in right next to the curb with precision, to perfectly fit between two vehicles. Father had been a master. Now I wouldn't be able to tell him in person how much I appreciated his expertise; I could no longer be mad at him for refusing to wear a seatbelt. In the blink of an eye, he had moved on. I'm just thankful that we became friends before his time here came to an end.

There were two important moments before Daddy died and both were when I was visiting Colorado. The first was when I asked him to take me to see my aunt Laura. She had been with Mother when she was dying and Mother told her about the "other woman." He didn't want to face Laura, but he finally agreed to take me. My aunt, much to his surprise, treated him with affection and kindness. I could see the muscles in his face relax and the fear leaving his eyes. On the way back to the airport, Daddy started talking about Grandma's best friend, a foreman for the biggest railroad in Colorado. His name was Jim Justice, and he and his wife, Sue, both admired my grandmother and her independent, rugged lifestyle on the ranch. They often looked out for Esther; Jim would come and kill a wild animal or snake she needed to be rid of. They checked on Grandma to make sure she was safe and looked after as a woman living alone. Just as my father mentioned his name, there was an exit with the name Justice. It was the marker along the way, letting us know we weren't alone on our journey.

The second moment happened the last time we were together. My father had taken me for a ride in Gardner. He had developed a need to return there. As we passed endless fields with bales of yellow hay, he pointed out the window to an old building. "This is where I went to school!" As the earth settled dust beneath my father's automobile, it told him how rich farm life had been for Grandma and me, how we could love it so much even though it had been a prison to him. I could see in his body language that something incredible had just happened. He felt the same joy.

My father had been pretty much alone as a child. He developed a secret life away from his parents in order to survive. With his mother sick with tuberculosis, he had no one to experience love with. There was no one to sing lullabies and his father was never around to teach him how to whistle.

Kids' brains develop rapidly during the early, crucial years. My father's learning was limited because his father took long trips away from home, too preoccupied with horses. His small son found that stupid. All of the racehorses his father had groomed were too slow. He and his schoolmates were hearing about something more exciting, faster! His knowing friends talked about the automobile.

G.I. Joe in war remained a child even through the role the government had given him. He was still a child when he got in his car at fifty-five years of age to go searching for his dad. The long trip took him to Fredericktown, Missouri, where he found my grandfather suffering from Alzheimer's — a father who didn't know who his grown son was but could remember the racehorses that he had trained and bet on when his son was a little boy. He talked about that.

Daddy's thrill in life came from the imaginary dreams of a child, the child that is forever embedded into the Holy Spirit of Jesus. God made us all in that fashion, uniquely different, but the same in this one holy way. The child remains no matter what age we become, and deserves respect and love. Through awareness we can learn to acknowledge, nurture, and take responsibility for that part of ourselves, never allowing anyone or anything the power to violate the openness of the young, innocent part of our being.

My father spent his last days on earth, not outside in nature but on the floor, inside next to his bed, with God, the God he didn't know growing up. I hope to someday have the sacred privilege to ask what was discussed during their time alone. With my father, driving was the holy endeavor. Now the Master was driving him home.

I carried the tattered Bible Pastor Jesse James had left behind into the Methodist church in Gardner, Colorado. It was big and heavy. A small one just hadn't been big enough for him. I referred to it periodically as I stood up at the pulpit in the exact same spot he had stood in his green alligator boots so long ago. Now I was doing Daddy's eulogy.

Sun peered through a stained-glass window, reflecting rainbow colors on the faces in the pews, the same place my grandmother had been every Sunday with miners, making different kinds of friends, like Peter Rabbit. The "orphans" on both sides of her had grown into young men. My father had been beside her too, a young boy growing older, developing his muscles by filling the fire belly of a steam engine train with coal so the wheels would turn on their tracks; later he would work long hours in a steel mill to feed his family before eventually becoming a car salesman. At Sheila's request, his name, Joseph William James, would be inscribed right next to Grandpa's under the same stained-glass window the sun was flirting with.

I went back outdoors carrying the old family Bible with our birth names written inside. I stared at the little white church and felt at home … so many memories. In the future, I would place the family Bible in my new home on Grandma's property.

The night flight into LaGuardia was filled with millions of beaconed eyes looking up at me from an upside-down midnight-blue sky. I got to thinking that it almost had the same magical quality as when I was five years old, sitting on Grandma's porch, seeing an explosion of shooting stars. My throat tightened as tears blurred my vision, melting New York into Colorado. I was now on a broader horizon with a new mission — to guard and protect, keep an eye on the reflective eyes staring back at me.

After 9/11, my New York City roots grew even deeper. I dug my heels into the heart of My City. It wouldn't be long before the Annual Evening with Friends of Charlie Parker — dedicated to battling the effects of substance abuse on family members — would come around again to raise money for the cause. Veritas Therapeutic Community Foundation on the Upper West Side was involved with the event. The evening would include Congressman Charles Rangel's gravelly voice mingling among jazz musicians who lovingly gave their talents and time to help.

Many had seen firsthand how the stubborn disease has toxic effects on parents, children, siblings, and friends.

That night I overheard musicians laughing, talking among themselves, and got a history of the Birdland — the original club opened in 1949 and was owned by "Joe the Wop" Cataldo, who caged finches inside its walls. Charlie "Yardbird" Parker, also known as "Bird," was a jazz virtuoso and a headliner at the club, which was a favorite haunt of stars like Frank Sinatra, Marilyn Monroe and Harry

Belafonte, and later Woody Allen and Bill Cosby. The musicians were inspired by the name of the club and used it in their work — John Coltrane's album *Live at Birdland* and George Shearing's song "Lullaby of Birdland" are examples.

Conflicts flared between competitive musicians when bebop was introduced by Charlie Parker and Dizzy Gillespie. It happened one night at a jam session when he discovered that twelve tones of chromatic scale can lead methodically to any key. Confines of simpler jazz soloing began breaking down. The story is that he was playing "Cherokee," a love song by Ray Noble, when the transformation occurred. Beboppers who followed him called the mostly older traditionalists moldy figs.

Sadly, Charlie Parker would turn into an old fig before his time. He was a heroin addict in his teens. He then turned to alcohol, eventually developing cirrhosis of the liver. He died when he was just thirty-four years old. Reportedly, the coroner mistook his body for that of a fifty-year-old.

The night of the Friends of Charlie Parker gala, Mr. Rangel, the politician-activist, asked for my phone number so we could meet for lunch. It never happened, but I ended up going to another Veritas event which Peter Jennings co-chaired at the Hammerstein Ballroom and included dinner, dancing, and jazz. I remember boldly walking up to Peter Jennings's table to introduce myself. I briefly told him about visiting another Veritas facility right down the road from me in Shohola and sharing my Bed of Trees project with the women there. I handed him a small card with a photo of *Bed Spring* on it. He thanked me for the information and we shook hands.

I turned away from the "pecking-order table" that was next to the stage Mr. Jennings would soon be speaking from. Manhattan society had separated me from him. I felt momentarily lost but the strong smell of Peter Jennings's cologne on my hand carried me back to where I was seated. I had heard he was quite the ladies' man. Was it a game, a pattern of his to place his scent on the palms of his hands so that his essence would linger? His fourth wife had been sitting at his table. I got a good look at her. She was considerably younger than he was and, as crazy as it sounds, looked a little like a younger, female version of him — dark hair, sophisticated, fine-boned. I had developed a girl crush on him after he spent seventeen intimate hours with me on television, giving blow-by-blow descriptions with relentless flashback images of the Twin Towers crumbling... crumbling ... crumbling.

I guess he must have taken trips to the restroom and eaten during commercial breaks during his extended time on the air following the 9/11 attacks. His ever-steady eagle eyes seemed to catch every subtle nuance about that terrible day. Stable presence, easy-on-the-eye charisma and sartorial splendor presiding over the horror ... white alpha-male Superman sexy. He had earlier brought in the millennium. One hundred and seventy-five million people had tuned in. Television critics called him superhuman because he stayed on the air for twenty-three hours straight, making it a marathon as we were holding our breath about a possible Y2K meltdown that didn't happen. What drove him to work so much harder than others? Was it because deep down he felt insecure because he hadn't finished high school and graduated from a prestigious college like Harvard? His accomplishments far exceed what a PhD would do next to his name. He and Todd Brewster authored *The Century*, a thick impressive coffee-table book on history, but I remember a remark made in an AA meeting that he had left Bill Wilson, the founder of AA, out of his work. Was it because his coauthor was connected to *Time* magazine where Bill W. had refused to be on the cover, but still got listed as one of the Most Important People of the twentieth century?

Peter Jennings would soon be celebrating a live Fourth of July special with ABC. Toby Keith was planning on singing "Courtesy of the Red, White and Blue," and apparently a conflict arose. Country and city-slicker culture collided behind the scenes about boot-up-your-ass phrasing within the song. I remember at the end of the broadcast watching Peter Jennings's body language change. His confidence deteriorated; his voice grew uneven and weak. His shoulders curved over like he wanted to hide, and I remember thinking, *What is going on with Peter Jennings?*

He had been out on the road *In Search of America* and did a segment that involved elk rutting at Rocky Mountain National Park. Dominant alpha testosterone with crashing horns. I wonder if he identified with them. My sister, Bobbie, had been there too, to see the elk and hear their bugle magnificence.

I caught a cab and passed where Peter Jennings lived, four blocks down from me on Central Park West. People from the past and present like Rock Hudson, Jerry Seinfeld, Isaac Stern, Diane Sawyer, Mike Nichols, and Beverly Sills had all lived there at various times. It is located near to the Museum of Natural History, a place no one should miss visiting.

Peter Jennings's musky, potent perfume went to bed with me that night, bringing on a High Order dream. I was lost in a large, canopied amphitheater wearing the fur coat my former husband bought me in Greece and using the same cosmetic bag to repeatedly freshen up in the bathroom mirror. Then I was outside following my sister Bobbie. She disappeared leaving me all alone. I was in a vast, lush green pasture and a long, well-tended log fence separated me from Peter Jennings, who was off in the distance. I remember being surprised that it wasn't greener where he was. I was standing on the same well-manicured carpet but I longed to go over to the other side. The fence that stopped me was made of smooth wood embedded with triangles of dazzling crystal that stood out from everything else, pointing upwards.

I am inviting you to interpret!

In late March 2004, Peter Jennings's voice was uncharacteristically gravelly as he informed us that he had lung cancer. "Yes, I was a smoker until about twenty years ago, and I was weak and I smoked over 9/11. But whatever the reason, the news does slow you down a bit."

How could this man who seemed to have all knowledge in the palm of his hand die from an addiction?

Mayor Bloomberg later designated the block on West 66th between Columbus and Central Park West, home to ABC News headquarters, Peter Jennings Way. We would also lose our

Hollywood Superman, Christopher Reeve, along with his lovely wife, Dana, who had cared for him. She died of lung cancer after never smoking a cigarette. Soon after, a Superman comic book from 1938 was found in a house wall and sold for one hundred seventy-five thousand dollars.

I would soon be shaking hands with a former CIA agent, the encounter taking me to the Rikers Island jail complex, right next to LaGuardia. I would be reading to inmates, teaming up with the Horticultural Society of New York. The training was extended to young people in public schools, combining specific guidelines with the healing presence of nature. Tony Smith presided over the society and focused on getting inmates not to return to Rikers Island.

We both knew the odds of recidivism in the United States — 65 percent. Two-thirds of people who have slipped through the cracks go back because of their partners in crime — alcohol and drugs. Over the course of eleven years, Tony Smith reduced recidivism to 15 percent for individuals connected to his well-thought-out program. He used a two-acre plot of land as an oasis for teaching students all they needed to know about horticultural techniques, science, botany and harvesting.

A book, *Doing Time in the Garden* by James Jiler, was a beacon of light over Tony's future interns. Tony filled the area with turtles, ducks, and birds not only to teach them needed skills, but also to have them experience what loving, healthy interdependence feels like between nature, people, and animals. This was while plotting a butterfly border and harvesting a crop of ripe peppers from the enclosed garden. The lucky ones graduating to the outside would go on to beautify grounds surrounding libraries and children's schools in Manhattan.

It was inside Rikers' two-acre plot, with a group of ten women, that I shared the story of my Bed of Trees. My goal was to have as much one-on-one communication as possible. I taught them how it was constructed, and we gathered branches, searched for wood, trees and root formations that would form the sculpture, putting what we could in a pile before sitting in a circle. I talked about one-day-at-a-time recovery from alcoholism; personal questions were asked. This was while we decided what kind of bed we would create and where to place it without violating the existing harmonious landscape that other inmates had preserved before us.

We decided on a bed with flowering morning glory vines climbing up into a canopy, weaving in and out of intertwining branches. The day ended with all of us on our knees, our bodies bowed to the ground, our hands kneading the soil to make seed germination easier while the sun graced our shoulders. James Jiler came to join us.

I remember glancing up, seeing the sun shining on the locked fence surrounding us, highlighting the circles of razor wire high in the sky. It didn't matter to us at that moment. We were living fully, happy, and free in spirit, if not physically free. Tony Smith made this experience possible through reactivating his old connections. He had been with the CIA for sixteen years before working under several mayors including John Lindsay and Rudy Giuliani.

The mission statement for the new planned bed was to provide support for healing the universe. Starting with the earth, the goal was to bring focus to the most urgent maladies within global warming. We were to educate the public collectively for hands-on help with a commitment to follow through to resolution. The *Morning Glory* bed was to be the focal point of communication, using the mattress area filled with earth as the picture frame for planting seeds that would grow into unique, healthy, living solutions. This was at a time when culture was weaving designs of its own volition. YouTube came into being on the internet, providing an opportunity to have fifteen minutes of fame, Andy Warhol style.

September 7, 2007, I was up again going to Rikers Island. I drove my truck to the bus station where I would then take a bus into New York City that was filled with commuters, some going to Wall Street. Most of us were sleeping. I got off at the Port Authority to catch the subway to Queens. It was on time and pleasant, with lots of room before rush hour reared its ugly head. I had made arrangements with James Jiler to meet at Starbucks. It was seven forty in the morning. I walked one block down the street after leaving the subway and it seemed like every nationality was taking in the morning sun.

I sat down to the smell of fresh coffee, next to a man who appeared to be German. He had several tools set out on a table inside Starbucks and was working on a large round antique clock. He was in tattered clothing that must have been quite expensive at one time because of the design. He had on a black top hat. I wondered if he had been an entertainer when younger, maybe in a cabaret in some far-out place in Paris. It seemed like he once carried an air of decadence about him, but it had frayed along with his clothing ... been misplaced with a past he was still holding onto. His silk brocade vest was inside out with a smartly tailored but faded shirt underneath. He was oblivious to everything going on around him except for repairing the magnificent old clock as morning ticked away.

James was late, but I had his book and began reading about life lessons through prison horticulture. I got to know him and his work even better through his writing. He helped the incarcerated make hammocks for animals at Staten Island Zoo from old fire hoses. I imagined there was still a big junk pile of donations somewhere that I could go through and create a surprise within our bed project.

On this particular day, James was tense. There had been an incident at the prison. The person approving our arrival was no longer answering his email. With that going on, I was thankful that we got clearance and there was no lockdown at Rikers. We finally arrived and walked through the fencing to the greenhouse after being picked up in a white van driven by a corrections officer. Today some of the garden was to be harvested.

I brought photos of my beds and all the animals from home. The inmates absolutely loved them and James kept coming up to show me work designs created from soap they had made from scratch, just like my grandmother had done so many years before in her kitchen.

One of the soap sculptures was made by a man named Angel. It was an etched pew with an open Bible on top. I was so taken by it, I asked James if I could work with Angel. He informed me that it wouldn't be possible because Angel had been caught with contraband. I asked if I could correspond with him, just to tell him how talented I thought he was as a sculptor.

As I was leaving Rikers, I shared that I kept my spiritual work anonymous for over ten years while I was in the country. James talked about one hand clapping in the woods. "It doesn't exist until someone sees or hears it."

I kept quiet, but wanted to say, "All Heaven responds with joy, it just seems not to exist here because it isn't on television."

"I know a place that is like the Museum of Modern Art, but that is never seen. It's a psychiatric ward where artists inside paint incredible scenes, they just don't talk about it." Voices from each patient's heart speak through their work … and He hears them, I thought.

He continued on with his disdain of senseless posturing within the art world. He gave it the finger-in-mouth gag gesture. I knew I would never forget this man. He was real and we were exploring new territory with one another in an unfamiliar forest. I was sure I would be working with him for a long time, but it wasn't to be. He mentioned his scheduled appearance on television right before he dropped me off at the Port Authority. That was the last time I saw him. Shortly after, he would no longer have his job at the Horticultural Society. Neither would Tony Smith. What happened? I heard that the powers that be were left out of too many press releases. We would soon all be gone except for the seeds we had planted … patiently waiting for their season to sprout.

Chapter 18
Unforeseen Forces

Back home, Muffin became the love of my life, but every fall I knew she would disappear like a bad boyfriend and I would be worried, wondering if she would come back when the first snowdrop flowers bloomed — that's when she returned the first time. I prepared a bed so she would hibernate under the porch, but Muffin never used it. I finally realized that bears don't like people around when they're sleeping in a log or cave. They want to be alone. She and her forest were on another frequency. She couldn't have cared less if one hand or two hands were clapping. When she was napping, she was on another planet!

For me, winter was always about waiting for Muffin to come home. The good news is, every year she reappeared from her secret hiding place, always much thinner. And hungrier!

We always had a great time being together, except when the air conditioner became a third party in our relationship. It was beside my bedroom window, right next to where she would tap to let me know she wanted me. It was part of our ritual. I would hear her tap and then place my hand against the window. Muffin would then place her paw on the window with the pane between us and we would make a paw-hand sandwich. That's how she knew she would soon be filled with cookies, berries and even ice cream!

When her order didn't arrive fast enough she would start jiggling the air conditioner, something she knew she wasn't supposed to do. She knew she was driving me crazy. I had warned her in the past and would give her mean looks accompanied with a couple of hard knuckle knocks on her forehead. She'd take off and then return to do the same thing, this time adding background noise … loud, breathy, black bear grunts of enthusiasm. She would shake the air conditioner up, down, sideways, everything but "Shake it Off." Taylor Swift's song of the future would have been perfect for Muffin. I was always surprised it didn't actually happen. I finally had strong hinges placed around the air conditioner with enough bear-proofing that she would have had to take the entire side of the house down. The triangle relationship ended when Muffin understood good behavior pays off and that I would be giving her Ben & Jerry's ice cream with marshmallows as a reward. She was one smart bear.

One day, I don't remember exactly when, our lives got turned upside down. It became against the law to feed bears in Pennsylvania. First, the changes started in New Jersey: too many knocked-over trash cans and news coverage of bear sightings. It wouldn't be long before bear-hunting season would be extended in both states. I hadn't seen this coming.

Muffin was a part of me. I took care of her. The relationships I build with animals mean more to me than almost anything. Sometimes when we looked into one another's eyes, there was the familiarity of an old best friend. It is a communication I don't fully understand, except that it's a love of the deepest kind.

She was a gift, my joy. We shared a life few people ever experience. We built a sacred trust through rituals, shared emotions, looking forward to seeing one another every day. We had the privilege of loving each other. How could I explain to a bear that because of a new law I could no longer feed her and be with her? I couldn't. I got sick to my stomach when I would hear her tap on the window. I wanted to disappear like I wasn't home, but I knew that Muffin would know I was in the house because of her keen sense of smell. The only thing that made life bearable, no pun intended, was that Muffin was healthy. When the sun was on her fur, it was so shiny and thick, it looked like it had been polyurethaned. I also knew she could take good care of herself without me. What I wasn't prepared for was her transition process. She started tap, tap, tapping on other windows in the neighborhood. They didn't know she wasn't going to kill them or harm their children.

Bobby Johnson, the game commissioner, called me. I had to explain to him that the reason she was causing so much trouble was because I was no longer feeding her. His false accusation that I was still feeding her ruined our close relationship. I was following the new, painful law that was passed.

One of my neighbors trapped Muffin with powdered sugar donuts, then called the game commissioner. Muffin got hauled approximately twenty miles from me to another wooded area before being released in Matamoras, Pennsylvania. After a few weeks, she found her way back home. She was not the same healthy bear I had known. She was near death, but made it to my window for one last paw tap. I went to her in my backyard. I, her stable mother, had to break the law to care for her.

It's 2008, I'm reading the Bible: "The mighty men of Babylon have forborn to fight, they have remained in *their* holds: their might hath failed; they became as women: they have burned her dwelling places; her bars are broken." (Jeremiah 51:30, KJV)

I'm having a great deal of difficulty identifying with these words. The God I talk with every day doesn't communicate that I am less courageous than men … a subliminal message of inequality.

The Lord says: "Thou art my battle axe and weapons of war: for with thee will I break in pieces the nations, and with thee will I destroy kingdoms; And with thee will I break in pieces the horse and his rider; and with thee will I break in pieces the chariot and his rider; With thee also will I break in pieces man and woman; and with thee will I break in pieces old and young; and with thee will I break in pieces the young man and the maid; I will also break in pieces with thee the shepherd and his flock; and with thee will I break in pieces the husbandman and his yoke of oxen; and with thee will I break in pieces captains and rulers." (Jeremiah 51:20-23, KJV)

These words didn't exist when my father spoke to me in the spring of 2008. Why? Jesus served and is serving as an example of how to be without warfare. Over two thousand years have passed and we still don't fully comprehend why He was sent down here in the nitty-gritty dirt of our existence. Many haven't taken the time to get to know the son that God sacrificed, to mirror Him. Instead, His behavior is considered effeminate, showing weakness.

Pope Francis has walked the streets of New York with an invisible Jesus at his side.

They are united in teaching us. They have planted seeds in Congress, musician's lyrics and in painter's visions. On September 26, 2015, the *Wall Street Journal* reported a sign in the heavens — a rainbow that appeared over people in Central Park waiting for Pope Francis's arrival. There was no storm or bad weather, only a clear sky with the signature of Christ. The event was quickly forgotten and replaced by the next big thing.

Many of us enjoyed our carefree ride before 9/11. We neglected personal accountability, we had no serious paybacks or consequences, and relinquished any concerns to the powers that be to prevent and/or defend us from disaster. It's an illusion that we can depend on the government to protect our children from guns in our schools, drugs in our neighborhoods, or unhealthy food in our stores and kitchens. We've been floating in the little private boats of our existence, believing things will take care of themselves without our involvement. We collectively must start accepting responsibility in different ways, to make our lives better in this age where technology is pushing us to the brink of mental decline, including further eroding the stock market with algorithms, flash trading, short covering and hedging — not only bets, but responses to each stage of descent. It impacts our lives whether we are in denial or not. One can't win in a rigged system. Invest in your own business, a venture that can nurture your life and the lives of others, including fairness to your employees. When your brand has developed, it can be made into an honest public company for other investors.

I struggled with documenting these next stories. I am torn between humility, the only path to truth, and wondering if disclosure is part of what He intended? I once again sought His guidance and direction, but didn't hear the answer right away. Then, finally: "Yes, my child, through my eyes small intimacies are big, you abandoned yourself for them. You listened. You trusted. You obeyed. That's how you found ME! Yes, they are part of the story, part of revelation."

For Thanksgiving, I went to Walmart and bought a comforter, blanket, some canned vegetables, things I thought someone might need. I remember being tired and not wanting to follow through with the inner urging, but I made it home. I also checked my pantry for goods I hadn't been using, including several cans of cat food I had gotten for a stray that no longer visited. I hesitated to put them with the other donations, fearful that maybe the yet-unknown person receiving them might try eating cat food if hungry enough. I pulled a bag of loose change I'd accumulated over the years and prepared a box to place everything in, after grabbing a large pink ribbon. The little voice kept telling me to put the cat food in. I did, then I closed the package and placed it in my truck and started driving, searching for just the right house.

After traveling over many narrow, unkempt roads without finding a place, I decided to go to a women's shelter where I had done spiritual work. Two women, without hesitation, said "Norman" at the same time. They told me how to get to him. I drove into Yulan and found the post office they had mentioned. He lived in a room in the back. I parked and took the package to a door at the end of the building, but saw no one. I knocked and decided to leave the package outside despite not wanting to. Somebody else might pick it up. As I was returning to my vehicle, a tall, thin man came out of the front of the post office. He had a little kitten following him. I asked the man if his name was Norman. "Yes."

I gave Norman the care package and drove away, taking one of the same roads back home, passing three home sites that I had considered buying at one time. Strangely enough, in front of each of the three properties, people were outside, waving to me. It was totally unexpected. How could this possibly be? But it happened.

One extension of the Beds of Trees project was having the pillow scroll printed onto greeting cards. It was a way to share the comfort of the beds with people who might not have an opportunity to see and feel them.

I went shopping and bought a soft Martha Stewart comforter which took up a lot of space and filled the rest of the box with small items. I can't recall now what they were, but this time I knew where they would be going. I wrote an anonymous note on the pillow-scroll card and placed it into the folds of the blanket. I remember writing, "You are so special in God's eyes. He wants you to have this."

Earlier I had gone to Narrowsburg, NY, to pick up grain at the feed store for the animals, and stopped at Peck's Grocery. On the way, I passed an old Victorian house across from railroad tracks, next to a graveyard that needed fixing. An elderly Black man was outside, trying to get to a chair on his front porch. It was difficult to watch because I could tell how much pain he was in, how sick he was, as he finally was able to sit down.

Shanda and Patrick were visiting then and, as we were driving, I told them what I had seen. We had the package in the truck. I returned to the old house near the tracks and put the box with a blanket and small items on the porch. I was glad the man wasn't home when we stopped by to give him the *God Calling* surprise package.

About six months later, I went to Peck's once again to pick up some groceries and was amazed at what I saw. The man's house was totally renovated. There were stained-glass windows with crosses framing the front porch. Two workers were outside the home, touching it up. I asked them if they had installed the stained-glass windows. "No, they were already there, we just cleaned them." I then asked who owned the house and they said that a Black man used to own it but he had died a few months earlier.

A year passed and once again I was in Narrowsburg, this time at an art gallery. I came across a brochure with a photograph of the old Victorian house. It was an aerial view with a big, wide rainbow over it. I took the photo home and stared at it for the longest time. The old man must be comfortable living in his new mansion in the sky ... I will know for sure, someday.

I pray that my home will be recognized with the glory of Yours, with patience, truth, and love. Now I know that you've placed me here to say. In June of 2009, I experienced the melding of King David's words and life with mine. "I waited patiently for the LORD; and he inclined unto me, and heard my cry. He brought me up also out of a horrible pit, out of the miry clay, and set my feet upon a rock, *and* established my goings." (Psalms 40:1-2, KJV)

A month later, I came across Maya Angelou's words from *I Know Why the Caged Bird Sings*: "There is no greater agony than bearing an untold story inside you," and I realized it was time to share my story. I did the unthinkable and purchased an Apple computer and built an office with a one-hundred-thousand-dollar inheritance from Grandma, Mom and Dad. "Funding pillars" had been put in place for the uphill battle. It now became harder not to write. I had to get my story out no matter what the circumstances or how long it might take.

Barely an hour after the decision was made, Harvey Goldman found me on the internet. I remembered the sixties and all the gifts Harvey had given me at that time, pursuing me while my then-boyfriend was a young doctor in San Francisco. It was Harvey's crush on me that was the catalyst for my former husband to propose. He must be powerful, I thought, placed back into my life now as a catalyst for my book journey.

In reconnecting I found out that Harvey had earned a degree in journalism from the University of Missouri and was a natural at connecting words. Writing for me takes forever, but Harvey and my brother-in-law, Patrick Sullivan, became angels of encouragement. Their gifts with language helped to shape my thoughts and memories into sentences. Many long hours of their time were spent on my behalf, but I still struggled.

Back on my knees I went: "God! Why are you having me do this? I don't know how to write."

This is true, my child. You are not a writer. I will provide the words. You are the words to be written.

The end of 2010 became one of the saddest times of my life. Muffin came around every day with her four cubs: M3 (Muffin the Great), Raspberry, Rascal, and Peanut, the smallest one. One afternoon I didn't want them to leave. Muffin and her babies had partially eaten, then carried pumpkins from a neighbor's house, placing them in our yard. I guess that might be called stealing! It couldn't have been worse because that particular neighbor was an avid hunter. I took a photograph of Muffin right before sundown and when I got the pictures back, I saw there had been a flaw in the film or some sort of malfunction. There was a red line that looked like a bullet aimed right into Muffin. I knew God was telling me that she would be leaving. It was bear season.

Three days later Muffin and three of her cubs were killed. Only Raspberry survived. His young face had turned old overnight, and his body language said it all when he came back to the window alone. He would look at me and then continually look behind him to make sure nothing was there. These days I can't get too near Chubby Cub Trail, where over the years Muffin established territory for her family. I can't bear sweet morning memories anymore. Only her black ghost remains.

I called Babe in Soho to tell him what had happened. So many years ago we shared our love of animals, how we would rescue and carry any kind of creature out on his terrace to save. Now we would be sharing pain. I climbed slowly up to his loft on the fourth floor and we spent the afternoon together. Both of us were struggling with health issues. Before leaving, he gave me an envelope containing seeds from an unusual tree he had discovered.

I said goodbye to Soho's Walker Street, caught the C train to go back uptown to 56th, where I lived part time. I sat on the train near an older Black man who was composing music on paper. He was all alone with his notes, oblivious to everything around him, just like the clock man at Starbucks in Queens. He would look up, reflect, and then add a B flat, E, then a C. I wanted to hear what he was creating. Sometimes his face had a gentle, endearing, childlike quality. I wanted to ask him some questions about music...

"Excuse me for interrupting your train of thought. I just started writing a memoir and have been thinking about how important music is in my life. I long to be able to do what you are doing."

I mentioned I had recently spoken to Marijke Jongbloed, a filmmaker friend of mine from Amsterdam who was in the process of producing a documentary on the musician Prince. She loved that he was self-taught and played twenty-four instruments. I was planning to meet with her the following week.

Suddenly I looked up and realized I was about to miss my stop. The gentleman next to me quickly tore a piece of paper from his music pad and scribbled *Dent* (his name) and his telephone number. I grabbed it as I ran off.

The following week, and several times after that, Denton and I spoke on the phone. He owned a Victorian home that he and his wife had lived in together until her recent death. They had been married twenty years and had a child now in her twenties.

Right before my first date with Denton, there was a terrible storm that closed the trains and buses down between Pennsylvania and New York. I almost didn't make it into the city. On top of that, my throat began tightening up, and it was almost impossible to get food or beverages down. The last thing on my mind was a relationship.

Denton picked me up on the West Side of Midtown and, with all the slushy snow, we traveled east by taxi to a concert at Gracie Mansion. We all went to a room in the basement where a woman by the name of Karen served us hors d'oeuvres. Her main concern was to check sound with the band in the large room on the first floor where the gathering was to take place. One of the band members, an older gentleman, didn't tolerate any fooling around with the setup. He followed Karen to the stage, enjoying being ahead of the game with sound control. He extended his trombone out nice and straight toward Karen and gave two soft toots followed by two blasts.

"What do you prefer?"

"The former." She was not amused.

"I will reluctantly adhere to your wishes." Musicians don't like people telling them how to perform.

It turned out to be a beautiful evening. Mayor Bloomberg spoke briefly. He had been on vacation during the storm that almost shut down the city, and now he seemed relaxed not having Marcia Kramer from CBS News nipping at his heels.

I shook hands with former Mayor Dinkins, and next to him was a beautiful golden retriever sitting in the middle of the crowd. I didn't know who his owner was, but I knew to leave him alone. I wanted so much to pet him ... soft sounds of dogs barking after 9/11 came back to my mind. I thought about all the dogs that eventually lost their lives. Right in the middle of the floor I said a silent prayer, thanking them.

A friend of Denton's told him afterwards that I was holy and he was spiritual, and that we looked good together. Can you imagine hotter words than that to jumpstart a relationship? I said goodbye to the press photographer, Donovan Gopie, who had taken a photograph of me with two beautiful Black women. Being white, I was in the minority that night. Donovan later took the time to send the photographs and share parts of his life journey with me. It was one of those unexpected moments, a mysterious déjà vu when strangers instantly become friends.

Denton was late on our second date. I waited four hours and couldn't reach him by phone. Finally, the maître d' notified me that he had called and was in the hospital. I had just spoken with him the night before and he seemed fine on the phone. In reality he had pneumonia.

Two days later I was in the hospital across town from him. I was again unable to swallow, due to scleroderma, or so I thought. Was this a red flag on what was to come? Was this how young love plays in older people?

While between tests in the hospital, Denton and I would talk by phone. He was on antibiotics and improving, while I was wasting away before a surgical procedure to help me eat.

I was thankful for his improvement but didn't want it to mean he would be visiting me while I was dressed in tubes and an oxygen mask. When younger, I had always managed to prance around in a new boyfriend's tuxedo shirt before sharing his bed. The last thing I wanted was for Denton to see me prancing around in a hospital gown. I had to get out fast!

I was diagnosed with achalasia. It is extremely rare to have scleroderma and achalasia at the same time. I wish I could explain the chronic disorder in a pretty way, but I can't. The disease makes it difficult for food and liquid to pass into the stomach. It's not a well-known disease and involves degeneration of nerves that control the muscle of the lower esophageal body and sphincter.

A procedure was performed to stretch the esophagus and inject it with Botox. Because of my medical history, a large group of caring doctors wanted to examine me. The doctors wanted to study and share the findings with medical students. They formed a large circle around me. A couple of students came and gently poked at my hands and face, looking at tissue that could turn all colors of the rainbow from Raynaud's syndrome, one of the symptoms of scleroderma. I was like some kind of an odd, fascinating creature. I am a patient with achalasia, scleroderma, pulmonary hypertension, AFib and non-Hodgkin's lymphoma. Yet, I'm still alive and look healthy.

During my stay I had a couple of interesting roommates who, from what I gathered, were on Medicaid. They did not understand the power of working and respectfully taking care of themselves. Instead, they'd come to the emergency room with some self-inflicted sickness to spend a few days in a crisply made hospital bed, served with food and given attention. One of them knew exactly where all of the light switches were and gave me a thorough breakdown of what to do to make my stay more pleasant. They were already friends with the nurses who brought them food from the outside because hospital food was so bad. I will say they knew everything, were charmingly clever and made my stay much easier.

Denton and I were both discharged and he invited me to Brooklyn. We decided to take the C train and he got down on his knees in front of everyone way before he was supposed to and asked me to marry him on the way to his home. Maybe this was God's will!

His house was filled with vibrant paintings.

I asked him, "What if I told you that each of these art creations strikes a different note in my soul and helps to compose the music of my life?"

This is how we talked in the beginning, when love was fresh and the canvas was clean. We confided to each other our innermost thoughts and feelings in the comfortable setting of his home. I was able to be completely myself, let my guard down, to share what weighed on my heart.

"When you told me that hunters killed Muffin, it was like they had killed a human being. That really got to me. I get really angry with certain things."

I bought him the *Good News Bible* and the book *God Calling*. In the beginning, we read them most every morning together and talked about how to keep our amorous love from fading because we were apart so much of the time.

Denton and I wanted to see Dave Brubeck when he was in town, so we arrived at the Blue Note three hours early and made friends with the people standing in line. We finally sat at the bar with our new friends in the last seats available. Finally we were able to hear "Pennies from Heaven," Brubeck's first song. There was an indescribable energy in the room that everyone felt during the entire concert. He had made it to ninety years of age with densely chorded, flawless tones. I started telling Denton about when I had met Brubeck and Paul Desmond in a bar in Basel, Switzerland, back in the sixties. Dave had sat back while Paul had done all the talking. They seemed very opposite. Paul was a drinker and was known as a womanizer. His airy, ethereal saxophone turned me on. Dave, in contrast, was a family man, brought up on a farm, and early on he had planned on being a veterinarian. One of our newfound friends had been listening to the conversation.

"Why don't you write him a note?" was the suggestion that came over my shoulder.

I placed my thoughts on a white paper napkin and was able to get it to him. *I met you briefly at a bar in Basel, Switzerland. It wouldn't have happened if it wasn't for your "Take Five" composer friend. Everyone in this room tonight is experiencing clean jazz from a cattle ranch family man. It comes through in your music. You are an inspiration. Thank you for "Pennies from Heaven." Sincerely, Penny James.*

I saw him leave in a black limousine. His silver hair and the white napkin he was holding next to his heart caught the light. I will never forget... "Life is not measured by the number of breaths you take, it's the moments that take your breath away." That was one of those moments for me.

He left us a short time later. Michael Jackson died around the same time, at a much younger age. The world paid a great price for Michael not giving up his drug addictions. He was our pop Mozart through the seventies and eighties. His musical style influenced musicians and performers all over the world.

America has so many people to look up to. Lance Armstrong overcame cancer and kept winning the race through the nineties. He was an icon until we all found out a few years later that he was on illegal steroids. The world continued to tick on, *60 Minutes* at a time, seeing more and more of America's naked underbelly through each passing decade.

Americans knock one another down at Walmart to get to Black Friday bargains like flat screen televisions. There seems to be no comprehension of what it means to be civil and logical. People want more and more, to look good and feel better. We expect endless markdowns. Businesses get back at us by selling junk products. Modern life is defined by endless relationships with things that need fixing. We've gone virtually mad with what it means to be natural, even with our teeth. If they aren't covered with caps they become undesirable.

Products are created and aggressively promoted so we can bleach them to shiny white perfection. No wonder they become overly sensitive! No wonder we have all become overly sensitive about appearance, in the quest for perfection that doesn't exist.

In the constant effort to achieve ideal beauty, it is easy to understand the corresponding need for numbing. Marijuana becomes legal to grow in the family backyard where croquet balls used to be. *Whoa!* Try fixing something and at the same time staying lit like a hippie! Bob Marley, youth, gambling, alcohol, bring it on!

The supporters of unhealthy indulgence got their wish. Recreational marijuana is now legal in Colorado with other states following. The ease of drug possession has been accepted, and gambling casinos are right around the corner in many residential areas. Obstacles to trouble have slipped away. Go out and have some fun.

We continue to buy into the shiny, Baby-Oil nudity and backward viewing of the Kim Kardashian brand empire, consuming her like a sponge. We are much less victims than we are aggressive pursuers of our own demise.

When I was growing up, George Orwell's *1984* was the book everyone was reading ... we were waiting for an ominous future, for that bomb to explode. He didn't get it exactly right, but look what Paul Harvey said on April 3, 1965, in a warning to America [radio broadcast]:

"If I were the devil ... I'd set about however necessary to take over the United States ... I would whisper to you as I whispered to Eve: "Do as you please." To the young I would whisper that "the Bible is a myth." ... I'd take from those who have and give to those who want until I had killed the incentive of the ambitious ... In other words, if I were the devil, I'd just keep right on doing what he's doing. Paul Harvey. Good Day."

Later, Morley Safer did another segment pertaining to capitalism and financial fraud. We still haven't learned. We are not following through on our responsibility to the process of evolution. We are stuck in unhealthy patterns and cycles of lawyers and loopholes. The 1 percent of our global society comprises legal power brokers who set up systems that protect their own goals while ignoring the greater good. It is absolutely imperative that we, every one of us, from the strong and capable to the challenged and compromised, stand up and demand change to the laws that defeat us.

We don't even know how to proceed in order to take care of ourselves. We are told that American staples — bread, butter, meat and potatoes — are not good for us. What's up with white Wonder bread? American life with all those colorful circles? A day comes when eggs are not good. Three years later they are called a superfood. Good. I love eggs. But we look at apples in a different way — maybe the skin is covered with pesticides. Organic foods. Some salmonella has slipped into them. There are outbreaks in restaurants and supermarkets. We know fish like tilapia is good for us, but we don't know where it came from and we're told if it comes from China, it's bad. Corn, soy products, sugar beets are all bad because of growth hormones, antibiotics, and Roundup. Canned foods, no good — bad tin or aluminum — anything processed, bad. Even the Teflon pans we are cooking on, no good — cancer, bad! Salmon and tuna, good — no, not good, because of mercury.

There's nothing we can eat, so why are so many people obese? The answer is many of us are eating garbage with additives that make us hungrier to eat more and more of the same. We go to bed having fructose and sugar nightmares rather than dreaming with natural sugar plums in our heads. And I just heard that my non-Hodgkin's lymphoma may have been caused by a polio vaccine I was given. This is reality, not reality television! Information is now in the open to consider and combat. We *can* do something. We know we've been duped by corporations, even Johnson & Johnson, with their smell-good talcum baby powder that some believe causes cancer if placed near open, vulnerable parts of our body.

THE GOOD: It is a fact that we are now having unimaginable breakthroughs, especially in the health industry. We are living longer; a woman recently died at 116 years old. Miraculous strides have been made in brain studies because cybernetics can explain the nature of the brain like never before. It is a science that compares studies of complex electronic machines with the human nervous system.

THE BAD: We are focused on both nuclear warfare and cyber warfare. We have not one enemy, but many. We are caught up in both personal and political storms with the capacity to cause wider damage than any bomb.

We are experiencing life where all information is fed through multiple computers and televisions in our homes. We are at the mercy of a World Wide Web that is constantly malfunctioning through viruses and glitches. The IBMs and Apples invented powerful equipment with the awesome responsibility to keep technology moving forward without destroying all of us. Tesla is now selling driverless cars. Where are we going? We are lost.

Chapter 19
Traveling Rainbows

My sister Shanda has been by my side since her birth. I don't know exactly why it happened this way, but she's always been the one beside me when I've really needed help. On March 28, 2012, I had to go back to the hospital for surgery. I had spent time in the past under better conditions, sitting comfortably in a doctor's lounge waiting for my former husband to finish his rounds. This day was different. The sensation I had been dreading had come true. I could no longer swallow at all.

I took a lot of time choosing the right doctor to operate on me. If I had only one ailment, the process of selection might have been simpler. But with the list of challenges I was facing, I had to exercise caution to find a physician who would treat me as a whole patient instead of only individual parts and needs.

The doctor I found was using a da Vinci surgery robot, the latest technology in the field.

When I woke up from surgery, I saw a woman's face … there was something about the way she was observing me.

"Was the surgery successful?" I asked. If it wasn't, I would soon be getting nutrition from a feeding tube in my stomach.

Her response had a sullen quality to it. She avoided looking into my eyes. "It went fine." I knew from her body language that something had gone terribly wrong. "Are you sure?" "Everything went fine. There is a button you can push if you're in pain."

"I don't like painkillers. I used to have a drug and alcohol problem."

"It's better for you to take it if you need it, just for a few days."

The next thing I knew, Shanda was next to me. She had been in the waiting room for several hours and no one had given her an update. Standard procedure is for the doctor to brief family once surgery is over, telling them when they can see the patient. She finally went to the nurse's station to find out what was going on.

My doctor was nowhere to be found.

Shanda had insisted that she be with me as an advocate. I was so glad she didn't listen when I said I'd be fine on my own. I was struggling and not receiving the help I needed. There had been a mix up with the dietician. I would get a menu, then receive no food to eat. Shanda had to go out to buy soup and soft foods, like cottage cheese, for a day and a half until my doctor finally arrived. He hadn't come to see me since the operation. He checked my progress only by X-ray and only for the area he had operated on. There was no physical examination. He sat in a chair near the hallway.

Shanda started asking him questions. "Why hasn't Penny received any food since her operation?"

He looked surprised. "I will take care of that."

The good news is that between Shanda's visits, I met several nurses who were loving and dedicated to their job. We became close. They quietly shared their disdain for the breakdown in healthcare and gave me coping skills when beepers never stopped at all hours of the night, the very hours when rest is needed for healing to take place. They constantly had to take blood tests while dealing with my sensitive skin from scleroderma.

It's so important to get names of dedicated people. Thank-you notes are a must. They need to know that they matter, hear how they are appreciated or else they burn out from a job that demands too much. This is a result of overwhelming paperwork, required record keeping, and endless protocols from fear of lawsuits, all in response to Medicare and Medicaid fraud.

Rich patients have private nurses and doctors. Those doctors are very well compensated and many don't accept Medicare. Then there are doctors who accept both Medicare and Medicaid, are barely compensated at all, and yet they treat each patient with loving devotion in spite of having to follow the same protocols and record keeping requirements.

When my doctor came to check me, I secretly wished he could be more like my cardiologist who has treated me for many years. He is a warm and caring man who stimulates the heart. When I had one particular crisis during my treatment, he even gave me his home phone number, something very rare in modern medicine. He has been written up in New York magazines, voted one of the best doctors by his patients. Our special relationship recognizes God as the Master Physician.

Shanda picked me up when I was discharged with a prescription for oxycodone, even though I said I didn't want or need it. I was completely exhausted from the ordeal my body had been through and the lack of sleep over those days in the hospital. It was a relief to finally be going to a peaceful place for quiet rest with no poking or beeping. We went to check into the Helmsley Hotel, domain of Leona Helmsley, the queen of mean. Soon after we arrived, of all things, the hotel fire alarm went off! It got resolved just as we started to evacuate, but those screeching alarms nearly did me in. The stress of everything was overwhelming. I needed a break.

That evening, Shanda got me into a cab and we took a ride across town to soak in some healing music. On the way inside, I ran into the owner of the club, a Middle Eastern man Denton knew. The man loved jazz, and on seeing him I recalled something Denton told me the owner said at an earlier time: "People are made from the earth. Angels are pure light. They are here; we just can't see them. They shine the brightest in the middle of fire."

Shanda and I sat down in the bar area and started sipping tonic water with slices of fresh lime. We felt as though we'd just escaped the hospital, a hotel fire, and a whole lot of other things. Angels must have been all around us. We were high on sisterly love without drugs or alcohol.

Three weeks later, I was scheduled to have a CT scan through my oncologist. The results came back showing a mass in my liver that hadn't shown on earlier scans. After speaking with the radiologist, my sister and I came to the same conclusion: it appeared that damage had been done to my liver during my surgery. The mass was in the same area.

We shook our heads. The last thing we wanted was to get involved with lawyers in a long, drawn-out fiasco wasting precious time, even though there were already lawsuits underway regarding the da Vinci robot malfunctioning. Apparently, ample testing was not done before the equipment was approved for use on patients. When too much pressure is placed on the robotic arm, the surgeon loses control. Not a good thing! We decided to retest the area, so I had to go through another long procedure.

June 6, 2012: "There is increased enhancement of the liver parenchyma surrounding this structure, which is thought to represent a hematoma. It is diminished in prominence in comparison with the recent examination."

I believe the hospital, the doctor, and the people around him, covered up the mistake. I knew the moment I woke up and saw the woman's face that something was wrong. I have a way of reading body language, and hers was perfectly clear. After doing some detective work, I found that many people expressed this doctor's less-than-professional manner with patients.

What can be done? Keep facts in a journal and have an advocate present at pre-op appointments and post-op examinations. Make sure all information is correct and then spread it like wildfire, far and wide. Just as important, when someone goes out of their way for you, does something unusual and good, spread the positive information like wildfire, far and wide. I saw on the news where a tarot card reader not interested in receiving money told "the truth" to a country singer — that he would die in his forties and be reincarnated as a quail. There aren't a lot of stories told about that particular bird. What would you do with information like that? Do you take it in and be true to who you are? Get on a rooftop, spread your arms before they become wings and shout out your future? Disinformation overload.

The bottom line is, one doesn't get to know who they are or where they're going from tarot cards, massive information on the internet or nonsensical news coverage. We are living through disinformation overload, and for those who are unable to hear or accept the hard truths of life, addiction becomes the misleading balm that we crave, although it destroys us. The numbing must stop. It's time to wake up. Death rates from drug addiction are the highest ever in American history. We are seeking truth in all the wrong places. Truth comes from within.

Who are you anyway? You are a universe, unique, unlike any other. A collection of experiences from birth becomes memories and forms perceptions that establish your handprint, also unlike any other. However, there is a common thread we all share. It comes from a mysterious longing, an energy we are always trying to connect with and claim as our own. Wisdom consists of an infinity of evolving wheels, turning, turning, turning to provide the combustible engines of our individual souls with enough power to bring us all together in one absolute voice of truth.

I went to my home away from home — to Big Fuji Apple, make it here, make it anywhere, New York City. I was out in the street, 7th Avenue and 56th on the way to the resurrected Ground Zero. Years had passed and I wanted closure. There was change in the air. It seemed like many people walking around had lost their footing, like, "What's going on here?" There was more scaffolding and noise than ever before. More falling cranes. The most recent one came down near Church Street and killed a man one block from where I was going to see the memorial.

I was shocked to see new buildings going up everywhere. It smacked of architectural egomania, each one trying to outdo the other. There was no sense of serenity with increased police presence on the ground. Instead, a sky filled with cranes and helicopters. The noise a constant invasion in a city already bustling. Anywhere you walked, there were orange cones and roped off sections marking pedestrian detours that extended into the streets, compromising space for the already limited traffic flow. Blaring taxi horns added to the cacophony, and we lived with trepidation that some piece of construction material could fall on our heads at any moment. Everyone at heightened awareness, looking up and down, watching every which way for any unattended luggage or misplaced debris.

The memorial turned out to be meaningful and magnificent. There was a formal introduction preceding it, a pathway with a cushion of green grass, and a man on his knees planting flowers. I saw cleansing, clear water moving down stark gray granite, softening the impact of the massive structure engraved with names of the fallen. The new Freedom Tower was formidable.

Shimmering rows of blue windows climbed to the sky with reflecting mirrors. I thought about the poster I placed on my terrace so many years ago … we did rebuild, and what went up is so much more inspiring than what was taken down.

I walked to St. Paul's Cathedral (the miracle church left standing after 9/11, along with one lone tree!) to pray, but found no pews. They removed them to make room for tourism in 2008. This is where so many of our finest came to sit quietly for a while, seeking comfort before returning to their rescue dogs. The commitment and sacrifice of the brave men, women and dogs who gave their very lives to clean up and rebuild lower Manhattan cannot be overstated. As many of the rescued and their families know, it was the dogs who saved them, who heard their cries from under the rubble and helped to dig them out. Many of those dogs have suffered with cancer and lost their lives as a result of their work at Ground Zero. They gave and gave without tiring, clearly understanding the urgency and the colossal task they faced with their handlers, as much as any of our human heroes.

I went back outside to Church Street, to the frenetic energy of building, to disconnection between people and environment, to a dystopian atmosphere from the aftermath of terror.

Ambiguity. What kind of society is this? What have we become? I thought about comparisons on both right- and left-wing political spectrums, what modern life really means, unsettled Ground Zero like a surreal Fellini film or Stanley Kubrick's *A Clockwork Orange*.

What became clear is that America must go a cut deeper than building impressive skyscrapers and doing body frisks, then charging thirty-two dollars to go to the observatory in the sky, a space where people were seen jumping and falling out of windows.

Let me be clear, money isn't bad. It has many functions, the most important to give us security. It's the addictive misuse of financial power that kills.

I stood there, looking up. I felt no security from these buildings. Observation from Ground Zero.

April 2015, I went to the Horticultural Society's annual New York flower show at The Pierre, 2 East 61st Street for cocktails, dinner and black-tie dancing. Without my awareness, omnipotent plans sat me down at pecking order's finest table. I was seated with Executive Director Sara Hobel, who had replaced Tony Smith. I had never met Sara before, but I got to know her that evening. She is down to earth, and admired by many. I wish everyone could cross into nature's path with her.

Also at the table was Hilda Krus, head of Greenhouse and Horticulture Therapy, whom I met at Rikers. When we first met, Hilda was James Jiler's assistant, and later on she replaced him. New York Park Commissioner Michael Silver was seated across from me. We spoke briefly about my Bed of Trees project. I was hoping I could now get into Central Park under the new administration. It wasn't long before it was mentioned that Michael has a daughter. I remember thinking she is lucky to have him as a father and that, with a man like him at the helm, maybe the long ban on statues of women in Central Park would be lifted. I left the reception early, wanting to walk home and enjoy recalling the evening's events. Outside there had been a change of weather, as often happens in April. It was like the winds of hell were trying to knock me off my feet. I was pretty much alone on the street except for the homeless huddled next to buildings for protection, so different from the cozy, uplifting atmosphere I just experienced.

That night, New York City's face was dark except for the light glowing from inside the Oak Room Bar at the Plaza Hotel. It was where I had stayed in the seventies, when a woman pulled up in a taxi filled with bags and asked me if this was the Plaza. The doorman replied: "If you don't know this is the Plaza Hotel, you shouldn't be staying here."

I passed to hear rowdy laughter coming from the imposing facade that would probably outlive all but my "interior castle." Memories of my past surfaced. It was the place I once had a tryst with cocaine in a rolled up hundred-dollar bill, accompanied by caviar, blinis, and a man with a handsome cleft in his chin that looked an awful lot like my father's.

Years later, Donald Trump would marry his second wife, Marla Maples, with fifteen hundred guests in the Grand Ballroom he once owned before filing bankruptcy and costing taxpayers money. Hemingway daiquiri fans would, over the years, drink themselves into oblivion, soaking in the decadence with oh so many torrid tales to tell.

Stories like former New York governor Elliot Spitzer who resigned after threats of impeachment due to a prostitution scandal. Before that happened, we all thought he was an upright, honest family man cleaning up Wall Street…

Despite these scandals associated with the famous landmark property, a sweet memory surfaced that night of my former husband taking my sister Shanda and me for tea and a pastry. I recall the three of us looking up at the big round heart of the Plaza Palm Court as the sun filtered through. Who I was and who I've become in the dance of life will always be present there.

My walk continued. A few blocks away is the London Hotel, where the rich buy one-thousand-two-hundred-dollar margaritas, tip not included. Not for middle-class bourgeoisie who are now struggling.

It was only a few months after the Horticultural Society benefit that I turned on the television in July to see New York Parks Commissioner Michael Silver saying that a statute had been lifted and statues of women would finally be allowed in Central Park: "The administration under Mayor de Blasio is fully committed to promoting gender equality across New York City and that includes the parks. I am thrilled to move this effort forward."

Women had no voting rights in Manhattan until 1917. Duke Ellington is the only statue of a Black man. All were white until he appeared in 1997. Progress has been slow.

Statues are being considered for Elizabeth Cady Stanton, Sojourner Truth and Susan B. Anthony. These suffragists were the most effective leaders of the largest nonviolent revolution in our nation's history. Their eventual success was a result of their longtime commitment to the cause and organizational prowess. We can only hope that their achievements will inspire generations of women to enlighten future generations of men with new thoughts.

I would love to see a sculpture of Dorothea Dix, born in 1802, who accomplished widespread reform on behalf of the mentally ill. She created thirty first-generation mental hospitals to care for those too often neglected and forgotten. In the future, we will know that there is equality when we consistently have several women instead of mostly men campaigning to be President of the United States, unlike the total male domination of our governmental systems over the last two thousand years. In Manhattan's Central Park, women heroes have not been represented, except by the Alice in Wonderland sculpture at the Children's Zoo.

Back home, I received a call from Michael Weisman with Quixotic Endeavors. The company was working on a documentary with Victor Skrebneski and asked if I would be available to participate. I planned to meet Michael at the Carlyle Hotel on East 76th Street, where Victor always stayed when visiting New York. Filming would take place in Bemelmans Bar. It has an Art Deco feel that Victor is very fond of, named after Ludwig Bemelmans, the creator of the classic children's books bearing his name. The walls are graced with charming large-scale murals of whimsical themes, picnicking rabbits, and ice-skating elephants. It's no wonder that years earlier President Kennedy didn't make it from the corridor all the way down to the bar to become part of the backdrop, frolicking around in his birthday suit!

We scheduled two different dates. Both were canceled. Mr. Weisman offered to send a crew to my studio in Pennsylvania before I had to leave for Colorado, but calendars could not be coordinated. I was not able to help Victor relive such an interesting time in history — but the sidewalk in Chicago where my high heels sank into wet cement in the sixties is now called Skrebneski Way.

Before going on my trip, I dialed a number from my hometown that had been around a long, long time. The man who answered was still living in Pueblo. John Harris had reached ninety years of age, been through World War II, and was from a family of successful farmers. I told John I was Sophie's daughter and that when we were both living on Overton Road I developed a crush on him. I was only eight years old and had dreams of marrying him!

I didn't tell him about seeing him holding my mother close outside in the parking lot of my school. I also remember that even Bozo, our cow, had broken the fence of our yard to get over to the Harrises' house to make love with one of his amorous bulls! Why had these memories lingered so long? The answer is haunting. John had been the one person who was able to do what I tried so hard to do as a child and failed. He was able to bring the light of love to my mother's eyes. He had also given a blood transfusion on my behalf along with his two other brothers when I was so sick at St. Mary Corwin Hospital. Now I can imagine him being on *Dancing with the Stars*, the oldest to win! I asked him many questions on the phone that day.

He knew about my mother's passing and had only one question for me. He ran into my father some time ago at the local barber shop, and wanted to know about him.

I thought again about my early life in Pueblo, all the people I'd met, the many influences even way before I was born … Pueblos were communal villages built by Zuni and Hopi tribes in the southwest United States. Their homes were flat roof structures of stone and adobe, many integrated in the natural terrain of cliffs and characterized as a peaceful, agricultural environment.

I read a feature story in the *New York Times* on April 7, 2016, about the drug lords in Pueblo. The gang members were mostly addicts and recruited children at libraries, many of them baby gangsters from the Mexican cartel. The epidemic began with prescription drugs and graduated to cheap heroin on the street because it's easier to get.

Photographer Nick Côte and writer Julie Turkewitz were sent out to cover the story. Pueblo has twelve murders per one hundred thousand people, the highest in the state of Colorado. It is three times that of New York City and twice that of Brooklyn, New York's deadliest borough. In the article, Dog Patch was mentioned, an area my father called seedy, which we used to drive by as children. Only the poorest people lived there. Shanda remembers John F. Kennedy driving a motorcade through that area from the airport in 1962, on his way to Pueblo high school stadium to discuss Colorado resource development programs. Unfortunately, the problem of gangs and drugs has spread throughout the United States, an ongoing epidemic.

I would soon be revisiting the Pueblo area. My brother-in-law Patrick climbed into his new red Ford F-350 Super Duty King Ranch truck with a diesel engine. He was a "super duty" pilot who served in the Vietnam War, flying a medivac to pick up his wounded brothers. He did this on his days off after flying helo gunships and SEAL ops in the Navy.

Patrick had a GPS as part of his F-350 cockpit, connected to iTunes. He still had the responsibility of getting his passengers safely to their destinations and providing them with entertainment. He started off with Marty Stewart gospel, then peppered it in with the audiobook *Agincourt*, a *New York Times* bestseller. The story is about one of the most famous battles ever fought, in a small town in France in 1415. The action intertwines with the play *Henry V*. Shanda and I wanted to nod off, but Bernard Cornwell was so good at weaving patron saints, Shakespeare, and the minds of meticulous, fine-tuned archers, that we became hooked, at least until the brutal slaughter-yard behavior involved horses.

I was driven cross country, thinking about people from apple-pie small towns who save the world by getting up each day and working hard at being American. We drove through areas where for fifteen years, Simon Cowell plucked young buds out of the fields to help them bloom, recognizing their talent and making their dreams come true. I wanted to feel grass roots again, without the influence of big-city commentators telling me what it's like. I longed to experience simple life again as I watched fresh green cornhusks sway outside the truck window.

I thought about what Patrick said years ago when taking a walk with Shanda and me at their Virginia home … he told me he had the responsibility of taking care of all of us. With Patrick, this is a big deal that he takes very seriously. In the war, during the days, he evacuated wounded soldiers and sailors to safer destinations, but at night while the rest of us lay sleeping on soft pillows, he was cleaning blood out of the helicopter and getting sick. He gave so much of himself in service, and yet has a passion for and fascination with war history.

Patrick's entire life was built around the military, as was his father's, with memories both good and bad. He spent time on the USS Enterprise, the first nuclear aircraft carrier, and was in charge of on-board filming, setting up early morning scenes in *Top Gun* with Tom Cruise. On two separate occasions Barbara Bush had asked for him to be her escort when she was on board with her husband, then vice president under the Reagan administration. I've seen photos of them together on our family walls.

Shanda and Patrick's home is a museum of swords, artifacts, uniforms, and more than a few civil war carbines that have blasted their way into one of Shanda's pink ribbon-and-bow guest rooms. It's in the basement, where real decorating battles took place between Guns N' Roses. They have been married for thirty-two years and we were in a big red mean vehicle, not able to go over sixty miles an hour because it was new! (New truck owners are advised to not exceed sixty miles per hour for the first five hundred miles.)

Going slow was not exactly Patrick's style. Eighteen-wheeler semi-trucks passed us, meeting up with August heat on the highway, shedding their rubber treads like snakeskin next to crosses on the side of the road. Motorcycles zoomed by, making their way to Mount Rushmore, to Sturgis, where anything goes. We drove past wind-energy transformers, fields of corn and also soybeans.

Jesus Loves You was on many passing license plates.

I spilled an Ensure on Patrick's leather seat and he became grouchy. I was thinking it was a good thing Denton wasn't with us. I had invited him, but it turned out that he had a work commitment and couldn't join us.

In truth, there was no room for Denton and his accumulation of meaningful must-haves. The huge Ford was already stuffed with two border collies that are not real and two very real, sweet long-haired dachshund dogs, Murphey and McCarty, plus dog bones, presents, camping gear, smashed cowboy hats, a giant Igloo cooler and a whole lot more. I wanted to hold on to Mom's pillow, the one filled with chicken feathers from our Overton Road home. Patrick also brought his mother's pillow, but in the packed car, neither of us could ever find either of them.

Each time we stopped to stay in a hotel, we had to separate and unload. Patrick and I argued and tried to avoid one another. He is unlike me in more than a few ways, but behind the plumage we are pretty much the same — except he is a member of Mensa, and when at home, he goes to church *every day*.

After arriving home in mid-August, he returned to the Therapeutic Riding Program in Clifton, Virginia. He volunteers there with army and marine vets teaching them to ride horses and healing both their visible and invisible wounds. Patrick has both a scientific mind and a spirit of allegiance to the flag. We both know war is born of ignorance and that bond between the two of us is unbreakable. I remember asking him if I could have one of his old anti-ballistic designs to place in my gallery. His answer was a roundabout no. "I would rather design a flower."

We were one day away from meeting up with Justin (Sheila's daughter's son, my great-nephew) and his caretakers at Rocky Mountain National Park. Justin was in an automobile accident and had a spinal cord injury similar to Christopher Reeve's, which left him quadriplegic. He is just amazing. He started attending college working on a degree in nutrition. He recently visited New York City to see a Broadway play on his twenty-first birthday. I was able to arrange for him to meet members of *The Lion King* cast backstage. It's something he will never forget.

Shanda and I were sitting in the backseat. She had a gentle wind blowing on her face. I thought about her a lot, even when she wasn't with me. She is my second skin and without a doubt the glue that keeps our family together. I'm going to be bold and declare her one of the angels. On earth in their visible form, angels are not prone to easy lives down here. At thirty-seven years of age, she developed weakness on her right side and had double vision. The diagnosis was multiple sclerosis. She is also a two-time survivor of breast cancer. The good news, if you can call it that, is that the chemotherapy seemed to keep her MS symptoms at bay. She is strong and healthy, except for periodic pain in her legs.

We met Bobbie at her home in Breckenridge and afterwards spent time with her and her friends, the mountain goats next to her property, before finally making it to Sheila's home in Gardner. We opened the door to a surprise birthday party that Sheila had planned for me. She looked so beautiful! She had homemade green chili and enchiladas, plus my favorite white cake with cream cheese frosting, which back in Pennsylvania had also been Muffin's favorite. The next day, Shanda and Patrick would be meeting the western singer-songwriter R. W. Hampton in Westcliffe, who had crossed over from his roots and performed "Unforgettable" by Nat King Cole at Daddy's funeral. I stayed behind, sitting in the middle of Grandma's meadow.

I've waited until now to fill you in on a surprise. Before my father's death, he helped me track down the owner of Grandma's property. A lease was eventually drawn up, which gave me rights to approximately forty-five acres of land, including her root cellars and garden. On July 3, 2004, I found out it was clear to start building a house on the upper pasture. Realizing I would spend a good deal of time back here in the future, I would need my truck. Sometime later, Patrick was good enough to drive my old, faithful Tundra from Shohola to Gardner for me.

I lifted the barbed-wire fence and briefly crawled into what used to be Grandma's garden. I could hardly believe I was back again, to be in innocence, to experience the joy I was born with.

Memories allowed my father to be present beside me as I sketched my name into an aspen. The scars on the huge aspen tree were carved from a small pocketknife he gave me when I was all of eight years old. The same knife that peeled sugar beets from our garden on Overton Road … transferred memories from his youth to ours of sugar beets picked from this garden by his mother and the dirt she dug into, shaping the root cellar into the perfect hill that would be their home, the property I stood on, alone.

My grandmother somehow knew it couldn't be too close to the aspen grove. What Daddy and I hadn't realized was that beneath the surface soil are complex aspen tree root formations that are well protected. It is their nature to grow so deep into the ground that they can even survive forest fires and thrive for as long as two thousand years. Unlike other trees, new shoots, up to forty feet away from the parent, can make new baby aspen trees without seed.

They say you can never go back and recapture the joy of childhood, but it's simply not true. There was an energy back then, and that same energy was with me that day. We mature and know that life is going to change for the better because we allow it to happen. After the long trip cross country, I was happy to be alone with my father once more.

Chapter 20
The Last Supper

Because of the trip to Colorado, Denton and I hadn't seen one another for several months, so for Thanksgiving I wanted to fix a holiday dinner, the first one in years, where we could sit down quietly to relax and enjoy one another. He planned on getting up early, crossing the George Washington Bridge to avoid delays, but he didn't arrive until four o'clock. I wanted the evening with him to be special so the turkey and I decided to tolerate time changes.

When he finally walked in the kitchen door, he looked great! I felt vulnerable, wanting to be pretty for him … wonderful for him that night. We hugged, but after that my plans for the evening derailed. When taking the turkey out of the oven, I placed two fingers on it before slicing. Denton quickly got me a fork and said he didn't want me touching the turkey. He then proceeded to tell me about people serving food in restaurants and how they wear rubber gloves. Before he came, I had been snapping fresh green beans from Walmart and crumbling crisp bacon and onion bits with my fingers, moving about cranberries and stuffing. He must have known I touched everything. He ate next to nothing.

Here the two of us were, together for Thanksgiving dinner, both unable to eat for different reasons. I live mostly on Ensure because of my challenges with swallowing, and it turned out he has a thing about cat germs. I have six cats. He must have been worried about the cats living in the main part of the house.

After dinner he unpacked his car and brought in a large keyboard, even though I have two pianos and had one tuned and ready for his visit. The next thing in was a big basketful of books, along with a large Apple desktop computer, and clothing. So much stuff! We both ended up exhausted and called it a night.

The next morning he went to Walmart and came back with his car filled with more stuff — goodies — fried chicken, thick fries, potato salad, bananas, orange juice, ice cream, a *National Enquirer* (with Charlie Sheen's face — HIV positive and not protecting his girlfriends) and tea. The pilot light on my stove wouldn't stay lit and the tea I fixed him was either too hot or too weak. He was cold, I was hot; he was hot, I was not.

The last time Denton and I had been together before this Thanksgiving visit, my dear friend Diana had been visiting me in New York City. The three of us had gone to dinner in Manhattan and we had a nice time. Before this holiday weekend, we all thought it would be fun to be together at my home in Pennsylvania but it turned out that Diana couldn't make it so it was just Denton and me.

He tuned my cello and decided to play it while I played the keyboard. That part of his visit was so much fun. He said he wanted me to pursue music because I had an aura around me when playing the piano and, with my ability, progress would come quickly. The first few simple pieces of music went beautifully. When it got more advanced, I started to struggle, counting to get the timing right. He told me to play with more feeling. I told him I couldn't do that and get the notes down at the same time. We started having a discussion about how brains work. It took us away from the beautiful groove we were in. Until that happened, two hours of bliss had seemed like two minutes.

I went to the kitchen to use my new NutriBullet Rx. I had seen it on television with its cutting blades that can liquefy anything in a matter of seconds. I put in a mango, orange juice, grapes, and arugula, thinking it would make a nice blend. I turned it on but didn't close the bottom of the container tight enough. Wow! It turned into a powerful spray gun. Mushy mango and green slime slid down the walls, garnished with flecks of grape skin. Imagine that on the air as an advertisement for NutriBullet!

After cleaning, I put together my usual Thanksgiving gift package. This time it was filled with Christmas tree lights, canned goods, some fudge, cookies my sister Sheila had baked, some extra pears, nuts, and grapefruit from Harry & David. I thought it would be fun for Denton and I to find a house together and drop it off as a surprise for someone while we were on the way to the Woodstock Museum. The present was big, heavy, and bright with a red bow.

Denton stayed away from it just like my food, and I ended up carrying it to the truck by myself … not what I had imagined.

We stopped at a house that was for sale a short distance away from mine. Denton was interested in real estate in the area. Some of his friends had even purchased summer getaways nearby at his suggestion. He fell in love with the inexpensive home and wanted to secure it by placing a down payment. I knew the owner and they talked nonstop. We were good!

Despite moments of discomfort between us, Denton and I still shared a strong spiritual bond. My heart had been blocked for many years in self-preservation but I was able to let myself love him. God had steered my path to wellness and I had grown enough that I was able to do away with barriers.

From Shohola it takes about forty-five minutes to get to Woodstock. The museum is filled with history and faces of musicians who will never be forgotten from the infamous, gigantic, musical mud bath extravaganza. Denton was all over the place. He became a flower-child guy, wanting me to photograph him driving a hippie bus — the brightest, most ornate one on display.

On the way home, we stopped at an art gallery in Shohola. I was having trouble spotting the right house to leave the gift basket and remembered reading in a local paper that the owner of this gallery was the same man who ran the women's rehab where I had done spiritual 12-step work. I figured he might know of someone who needed a surprise gift, but when we got there, Denton started chatting with him and once again lost track of time. I was tired and mentioned to Denton that I wanted to leave. He then did an odd thing, he said he was tired too and sat in the only chair in the room! I went to my truck and rested next to my neatly ribboned package and waited for him. The day certainly hadn't gone the way I had imagined.

We made it home. He had promised to eat turkey, gravy, stuffing and maybe a few leftover green beans. We sat down together but, oh, there was another visitor, his computer. Instead of us sharing the meal in each other's company he focused on reviewing the Woodstock photos staring at the screen. Finally, he got up and went to the refrigerator for some Italian dressing, then poured it over the turkey and beans.

Sunday morning I was up early and noticed a dark-brown splatter, what looked like a teeny tiny turd on my rainbow steps going downstairs. I waited for Denton to wake up. I felt awful … had he gotten ill from eating my cooking and couldn't make it to the bathroom upstairs?

"Did you get sick last night?"

"No."

Was I relieved!

"There's a brown area on the steps going downstairs. Did you bring something up to eat and maybe spilled it?"

"No."

He went down and looked at it, then looked up at me. "Maybe it's your gravy."

I looked down at him. "My gravy is lighter than that."

"Oh! I brought up chocolate ice cream. Don't worry, I'll clean it up." He meticulously mopped up and down the rest of my house.

God's ironic humor is divine comedy. "Send in the Clowns" — Denton had completely missed the Stephen Sondheim sheet music I had placed on the piano upstairs. It turned out we didn't need to read the notes; we had played out the lyrics perfectly.

I started watching a spiritual program. Denton came to join me with his computer. He sent me an email message that we make a charming couple. This was while we were sitting on the same couch. He mentioned that he had realized overnight that he made a bad judgment call in wanting the house down the road and should call the man and tell him that he had decided against it.

A short while later, I stood at the top of my stairs outside, like my grandmother had done on hers so many years ago, and waved goodbye to Denton. He is someone I will always care for, admire and respect; a man with a kind, gentle heart. But we are different people, separate in love. It was not meant to be.

It was a while before discovering that nothing would stop *How Nature Healed a Broken Soul* from being written. Despite delays and my impatience with His timing, I was given fresh energy to finish. The last chapter in the ghost forest tale Grandma shared with me in childhood was completed when Muffin crossed over to Rainbow Bridge, the image used in my book *Muffin* when she crossed over to Heaven. Imagination and reality had merged, blending into a true story of life.

Even *Sesame Street* joined in the serendipitous pattern of ironic humor. One of my early *Playboy* covers must have been in Jim Henson's mind, because one muppet, Delbert the La Choy Dragon, was apparently sexier than I was on a cover of *Playboy*. It was around this time that an advertising piece surfaced with my photo next to an image of the muppet. Even Kermit's mansion got decorated with a *Playboy* cover. Jim Henson's characters were the cast of one of the longest-running shows in television history. *Sesame Street* received multiple Emmy awards, is televised in one hundred and twenty countries, and known as the world's most highly regarded educational program for young people.

If only we could all maintain the open, developing mindset of early childhood learning. Is it possible that virtual reality could be used in the future to help global government leaders tap into their childlike innocence and generosity? It would be wonderful if advanced electronics could combine imagination with environment, offering another reality to prevent the threat of war and achieve peace.

Chapter 21
The Full Circle

It's the autumn of my writing. The leaves from the tree of me are falling. A lifetime of words got stored in my trunk from lots of other people, then became the resin of me.

A year has passed. I'm back in my gray thundercloud 2002 Toyota Tundra, the truck I use at my home in Colorado. Darius Rucker's *Learn to Live* CD is waiting to be played once again. I stop for a mother goose waddling across the road with her ducklings, looking like they are going to walk right up the steps of what was once Grandpa's church. I pass the old candy store; there is something missing. The lone filling station is gone! A vibrating arrow pierces my heart. Why does that bother me so much? I watch quietly as a weed tumbles past the empty space. I will never again see my father here or be with my grandmother going to the station that I knew as a child. All has vanished into thin air. What is left? Me. I am the feather that rides the wind of faith along with the aeolian harp and the rolling tumbleweed.

What if there was a supernatural filling station where people could go and fill up their engines with faith, hope and joy, then ride off into the sunset with their Daimlers, RVs, Ford pickups, eighteen-wheelers, and fuel-emission-rigged Volkswagens, before coming back for more? A few buildings away, one bar is still open (since the sixties) that was known for yummy bacon cheeseburgers and fries. Allen Ginsberg once visited there. I wonder if they still serve food.

I walk in to find a large, uncluttered room, immaculately clean and tastefully decorated, and think to myself, *What a perfect setting for a magical, starlit Saturday open mic night in Gardner, Colorado.*

An elderly woman, Bertha Trujillo, emerges from behind a closed curtain. I briefly notice her living space behind the bar. She is standing with crutches. I introduce myself. She knew Grandma Esther well, knows her entire history and graciously shares some time with me, talking about the old days. In these moments, I can see my grandmother as a young woman, feel close to her again even though she is gone. This brief exchange with Bertha is a gift, but she can't help with much information on Ginsberg, except remembering him once reciting poetry with two friends.

I think about this woman in front of me. She is now close to one hundred, but was young back then, with a strong presence, tough and vulnerable at the same time. I know for sure, she is a survivor! I thank her and go back to my truck with new words forming in my head. Everyone has a beautiful song inside of them. Mine is *broken* "Hallelujah" by Leonard Cohen. My comfort zone is with once-broken friends who pick themselves up every day to take better care of their hearts ... sometimes the children the world breaks are the ones who grow up to save it.

Leonard Cohen and Allen Ginsberg hung out in Manhattan's West Village in the sixties, with folk musicians Judy Collins, Bob Dylan, and Ramblin' Jack Elliott. For a short time, on the outer fringe, this colorful mix included Andy Warhol and names like the Velvet Underground, Richard Pryor, Barbra Streisand, and Pete Seeger. They also moved in circles with Gloria Steinem, Peter, Paul & Mary, the Black Panthers and Lily Tomlin. Imagine them all together, influencing one another while under surveillance by the FBI through both President Johnson and Nixon for un-American activities. It happened! It was sex, drugs and rock and roll, a diverse representation of creative genius on Bleecker Street, against the status quo.

Will left and right wings ever learn to balance themselves out? Ramblin' Jack is still out on the road and frequents the National Cowboy Poetry Gathering in Elko, Nevada, where Shanda and Patrick attend. It's made possible through the Folklife Center, where Patrick is a member of the board of directors. Shanda and Patrick called Ramblin' Jack this past July to wish him a happy birthday. He is eight-five years old now, with the energy of a teenager. What many artists who get together have in common, including poet Paul Zarzyski, is that they all love Shanda. Ask each and every one of them. She's just happened to be there when they've needed support.

I have a deep, triangular pathway that I call my residential holy trinity, between Shohola, Manhattan, and Gardner — my one big home of three. Gardner is at the top of the pyramid, transmitting spiritual energy to Manhattan and Shohola on the ground floor, through the dark and light of life so that all colors surface and bloom.

Deer and turkey are staring in from outside my home at my dear friend and employee, Sandy. Six once-orphaned cats wanting attention periodically jump on the windowsill of my now 107-year-old farmhouse. It's 2016 and we have finally finished writing *How Nature Healed a Broken Soul* and sent the manuscript to Beth Kallman Werner, owner of Author Connections, for editing and marketing.

Beth and I once met at the Village Diner outside of Milford where they serve the best cherry pies. She told me writing is only the first part; it can take up to two years to publish the traditional way, but if you self-publish it can take far less time, you keep all of the rights and marketing can begin early. She gave me a list of what I needed to do.

I feel the familiar weight of responsibility attached to this project. The small lumps around my throat and neck have increased. I am tired. I am overwhelmed. I am in a meltdown. Spiritual energy has sustained me throughout the quiet writing from my cushioned couch in Shohola, but I am not prepared for the next chapter. My body feels taxed and heavy. It's getting harder and harder to get food and water down. My knees are sore, but I make my way home and get on them anyway. I have learned time and again to rely on Him when my body is no longer reliable.

"I need a miracle before I run out of time." An answer comes swiftly back.

Dear child, you are the miracle that will never run out of time. You are open enough to break once again. You will know your power. It is mine. I hear broken wings. Yours can become the strongest of all. Only when broken can you heal other broken hearts. Blessed with me whose broken heart of love will heal the world. Heaven doesn't carry death. It doesn't fly here. I'm giving you the opportunity to persevere in pressure while you lean in hard on me. This time I pull the arrow out of you almost to the breaking point, to help you release my perfume.

I don't think about my pain; instead, I focus on the painter Seurat's dots. They are colorful and organized. What if the naked eye couldn't see them and perceived only irregular black spots? The surrounding white light contains every hue of the color spectrum along with all wavelengths of sound making music the ultimate form of communication. We bask in the miracle of melody and lyrics when a moment reaches perfection; you and me, wild and free. It's transcendent, like when we attend a concert and move as one with fifty thousand strangers because the songs unite us.

It is no accident that love and sex are so often directly linked to music. When we feel an orgasm coming on, we want to keep the waves of pleasure rocking us over and over. The peak of a sexual encounter is the very foundation of procreation, His hand in perpetuating human existence. Unforgettable songs like Donna Summer's "Love to Love You Baby" are expressions of the ending climax.

Dutch poet and preacher Eliza Laurillard wrote, "The whole of God's creation is music, and the notes are sun and cloud, mountain and stream, tree and flower, man and beast. It is one great symphony!"

No one did movies better than Walt Disney in his early years. He made cinema the visual soundtrack of our lives with many of the greatest stories on earth. They are an endless source of kindling in the furnace of dreams around the world.

There are countless examples of how movies have both shaped and shared the human condition. From animated shorts like the Mickey Mouse cartoons during the Great Depression to Julia Roberts in her red velvet gown and stunning Harry Winston jewels in *Pretty Woman*. And I'm sure I don't even need to mention the impact of *The Godfather*, *Jaws*, *Apocalypse Now* and *Vincent and Theo* (the boutique art film about Van Gogh's life), along with so many others that have become classics across screens around the globe.

Now I reflect on the screenplay of my life. I've spent endless hours over the years, not with American royalty, but with addicts. I am keenly aware of the physical impact on the body. The lumps in my neck aren't getting better so I call my oncologist. On top of concern over the inflamed lymph nodes in my neck, there is a recurring pain in my lower abdomen, which I believe is tied to the cancer. I call my doctor's office for more than a week, trying to make an appointment to see her as soon as possible. After much back and forth with no luck, I ask to be booked with another doctor. I meet his nurse first and am told that my doctor died unexpectedly, the day before. She hid her own illness from everyone around her. Those close to her are both shocked and deeply affected by her passing. She was a pioneer in the study of hematology.

At that first visit with my new doctor, I explain that my cancer, non-Hodgkin's lymphoma, was previously slow growing but is now advancing rapidly. He speaks about chemotherapy, about the drug Rituxan, thinking it will be an ideal base to start with because one of his other patients also has scleroderma and it helps both the cancer and autoimmune disease. I see his eyes light up, and it's a wonderful moment because it's clear he believes he can help me. A PET scan is scheduled and the results will determine what other medications I need.

I leave the doctor's office and catch the bus on 5th Avenue going south to 56th Street. New York City is under a heat wave, up to 105 degrees. It's comfortable on the cool bus and I enjoy the ride past the trees that line Central Park until we run into a major traffic jam at 58th Street. All of a sudden there are police cars, ambulances, and chaos. We have to get off the bus. I have no idea what's going on and don't care. It's so hot, it's hard for me to breathe. I walk and find a deli with an eating area where I can sit down and cool off. Then a Starbucks. Then Dean & DeLuca's until I'm finally able to get home.

Up in my apartment, I look out above the noise of the street. Carnegie Hall's rooftop is solar and green. I love looking outside my window high in the sky ... it soothes me. I'm thankful to be inside with the air conditioner, enjoying the view. When I turn on the television, the area I got off the bus in is on the screen. The mess is caused by a man from Virginia who suction-cupped his way up Trump Tower and was beating on Trump's windows in protest. This is real life in the twenty-first century. Welcome to NYC!

Thursday, the day before the scan, I stay off my feet, no carbohydrates for twenty-four hours, and then fasting on water only for six hours before the procedure. Friday comes, and ten minutes before leaving for my appointment, the telephone rings giving notice that the scan has been canceled because the new, state-of-the-art machine they purchased broke down.

I don't have the luxury of simply being sick. It seems excellent health is required to manage getting from A to B in order to recover. Then I hear a quiet voice: *I'm in perfect health.*

I finally have a day off. On August 18, I receive a letter from Bon Secours, the hospital near my home in Shohola. I asked about possibly having my scans done locally, and I think, *Wow, this is a miracle they've replied so fast!* But the letter isn't about cancer treatment. I went there last year for a CAT scan for a shoulder problem, they are notifying me that their records have been hacked. Mine were included, along with my social security number. They offer a free year of security protection if I contact the company, fill out paperwork and answer some questions in order to receive protection.

The same day my sister Sheila calls from Gardner. She received a telephone call from Jerry Smith, the man I am leasing my Gardner property from. He said he must get into my house because there's a hole all the way through one wall above my entranceway with a gap a few feet wide in the loft area on the north side of the building. The wood is damaged, and a burn area around the edges indicates there was a fire. Either there was an explosion from the inside or lightning from the outside. It turned out lightning struck the house!

I have not been to Colorado yet this year … maybe in a few months, when chemotherapy is over.…

After a long winter, my cancer subsides and I finally make it back to Colorado. It is early summer again. I crawl between two rows of barbed-wire fence, once again. I lie down on a blanket of grass with the sound of Spring Branch Creek in the secret garden of my grandmother. I've been waiting to be back here — it seems like forever. The deepest part of me lives on this small plot of land.

Grandma Esther Flora's heart is next to me outside the fence she constructed so many years ago. She's on the road, riding Browny Red. I'm safe and happy here. It's the spirit place where Monsanto doesn't have power to alter seeds. Illness vanishes, sorrow is nowhere to be found. I'm reminded of the "vital effluence" D. H. Lawrence speaks of in *In the Spirit of Place*.

The Sangre de Cristos are watching over me. This is where Heaven and earth meet. God and I talk about my Facebook friends like Susie Chinn and Dan Smith, whom I have never met in person. We discuss my friends who have already passed on, like William Kelley, Cheryl from Jr. High, and Miss Pinkerton from grade school.

"I know they're with me, but I long to see them again."

You will, my child. We will all be meeting you on Rainbow Bridge. Those you've cared for will always be with you and there will be so many waiting, you won't be able to count them.

Then He says a really crazy thing — His logic differs greatly from mine: *It would give me great pleasure if you read your story of Muffin to baby Jesus. Although he was surrounded by loving animals, the little black cub I love so much wasn't among them.*

With God it's always the unexpected. Why would He want me to do this now, in answer to something that happened over two thousand years ago? He communicates on a level that transcends earthly conversation.

I delight in you as you delight in all of my creatures. I am fascinated by my creation of you. You know the order of things. You have searched my heart and know the mind of the spirit. You are my song in the garden.

"What I don't understand is that You have a dream for me that isn't mine. My dream has always been to be a singer, but You have guided me to write."

Yes! And you have completed them against your own will. I wanted you to tell the story of us together. I am honored by your unconditional love.

"I will finish these books for Jesus. I still desire singing but my illness has compromised my vocal cords. I've pursued voice lessons for so long and haven't been able to sing."

That will pass. Soon you will experience what sounds from your voice can be. Your power and mine are the same. I see you singing to birds; they love your voice and hear how good you are. They should know, because I have them singing all over the world.

I honestly never know what might start growing next. It's thrilling! It's been a humming long and lazy afternoon. I don't want to leave.

Not far from Gardner, Forbes bought Trinchera Ranch in 1969 for $50 an acre. He sold the property in 2007 (before the stock market crash) for over twenty times what he paid for it. The new buyer was Louis Bacon, a hedge-fund manager. Bacon purchased it for $175 million and the package includes the Sangre de Cristos — beautiful, untouched land framing my grandmother's. It will be left whole and undeveloped, at least for now. He wants to keep it untouched, and I am grateful.

My home in the meadow is held up in the center by one massive tree. I call it the Tree of Trees. All the walls surrounding it are exposed with no covering. The tree survived the lightning strike, three times hotter than the sun, which burned a hole through the loft bathroom before going out — fire and water synergy. The great room is a two-story space, open to the high ceiling with branches reaching the end of the beginning … from the ground up. I look outside. Nearby, the forest of white bark mixed with the smell of pine trees is my fortress. What is it about trees that makes me feel safe and protected?

One morning, I have chipmunks scampering all around me, eating Cheerios with me for breakfast. I get a bowl, they get a bowl. Cows lick dust off my truck's windows. (Their tongues are not the best windshield wipers!) And yes, I sing to birds every morning.

It's time to sort through personal things. I find a huge scrapbook filled with photos, posters and articles written about me that I no longer remember. Mother had saved photos I thought I would never see again, thinking they had been lost forever in the Larchmont fire.

She hadn't gone to my pageants but she had kept newspaper articles from interviews I don't even remember doing. All those scraps of paper were meaningful to her. I'm seeing that now and embrace what she was so proud of. I had made it in her eyes, and perhaps society's, at least for a while. Her dream was to be financially independent and start a successful business to experience freedom. My idea of success now differs greatly from hers in that time because I was born when life was easier and able to do things she couldn't.

Now I see Mom as successful. In my memory, she is the smell of lilacs sending me off to school, lunch every day with a peanut-butter-and-jelly sandwich. I continue to carry the sweet pocket of faith, connecting us in another existence. Newspaper clippings are clutter that will eventually disintegrate. What is lasting? Simply being aware of blessings and acting on them every day, with grace.

I'm approximately the same age now that Mother was when she left us. I realize it was Sophie's wisdom that made it possible to complete my calling as an adult. My mother suffered from lack of opportunity, education, and equal rights but in using me as a child messenger in the schoolyard of her life, demonic depression did not prevail. How ironic that Mom never liked her name but now it is on the most popular list. The generational curse is broken. Leadership is evolving as female roles and influence continue to grow in schools that finally educate girls, something that hardly existed in Sophie's time. Seeds of peace are being sown by women in gardens all over the world. A new story is beginning.

> Listen, O isles, unto me; and hearken, ye people, from far; The LORD hath called me from the womb; from the bowels of my mother hath he made mention of my name. And he hath made my mouth like a sharp sword; in the shadow of his hand hath he hid me, and made me a polished shaft; in his quiver hath he hid me; And he said, It is a light thing that thou shouldest be my servant to raise up the tribes of Jacob, and to restore the preserved of Israel: I will also give thee for a light to the Gentiles, that thou mayest be my salvation unto the end of the earth. (Isaiah 49:1-2, 6; KJV)

I'm back in the middle of the meadow. The old homestead and root cellar are on either side of me, to the right and left. Grandpa Jesse's Bible sits proudly on my knees.

In closing, having you read these pages means the world to me. This is the reason why I'm here. Hold onto these words and never allow them to fall away. Tattoo them on your heart: You are special. You are chosen. You are not alone. The world needs you. I need you. Your love is real and your energy is felt. Yes, I'm listening. The fresh teardrop, the rain, the stream you hear is listening. The moments shared together are forever connected with *How Nature Healed a Broken Soul.*

~

NATIVE AMERICAN PROVERB

Listen to the wind,
It talks.

Listen to the silence,
It speaks.

Listen to your heart,
It knows.

Questions from Readers

Q: *The book is an autobiography, yet you go through your mother's childhood as if you've been there. Example: Writing about the movement of the sun and shadows through the trees. Isn't an autobiography supposed to be totally nonfiction?*

A: After gaining as much research as I could from Aunt Gen and others, I got on my knees and asked for a detailed reenactment, then wrote down what was revealed. This process goes deeper than earthly history and imagination. The content is only concerned with the reality of the moment. Getting to this place in writing did not happen overnight and required long periods in solitude with God.

Q: *Why do you find it necessary to go into so many intimate details concerning your former husband?*

A: The collection of details surrounding my marriage was the big white elephant in the room not dealt with. Only when I had the courage to write the truth was I able to face reality and change. Hiding feelings that are so unsettling creates a lie in the story of life. Hidden secrets and thoughts need to surface, placed in the light *in all of life* before healing can take place. Divorce puts both parties in the middle of a fire where character is at stake. The past cannot be changed. In many ways, one might say I failed the test and serve as an example of wife-school graduation.

However, observing my attitudes and behavior at that time, almost as a third person looking in from the outside, gave me the gift of objectivity. I needed a transformation to take place. I deliberately refrained from using my former husband's name because of the raw, embarrassing circumstances in the nature of our intimacy. There is obviously a window of transparency for any reader who chooses to look deeper, but

I have no interest in character judgment. This is strictly about my own journey and lessons learned.

Q: *Why didn't you go into family history on your father's side like you did on your mother's?*

A: DNA from my father's side is connected to Jesse in the Bible. Grandpa always said he was a distant cousin to the outlaw, Jesse James. Grandma said he was making it up. I chose to believe her. I don't want to have a DNA test. It's a waste of precious time, and in reality, to research and discuss both bloodlines would have taken more energy and bandwidth than I was able to commit.

Q: *What is the most important thing you've learned?*

A: Mmmm, there are many. It has been my experience that the roots of darkness and evil can only exist on the hard surface brought about by wounds left unattended. We are a part of the earth, to be tilled, softened, and given nutrition until health emerges. Most people don't realize that if we simply keep digging underneath the tough topsoil we will find the hidden treasure, the well of still, deep water reflection called sacred. That is who you and I really are.

"Give what you have to somebody,

it may be better than you dare to think."

~ Henry Wadsworth Longfellow

Reflections

Windshield wipers zigzag across the window over the course of a lifetime.

As a child, I felt the weight of the world on my shoulders.
I've gotten older and I am in the driver's seat now.
Through the years, the weight feels lighter, but not by much.

It's night in the middle of a storm.
I'm searching outside a teared window for the underdogs.
My soul will never silence till I find them. It is only for them that I got to the finish line.
My eyes blink for clear vision to find the ones most broken who require cheering on to win in the game of life.
I wait…

The storm this night is not yet over.
I long for their voices to be heard above the sound of the pouring rain.

One life encompasses the entire universe.
Our actions, good and bad, shift and alter the entire world.
To think otherwise is an illusion.

Being able to endure the fire of living through paradoxical experiences melts away the dross of unforgiveness, fantasies and judgments.

The world begins to shine in a more realistic way.

Leadership emerges.

If you enjoyed this book, please leave a review! It really helps get the word out. https://amz.run/5xVI

For more information about Penny James or her books, contact Beth Kallman Werner at Author Connections.
1-570-686-1214 or beth@authorconnections.com